Ian Allan abc

1989

BR…

M… …TS

LONDON

IAN ALLAN LTD

Introduction

New to this edition is the current BR Director of Mechanical Engineering's (DMEE) full Design Classification for each vehicle. Network SouthEast's Regional Traction & Rolling Stock Engineer also has a separate design reference inherited from, and used in conjunction with, all Southern Region-operated electric units. Whilst both are listed herein there are examples where the two records do not agree, in which case this book shows the revised DMEE reference.

The most significant factor during 1988 was the continued growth of passenger traffic which stretched the rolling stock resources of BR. Due to this, although new units were delivered, stock that was in a reasonable condition that was planned for condemnation in fact received a light overhaul at a BRML Level 5 depot.

Regrettably BR continued to experience serious problems with some of its new units. The Pacer DMUs suffered numerous gearbox failures and a programme of replacing many SCG boxes with Voith units, a type proven on BR's Sprinters, has greatly improved availability. Problems with the sliding plug doors caused all Class 155 Super Sprinters to be 'grounded' at Cardiff and Leeds in mid-December. Luckily Metro-Cammell had been ahead of schedule with delivery of Class 156 units and Provincial Sector management was able to draft 20 of these to Cardiff, and make small adjustments elsewhere to cover their duties, some reverting to locomotive-hauled coaches.

By October 1989 sufficient new 'Express' Class 158 units are due to be delivered by BREL '88 Ltd for ScotRail Express (Glasgow/Edinburgh/Aberdeen) services in place of locomotive-hauled trains. Some duties at present formed of Class 156 units will later be operated by Class 158s and cascading will allow old DMUs to be withdrawn. However it will be at least 10 years before all the 1960s-era units can be eliminated, and therefore a limited programme of second life-extension overhauls will commence this year, particularly on Class 108 vehicles.

Network SouthEast received Government authority for new Networker Turbo DMUs for Chiltern Lines duties which will replace Marylebone route Class 115s. Generally NSE is awaiting feasibility studies and Government approval before investing in the Paddington-Oxford, Reading-Tonbridge and Waterloo-Exeter routes.

Subject to Government authority Birmingham's Cross-City line (Lichfield-Redditch) will be electrified and operated by new units. ScotRail's Class 311 and unrefurbished Class 303 units will be replaced by the new Class 320 series on order with BREL at York.

Thameslink's 60 Class 319 EMUs have already proved a tremendous success and a further 20 are on order to cover traffic growth on both sides of the Thames. The new Anglia Class 321 EMUs are being delivered at the rate of two per week and are generally augmented rather than directly replacing old units. The compartment-style Class 302s retained primarily for peak-hour duties will gradually be withdrawn.

By the end of 1988 two Class 442 Wessex Electric units had still to enter service and two more had already been involved in incidents, one as a result of vandalism. Traffic growth meant that BR decided to overhaul three of the Class 432 4-REP tractor units, but one was written off in the Clapham tragedy last December, the worst accident on BR in 20 years. Thus NSE has retained the Class 492/8 and additional Class 438 units on a short-term basis. 'New' stock, in the form of 1938 London Underground life-expired trains, has been purchased for the Isle of Wight and should enter service in 1989 after overhaul and modifications at BRML Eastleigh. Refurbishment of other slam-door Southern Region stock this year is expected to be confined to Class 423 4-VEP units. Kent suburban services are scheduled for new Networker trains in 1991, an order for over 700 vehicles is sure to be subject to very keen tendering by at least BREL and Metro-Cammell, with Brush and GEC seeking type approval of new ac traction motors installed in EMU Nos 7001 and 5920 respectively.

Multiple-units do not have the enthusiastic following of locomotives, but from an economic viewpoint they form the only way forward for BR's short- and medium-distance routes. The future for locomotives on BR will be confined to the long-distance International routes via the Channel Tunnel, East and West Coast main lines, plus freight and engineering duties.

Roger Wood, Editor
March 1989

Sector Codes

Multiple-unit stock is used by five of BR's six Sectors, Railfreight having no normal use for such stock. BR's policy is to allocate all costs of stock to a financial pool to be funded from service income and national and local Government grants. The Pools in use at the time of going to press are:

InterCity

IVGA Gatwick Express

Network SouthEast

NCH Charter services
NGB Gospel Oak-Barking line
NGE Great Eastern lines (Anglia East)
NGN Great Northern lines
NKC Kent Coast routes
NKS Kent suburban routes
NMY Chiltern Lines (Marylebone)
NNE Northeast routes (Anglia West)
NNL North London lines
NNW North Western lines
NSB Surrey and Berkshire
NSL South London lines
NSS Solent and Sarum
NST London, Tilbury & Southend line
NSX Sussex routes
NWR Western Region
NXX Spare
NXXZ Authorised for condemnation

Provincial

This Sector ceased to use area and route codes with effect from 1 April 1989. All stock is financially controlled based on maintenance depot allocation, the cost of work effected at other than home depot being charged to the current recorded DMEE Rolling Stock Library allocation (eg Newton Heath based stock has a Sector code of *PNH* etc.)

PXX Spare
PXXZ Authorised for condemnation

Parcels Sector

RPMA AC electric multiple-units
RPMD DC electric multiple-units
RPXN Diesel multiple-units
RXXX Spare or authorised for condemnation

Departmental

DXXZ Captial stock awaiting transfer to Departmental service, or authorised for condemnation

Special Characteristics

- **D** Additional dc lines collection shoe (Euston-Watford route)
- **E** Express gear ratio on suburban stock
- **L** Headlight/Spotlight fitted
- **F** Facelifted units, not standard to class
- **G** Through gangway fitted, not standard to class
- **M** Driver only operation, cab-signalling centre communication
- **O** Open type accommodation, normally non-corridor compartments
- **R** Radio Electronic Token Block signalling system
- **V** Voith transmission (other SCG)
- + AEC engines (others in class Leyland)
- # Asbestos insulation

Liveries

- **L** London & South Sector ('Jaffa-Cake')
- **M** Greater Manchester PTE
- **N** Network SouthEast
- **P** Provincial blue
- **RR** Post Office red
- **S** Strathclyde PTE
- * Special, see class heading

Acknowledgements

This stock is a very difficult area to maintain accuracy of records. The five Regions have, to varying degrees, issued their own records but not ensured that the main BRB records were similarly revised.

The editor wishes to thank the staff of RSL Derby, the responsible officers of the five Regions, and also, Alan, Brian, Dave L, Dave T, Lawrie and Peter for their invaluable assistance.

Level of Repair and Maintenance Facility

In April 1987 BR introduced a new maintenance policy for all traction and coaching stock. Under the scheme, depots and workshops are classified on a scale of 1 to 6, called Levels, determined by the facilities available and work effected at each location.

The larger establishments, Level 5, normally have separate workshops to carry out this category of repair and are not necessarily answerable to the Sector which 'owns' the main depot.

Definition

Level	*Facility*	*Description*
1	Fuel point	Facility for dispensing fuel, oil and water to diesel locomotives and/or DMUs. Minor servicing to EMUs. Manned by unskilled staff.
2	Servicing	Capable of undertaking 'A' exam work and occasional 'B' exams on locomotives and multiple-units together with work arising and brake blocking also full maintenance for diesel shunter locomotives. For coaching stock some cleaning, chemical emission toilet disposal, environmental checks, two daily exams, weekly exams and brake blocking. The facility will have a covered pit, a small store and be manned by skilled staff.
3	Maintenance	This facility will have a Traction and Rolling Stock allocation and be capable of carrying out all levels of exams and the majority of repairs arising. It will have covered pits, staff accomodation, light lifting and jacking facilities. A full range of equipment will be available to meet all exam requirements. Multiple-units and coaching stock all levels of exams, code 'C' cleaning, patch painting and some body repair.
4	Maintenance and repair	As for level 3 but having an additional capability for heavier repairs. The depot will be well equipped with cranes and/or heavy lifting jacks for bogie removal and possibly a wheel lathe.
5	Heavy repair	A facility capable of undertaking unplanned heavy repairs and collision damage. May also have the facility for lower level of classified repair, limited component refurbishment and half life component exchange. Fuelling facilities are not necessarily provided.
6	Workshop	A main workshop with full facilities for undertaking all levels of classified and unclassified repairs.

	Level DMU	EMU		Main Sector(s)	Full Maintenance Classes Allocated
AF	2/5*	2/5*	Ashford, Chart Leacon T&RSMD	N	—
AN	2		Allerton SD	P	—
AY	2		Ayr SD	P	—
BD		4/5*	Birkenhead North EMUD	P	508
BE	1	1	Bedford	N	—
BI		4	Brighton T&RSMD	N	421/1, 421/3, 421/4, 422/1, 422/2, 423/0, 423/1
BM		4	Bournemouth West EMUD	N	423/0, 423/1, 431, 432, 438, 492/8
BQ		4	Bury EMUD	P	504
BP	1		Blackpool	P	—
BR	2		Bristol Bath Road TMD	P	108
BX	2		Buxton TMD	P	108
BY	4	4	Bletchley TMD	N	104(T), 108, 115, 310, 310/1, 313, 317 (321)
CA	4		Cambridge (Coldhams Lane) TMD	R	101, 105, 114, 128
CC		4	Clacton EMUD	N	309/1, 309/2, 309/3, 309/4, 312/0, 312/1, 313
CE		2	Crewe ETD	P	—
CF	4		Cardiff Canton TMD	P	101, 116, 119, 155
	5	5	Cardiff Cathays RSMD	—	
CH	2		Chester TMD	P DMUs to cease asap	101, 108
CK	1	4	Corkerhill SD	P	156
CL	1		Carlisle Upperby RSMD	P	
CP	1		Crewe RSMD (all stored)	P	101, 104, 115, 116, 127
DL	5	5	Doncaster Major Depot, BRML	—	
DY	4		Derby, Etches Park T&RSMD	P	150, 150/1, 151, 154
ED	4		Eastfield, Glasgow TMD	P DMUs to Level 2 soon	101, 104, 107, 108

	Level				Full Maintenance
	DMU	EMU		Main Sector(s)	Classes Allocated
EH	4		Eastleigh T&RSMD	N	205
EM		4	East Ham EMUD	N	302, 308/1, 310
EX	1		Exeter St Davids SD	P	
FR	2	3	Fratton T&RSMD	N	411/5, 412, 421, 423/0, 423/1
GI		2	Gillingham EMUD	N	—
GW		4	Glasgow, Shields EMD	P	303, 311, 314, 318
HA	4		Haymarket TMD	P	101, 107, 108, 110(T), 120, 150/2, 156, (158)
HE		4	Hornsey EMUD		313, 317/1, 317/2
HR		3	Hall Road EMUD	P	507
HT	4		Heaton T&RSMD	P	101, 111(T), 142, 143
IL		4/5*	Ilford EMD	N	302, 305/1, 305/2, 307, 308/1, 308/2, 315, 321
IP	1		Ipswich HS	F	—
LA	4		Laira TMD	P	101, 118, 121, 122
LE	4		Landore TMD	P	101, 108, 116(T), 118(T)
LG		4	Longsight EMD	P	303, 304
LO	2		Longsight TMD	R	127
ME	2		Marylebone TMD	N	—
MN	1		Machynlleth	P	—
NC	4		Norwich, Crown Point T&RSMD	P	101, 111(T), 156
NH	4		Newton Heath TMD	P	100, 101(T), 104, 105, 108, 142, 142/1, 150/2
NL	4/5*		Neville Hill T&RSMD	P	101, 108, 110, 111, 141, 141/1, 142, 144, 150/2, 156
OO	4		Old Oak Common HSTD	N	101, 104, 116, 121
ON		3	Orpington HS	N	—
PB	1		Peterborough SD	N	
PE	1	1	Peterborough CS	R	

	Level DMU	EMU		Main Sector(s)	Full Maintenance Classes Allocated
RE		4	Ramsgate EMUD	N	411/3, 411/4, 411/5, 413/2, 413/3, 414/2, 419, 423/0
RG	4		Reading TMD	N	101, 117, 119
RY		4/5	Ryde, Isle of Wight EMD	N	(483), 485, 486
SG		4/5*	Slade Green T&RSMD	N	415/1, 415/3, 415/4, 416/2, 416/4
SH	—	‡	Strawberry Hill	—	—
SL		4	Stewarts Lane T&RSMD	I	488/2, 488/3, 489
SU	4/5*	4/5*	Selhurst T&RSMD	N	319, 415/3, 415/4, 416/2, 416/3, 455/8
	1		Stirling	—	
TS	4		Tyseley TMD	P	101, 108, 111(T), 115(T), 116, 121, 127(T)
WC		4/5*	Waterloo (Waterloo & City) EMUD	N	487
WD		4	East Wimbledon EMUD	N	414/2, 414/3, 423/0, 455/7, 455/8, 455/9
WN		1	Willesden TMD	N	
ZG	6	6	Eastleigh BRML		
ZH	5	5	Springburn BRML		
ZN		5	Wolverton BRML		
BREL Works:					
ZD			Derby Carriage CEM (under contract)		
ZR			York Carriage		
British Railways Board:					
ZQ			BRB Headquarters (stock on acceptance)		

Sectors:
I: InterCity
P: Provincial Services
N: Network SouthEast
R: Parcels

* Level 5 Workshop for specific work only
‡ Specialist repair workshops

Diesel Multiple-Units

Class 119 — Driving Motor Brake

Built: Gloucester RC&W Co 1958

Diagram	Type	Weight	Seats 1st	Seats Std
DQ3.02.0B	DMBC	37.5t	18	16
DQ2.--.--	DMBS	37.5t	—	34

Engines: Two Leyland 150bhp (112kW) 6-cyl horizontal

Transmission: Four speed epicyclic gearbox/ carden shaft

Dimensions: 19.66m L × 2.74m W × 3.86m H. Gangway within unit

Maximum speed: 70mph

Brakes: Vacuum

AWS: Fitted

Veh No	*Dia*	*SC*	*Liv*	Pool	Dep
51057	2----			*PCH*	CH
51060	3020B			*NSS*	RG
51062	3020B	#	N	*NWR*	RG
51065	3020B	#		*NSB*	RG
51066	3020B		N	*NSS*	RG
51071	2----			*PCH*	CH
51073	3020B		N	*NWR*	RG
51074	3020B			*NWR*	RG
51076	3020B			*NWR*	RG
51079	3020B			*NSS*	RG

Class 119 — Driving Motor

Built: Gloucester RC&W Co 1958

Diagram	Type	Weight	Seats	Toilet
DP2.03.0C	DMS(L)	38.5t	68	2

Engines: Two Leyland 150bhp (112kW) 6-cyl horizontal

Transmission: Four speed epicyclic gearbox/ carden shaft

Dimensions: 19.66m L × 2.74m W × 3.86m H. Gangway within unit

Maximum speed: 70mph

AWS: Fitted

Veh No	*Dia*	*SC*	*Liv*	Pool	Dep
51086	0C			*NWR*	RG
51088	0C			*NSB*	RG
51090	0C	#	N	*NWR*	RG
51094	0C		N	*NSS*	RG
51095	0C	#		*PCH*	CH
51099	0C			*NWR*	RG
51101	0C	#		*PCH*	CH
51103	0C	#		*NSB*	RG
51104	0C		N	*NWR*	RG
51107	0C		N	*NSS*	RG

Class 116 — Driving Motor Brake

Built: British Railways, Derby Carriage Works 1958

Diagram	Type	Weight	Seats	Note
DQ2.30.1A	DMBS	36.5t	65	Gangwayed
DQ2.30.2B	DMBS	36.5t	65	Refurbished and Gangwayed

Engines: Two Leyland 150bhp (112kW) 6-cyl horizontal
Transmission: Four speed epicyclic gearbox/ carden shaft
Dimensions: 20.29m L × 2.82m W × 3.86m H. Gangwayed within unit, with side doors to each seating bay as shown
Maximum speed: 70mph
AWS: Fitted

Veh No	*Dia*	*SC*	*Liv*	Pool	Dep
51128	2B	LG		*PCF*	CF
51129	2B	G		*PTS*	TS
51130	1A	G		*PTS*	TS
51131	2B	G		*PTS*	TS
51132	2B	LG		*PCF*	CF
51133	1A	G		*PTS*	TS
51134	2B	LG		*PCF*	CF
51135	2B	LG		*PCF*	CF
51136	2B	G		*PTS*	TS
51138	2B	G		*PTS*	TS
51139	2B	LG		*PCF*	CF
51140	2B	LG		*PCF*	CF

Series continued with No 53050.

Class 116 — Driving Motor

Built: British Railways, Derby Carriage Works 1958

Diagram	Type	Weight	Seats	Note
DP2.20.1A	DMS	36.5t	89	Gangwayed
DP2.20.2B	DMS	36.5t	89	Refurbished and Gangwayed

Engines: Two Leyland 150bhp (112kW) 6-cyl horizontal
Transmission: Four speed epicyclic gearbox/ carden shaft
Dimensions: 20.29m L × 2.82m W × 3.86m H. Gangwayed within unit, with side doors to each seating bay as shown
Maximum speed: 70mph
Brakes: Vacuum
AWS: Fitted

Veh No	*Dia*	*SC*	*Liv*	Pool	Dep
51141	2B	LG		*PCF*	CF
51142	2B	G		*PTS*	TS
51143	2B	G		*PTS*	TS
51144	2B	G		*PTS*	TS
51145	2B	LG		*PCF*	CF
51146	1A	G		*PTS*	TS
51147	2B	LG		*PCF*	CF
51148	2B	LG		*PCF*	CF

Veh No	Dia	SC	Liv	Pool	Dep
51149	2B	G		PTS	TS
51151	2B	G		PTS	TS
51152	2B	LG		PCF	CF
51153	2B	LG		PCF	CF

Series continued with No 53092.

Class 101 Driving Motor Brake

Built: Metropolitan-Cammell 1958

Diagram	Type	Weight	Seats	Engine	Note
DQ2.02.1A	DMBS	32.5t	52	AEC	—
DQ2.02.2B	DMBS	32.5t	52	AEC	Refurbished
DQ2.02.2E	DMBS	32.5t	52	Leyland	Refurbished
DQ2.32.0A	DMBS	32.5t	49	Leyland	Refurbished

Engines: Two AEC or Leyland 150bhp (112kW) 6-cyl horizontal
Transmission: Four speed epicyclic gearbox/carden shaft
Dimensions: 18.49m L × 2.82m W × 3.85m H. Gangwayed within unit
Maximum speed: 70mph
Brakes: Vacuum
AWS: Fitted

Veh No	Dia	SC	Liv	Pool	Dep
51174	022E			PHA	HA
51175	022B	†		PNL	NL
51177	022E			PNC	NC
51178	022B	†		PNC	NC
51179	022E			PLA	LA
51180	022E			PNC	NC
51181	022E			PLA	LA
51182	022E			PHA	HA
51183	022E	#		PNL	NL
51184	022E			PNC	NC
51185	022E			PNC	NC
51187	022E			PNC	NC
51188	022E			PNC	NC
51189	022E			PNC	NC
51190	022E			NSS	RG
51191	022E			PNC	NC
51192	022E			PNC	NC
51194	022E			PNC	NC
51197	021A	#		PHT	HT
51201	022E			PNC	NC
51203	022E	#		PHT	HT
51205	022E			PLA	LA
51206	022B	#†		PNH	NH
51207	022E		N	NGE	CA
51208	022E		N	NGE	CA
51210	022E			PHA	HA
51211	320A	L		NSS	RG
51212	022E		N	NWR	OO
51213	022E			PNC	NC
51215	022E	#		PNL	NL
51216	022B	#†		PHT	HT
51217	022B	#†		PHT	HT
51218	022E			PNC	NC
51219	022E			PLA	LA
51220	022E		N	NWR	OO
51221	022E			NWR	OO
51222	022E			PCF	CF
51223	022E			PLA	LA
51224	022E			PED	ED
51225	022E			NWR	OO
51226	320A			NSS	RG
51227	022B	#†		PNH	NH
51228	022E			PHA	HA
51230	022E			PNC	NC
51231	022E			PHA	HA
51234	022E			PHA	HA

Veh No	Dia	SC	Liv	Pool	Dep
51241	022E			PHA	HA
51243	022B	#†		PNH	NH
51244	022E			PHA	HA
51245	022E			PHA	HA
51246	022E			PLA	LA
51247	022E			PNC	NC
51249	022E		S	PED	ED
51252	022E			PNC	NC
51253	022E			PHA	HA

Series continued with No 51425.

Class 118 — Driving Motor Brake

Built: Birmingham RC&W Co 1960

Diagram	Type	Weight	Seats	Toilet
DQ2.20.0A	DMBS	36.5t	65	—
DQ2.20.1D	DMBS	36.5t	65	Refurbished

Engines: Two Leyland 150bhp (112kW) 6-cyl horizontal
Transmission: Four speed epicyclic gearbox/carden shaft
Dimensions: 20.45m L × 2.82m W × 3.86m H. Gangwayed within unit, with side doors to each seating bay
Maximum speed: 70mph
Brakes: Fitted
AWS: Fitted

Veh No	Dia	SC	Liv	Pool	Dep
51305	0A	#		PLA	LA
51306	1D			PTS	TS
51307	0A	L		PCF	CF
51310	0A	#		PCF	CF
51312	0A	#		PCF	CF
51314	0A			PTS	TS
51315	0A	#		PCF	CF
51316	1D			PTS	TS

Class 118 — Driving Motor

Built: Birmingham RC&W Co 1960

Diagram	Type	Weight	Seats	Note
DP2.21.0B	DMS	36.5t	89	—
DP2.21.1D	DMS	36.5t	89	Refurbished

Engines: Two Leyland 150bhp (112kW) 6-cyl horizontal
Transmission: Four speed epicyclic gearbox/carden shaft
Dimensions: 20.45m L × 2.82m W × 3.86m H. Gangwayed within unit, with side doors to each seating bay
Maximum speed: 70mph
Brakes: Vacuum
AWS: Fitted

Veh No	Dia	SC	Liv	Pool	Dep
51319	0B		N	NWR	00
51320	0B	#		PLA	LA
51321	1D			PTS	TS
51325	0B	#		PCF	CF
51327	0B	#		PCF	CF
51329	0B			PTS	TS
51330	0B	#		PCF	CF
51331	1D			PTS	TS

Class 117 Driving Motor Brake

Built: Pressed Steel Co 1959

Diagram	Type	Weight	Seats	Note
DQ2.20.1C	DMBS	36.5t	65	Refurbished

Engines: Two Leyland 150bhp (112kW) 6-cyl horizontal
Transmission: Four speed epicyclic gearbox/ carden shaft
Dimensions: 20.45m L × 2.82m W × 3.86m H. Gangwayed within unit, with side doors to each seating bay
Maximum speed: 70mph
Brakes: Vacuum
AWS: Fitted
Special livery: GWR: 51368

Veh No	*Dia*	*SC*	*Liv*	*Pool*	*Dep*
51332	IC			*NWR*	RG
51333	IC		N	*NWR*	RG
51334	IC			*PTS*	TS
51335	IC		N	*NWR*	RG
51336	IC		N	*NWR*	RG
51337	IC			*NWR*	RG
51338	IC			*PTS*	TS
51339	IC			*PTS*	TS
51340	IC		N	*NWR*	RG
51341	IC		N	*NWR*	RG
51342	IC		N	*NWR*	RG
51343	IC		N	*NWR*	RG
51344	IC		N	*NWR*	RG
51345	IC			*NWR*	RG
51346	IC		N	*NWR*	RG
51347	IC		N	*NWR*	RG
51348	IC			*PTS*	TS
51349	IC		N	*NWR*	RG
51350	IC		N	*NWR*	RG
51351	IC		N	*NWR*	RG
51352	IC			*PTS*	TS
51353	IC			*PTS*	TS
51354	IC		N	*NWR*	RG
51355	IC		N	*NWR*	RG
51356	IC		N	*NWR*	RG
51358	IC		N	*NWR*	RG
51359	IC		N	*NWR*	RG
51360	IC			*PTS*	TS
51361	IC			*NWR*	RG
51362	IC		N	*NWR*	RG
51363	IC			*NWR*	RG
51364	IC			*PTS*	TS
51365	IC			*PTS*	TS
51366	IC		N	*NWR*	RG
51367	IC		N	*NWR*	RG
51368	IC		★	*PTS*	TS
51369	IC			*PTS*	TS
51370	IC			*PTS*	TS
51371	IC			*PTS*	TS
51372	IC			*PTS*	TS
51373	IC			*PTS*	TS

Class 117 Driving Motor

Built: Pressed Steel Co 1959

Diagram	Type	Weight	Seats	Note
DP2.21.1C	DMS	36.5t	89	Refurbished

Engines: Two Leyland 150bhp (112kW) 6-cyl horizontal
Transmission: Four speed epicyclic gearbox/ carden shaft

Dimensions: 20.45m L × 2.82m W × 3.86m H. Gangwayed within unit, with side doors to each seating bay
Maximum speed: 70mph
Brakes: Vacuum
AWS: Fitted
Special livery: GWR: 51410

Veh No	*Dia*	*SC*	*Liv*	*Pool*	*Dep*
51374	IC			*NWR*	RG
51375	IC		N	*NWR*	RG
51376	IC			*PTS*	TS
51377	IC		N	*NWR*	RG
51378	IC		N	*NWR*	RG
51379	IC			*NWR*	RG
51380	IC			*PTS*	TS
51381	IC		N	*NWR*	RG
51382	IC			*PTS*	TS
51383	IC		N	*NWR*	RG
51384	IC		N	*NWR*	RG
51385	IC		N	*NWR*	RG
51386	IC		N	*NWR*	RG
51387	IC			*NWR*	RG
51388	IC		N	*NWR*	RG
51389	IC		N	*NWR*	RG
51390	IC			*PTS*	TS
51391	IC		N	*NWR*	RG
51392	IC		N	*NWR*	RG
51393	IC			*NWR*	RG
51394	IC			*PTS*	TS
51395	IC			*PTS*	TS
51396	IC		N	*NWS*	RG
51397	IC			*NWR*	RG
51398	IC		N	*NWR*	RG
51399	IC			*NWR*	RG
51400	IC		N	*NWR*	RG
51401	IC		N	*NWR*	RG
51402	IC			*PTS*	TS
51404	IC		N	*NWR*	RG
51405	IC			*NWR*	RG
51406	IC			*PTS*	TS
51407	IC			*PTS*	TS
51408	IC		N	*NWR*	RG
51409	IC			*NWR*	RG
51410	IC		★	*PTS*	TS
51411	IC			*PTS*	TS
51412	IC			*PTS*	TS
51413	IC			*PTS*	TS
51414	IC			*PTS*	TS
51415	IC			*PTS*	TS

Class 108 Driving Motor Brake

Built: British Railways Derby Carriage Works, 1960

Diagram	**Type**	**Weight**	**Seats**	**Note**
DQ2.13.1A	DMBS	29.5t	52	—
DQ2.13.2B	DMBS	29.5t	52	Refurbished

Engines: Two Leyland 150bhp (112kW) 6-cyl horizontal
Transmission: Four speed epicyclic gearbox/ carden shaft
Dimensions: 19.84m L × 2.82m W × 3.87m H
Maximum speed: 70mph
Brakes: Vacuum
AWS: Fitted

Veh No	*Dia*	*SC*	*Liv*	*Pool*	*Dep*
51416	2B			*PCF*	CF
51417	2B			*PCH*	CH
51418	2B			*PCH*	CH
51419	1A			*PCH*	CH
51420	2B			*PNH*	NH
51421	2B			*PCH*	CH
51422	2B			*PCH*	CH
51424	2B			*PCH*	CH

Series continued with No 51901.

Class 101 — Driving Motor Brake

Built: Metropolitan-Cammell 1959

Diagram	Type	Weight	Seats	Engine	Note
DQ2.02.2E	DMBS	32.5t	52	Leyland	Refurbished
DQ2.32.0A	DMBS	32.5t	49	Leyland	Refurbished

Full details see series commencing No 51174.

Veh No	*Dia*	*SC*	*Liv*	*Pool*	*Dep*
51425	022E			*NSS*	RG
51426	022E			*PHA*	HA
51427	022E			*PNC*	NC
51428	022E			*PNC*	NC
51429	022E			*PNC*	NC
51431	022E			*PNC*	RG
51432	022E			*NSS*	RG
51434	320A			*NSS*	RG
51435	022E			*PNH*	NH
51436	022E	#		*PNL*	NL
51437	022E			*NSB*	RG
51438	022E		N	*NNE*	CA
51442	022E			*PNC*	NC
51443	022E		N	*NWR*	OO
51444	022E		N	*NGE*	CA
51445	022E		L	*PNL*	NL
51446	022E		L	*PNL*	NL
51449	022E		L	*PNH*	NH
51450	022E		L	*PNL*	NL
51454	022E			*PNL*	NL
51455	022E			*PNL*	NL
51456	022E	#		*PNH*	NH
51458	022E			*PHT*	HT
51462	022E		L	*PCF*	CF
51463	022E		L	*PNL*	NL
51465	022E			*PNL*	NL
51467	022E			*PHT*	HT
51468	022E			*PED*	ED

Series continued with No 51795.

Parcels Sector vehicles in this series.

Class 101 — Driving Motor

Built: Metropolitan-Cammell 1959

Diagram	Type	Weight	Seats 1st	Seats Std	Toilets	Note
DP2.10.1D	DMS(L)	32.5t	—	65	1	Mk 3 Bogies
DP2.10.2F	DMS(L)	32.5t	—	65	1	Mk 3 Bogies Refurbished
DP2.10.2H	DMS(L)	32.5t	—	65	1	Mk 2 Bogies Refurbished
DP3.04.2H	DMC(L)	32.5t	12	53	1	Mk 3 Bogies Refurbished
DP3.17.0D	DMC(L)	32.5t	12	46	1	Mk 3 Bogies Refurbished

Engines: Two Leyland 150bhp (112kW) 6-cyl horizontal
Transmission: Four-wheel epicyclic gearbox, carden shaft
Dimensions: 18.49m L × 2.82m W × 3.85m H
Maximum speed: 70mph
Brakes: Vacuum
AWS: Fitted

Veh No	Dia	SC	Liv	Pool	Dep
51495	2101D			PNL	NL
51496	2102F			PHA	HA
51498	3042H			NSS	RG
51499	3170D			NSS	RG
51500	2102H			PNL	NL
51501	3042H			NSS	RG
51503	3170D			NSS	RG
51504	3042H			NSS	RG
51505	2102F			PCF	CF
51506	2102H	LR		PNC	NC
51508	2102H	LR		PNC	NC
51509	2102F			PCF	CF
51510	2101D			PNL	NL
51511	2102F			PCF	CF
51512	2102F			PNL	NL
51513	2102F			PCF	CF
51515	2102H	L		PHT	HT
51516	2102F			PHT	HT
51517	2102H	L		PNL	NL
51519	2102F	L		PNL	NL
51522	2102H	L		PHT	HT
51523	2102H	L#		PNL	NL
51524	2102F			PNL	NL
51526	2102F			PNL	NL
51529	2102F			PNL	NL
51530	2102F	L		PLA	LA
51531	2102F			PHA	HA
51532	2102F	#		PNH	NH
51533	2102F	L		PNL	NL
51538	2102F			PNL	NL

Series continued with No 51803.

Class 108 — Driving Motor

Built: British Railways Derby Carriage Works, 1959

Diagram	Type	Weight	Seats		Toilet	
DP2.26.0A	DMS(L)	28.5t	—	64	1	Refurbished
DP3.11.1B	DMC(L)	28.5t	12	52	1	Refurbished

Engines: Two Leyland 150bhp (112kW) 6-cyl horizontal
Transmission: Four speed epicyclic gearbox/carden shaft
Dimensions: 18.49m L × 2.79m W × 3.87m H. Gangwayed within unit
Maximum speed: 70mph
Brakes: Vacuum
AWS: Fitted

Veh No	Dia	SC	Liv	Pool	Dep
51561	2260A	L		PLE	LE
51562	2260A	L		PLE	LE
51563	2260A	L		PLE	LE
51565	2260A	L		PLE	LE
51566	2260A	L		PHA	HA
51567	2260A	L		PLE	LE
51568	2260A			PBX	BX
51569	2260A			PBX	BX
51570	2260A			PLA	LA
51571	3111B			NNL	BY
51572	3111B			NNL	BY

Series continued with No 52038.

Class 115 — Driving Motor Brake

Built: British Railways, Derby Carriage Works 1960

Diagram	Type	Weight	Seats	AWS	Note
DQ2.18.0A	DMBS	38.5t	78	Fitted	—
DQ2.18.1A	DMBS	38.5t	78	Fitted	—
DQ2.18.2B	DMBS	39t	78	Fitted	Refurbished
DQ2.18.3B	DMBS	39t	78	—	Refurbished
DQ2.33.1B	DMBS	39t	78	Fitted	Refurbished and Gangwayed

Engines: Two Leyland Albion 230bhp (172kW) 6-cyl horizontal
Transmission: Four speed epicyclic gearbox/ carden shaft
Dimensions: 20.45m L × 2.82m W × 3.87m H. Built non-gangwayed, side doors to each seating bay semi-open. Gangways within unit fitted where shown (G)
Maximum speed: 70mph
Brakes: Vacuum

Veh No	*Dia*	*SC*	*Liv*	*Pool*	*Dep*
51651	331B	G		*NMY*	BY
51652	181A			*NMY*	BY
51653	182B			*NMY*	BY
51654	331B	G		*NMY*	BY
51655	182B			*NMY*	BY
51656	331B	G		*NMY*	BY
51657	331B	G		*NMY*	BY
51658	182B			*NMY*	BY
51659	182B		N	*NMY*	BY
51660	183B			*NMY*	BY
51661	181A			*NMY*	BY
51662	331B	G		*PTS*	TS
51663	182B			*NMY*	BY
51664	182B			*NMY*	BY
51665	182B			*NMY*	BY
51666	182B		N	*NMY*	BY
51667	182B		N	*NMY*	BY
51668	181A			*NMY*	BY
51669	182B			*NMY*	BY
51670	182B			*NMY*	BY
51671	181A		N	*NMY*	BY
51673	182B			*NMY*	BY
51674	180A			*NMY*	BY
51675	181A			*NMY*	BY
51676	331B	G		*NMY*	BY
51677	182B			*NMY*	BY
51678	183B	G		*NMY*	BY
51679	331B	G		*NMY*	BY
51680	182B			*NMY*	BY

Series continued with No 51849.

Class 101 — Driving Motor Brake

Built: Metropolitan-Cammelll 1959

Diagram	Type	Weight	Seats	Engine	Note
DQ2.02.2E	DMBS	32.5t	52	Leyland	Refurbished

For full details see series commencing No 51174.

Veh No	Dia	SC	Liv	Pool	Dep
51795	022E			PNL	NL
51798	022E	#		PNH	NH
51799	022E	L		PNL	NL
51800	022E			PHA	HA
51801	022E	L		PNL	NL

Class 101 — Driving Motor

Built: Metropolitan-Cammell 1959

Diagram	Type	Weight	Seats	Toilet	Note
DP2.10.2F	DMS(L)	32.5t	65	1	Mk 3 Bogies Refurbished

For full details see series commencing No 51495.

Veh No	Dia	SC	Liv	Pool	Dep
51803	2102F			PED	ED
51804	2102F			PNL	NL
51808	2102F	L		PNL	NL

Class 110 — Driving Motor Brake

Built: Birmingham RC&W Co 1961

Diagram	Type	Weight	Seats	Note
DQ2.—.—*	DMBS	32.5t	45	*Official code DQ3.01.0B. Refurbished

Engines: Two Rolls-Royce 130D of 180bhp (134kW), 6-cyl
Transmission: Four speed epicyclic gearbox/ carden shaft
Dimensions: 18.48m L × 2.82m W × 3.84m H. Gangway within unit
Maximum speed: 70mph
Brakes: Vacuum
AWS: Fitted

Veh No	Dia	SC	Liv	Pool	Dep
51809				PNL	NL
51812				PNL	NL
51813				PNL	NL
51817				PNL	NL
51823				PNL	NL
51827				PNL	NL
51828				PNL	NL

Series continued with No 52066.

Class 110 — Driving Motor

Built: Birmingham RC&W Co 1961

Diagram	Type	Weight	Seats	Toilet	Note
DP2.—.—*	DMS	32.5t	66	1	*Official code DP3.13.1B. Refurbished

Engines: Two Rolls-Royce 130D of 180bhp (134kW), 6-cyl
Transmission: Four speed epicyclic gearbox/ carden shaft
Dimensions: 18.48m L × 2.82m W × 3.84m H. Gangway within unit
Maximum speed: 70mph
Brakes: Vacuum
AWS: Fitted

Veh No	Dia	SC	Liv	Pool	Dep
51829				PNL	NL
51830				PNL	NL
51834				PNL	NL
51835				PNL	NL
51840				PNL	NL
51842				PNL	NL
51843				PNL	NL
51847				PNL	NL

Series continued with No 52077.

Class 115 — Driving Motor Brake

Built: British Railways, Derby Carriage Works 1960

Diagram	Type	Weight	Seats	AWS	Note
DQ2.18.1A	DMBS	38.5t	78	Fitted	
DQ2.18.2B	DMBS	39.0t	78	Fitted	Refurbished
DQ2.18.3B	DMBS	39.0t	78	—	Refurbished
DQ2.33.0A	DMBS	38.5t	78	—	Gangwayed
DQ2.33.1B	DMBS	39.0t	78	Fitted	Gangwayed, Refurbished

For full details see series commencing No 51651.

Veh No	Dia	SC	Liv	Pool	Dep
51849	331B	G		NMY	BY
51851	330A	G		PTS	TS
51852	331B	G		PTS	TS
51853	331B	G		PTS	TS
51854	331B	G		PTS	TS
51855	331B	G		NMY	BY
51856	331B	G		PTS	TS
51857	182B		N	NMY	BY
51858	331B	G		PTS	TS
51859	331B	G		PTS	TS
51860	331B	G		PTS	TS
51862	331B	G		PTS	TS

Veh No	Dia	SC	Liv	Pool	Dep
51863	183B			NMY	BY
51865	330A	G		PTS	TS
51866	331B	G		NMY	BY
51867	330A	G		PTS	TS
51868	331B	G		PTS	TS
51869	331B	G		PTS	TS
51870	330A	G		PTS	TS
51871	182B			NMY	BY
51872	182B			NMY	BY
51873	182B		N	NMY	BY
51874	182B			NMY	BY
51875	182B			NMY	BY
51876	331B	G		PTS	TS
51877	331B	G		PTS	TS
51878	331B	G		NMY	BY
51879	182B		N	NMY	BY
51880	331B	G		PTS	TS
51883	182B			NMY	BY
51884	331B	G		PTS	TS
51885	181A			NMY	BY
51886	181A			NMY	BY
51887	182B			NMY	BY
51888	181A			NMY	BY
51889	181A		N	NMY	BY
51890	182B			NMY	BY
51891	182B			NMY	BY
51892	331B	G		PTS	TS
51893	331B	G		NMY	BY
51894	182B			NMY	BY
51895	331B	G		NMY	BY
51896	182B			NMY	BY
51897	331B	G		PTS	TS
51898	331B	G		PTS	TS
51899	183B			NMY	BY
51900	182B		N	NMY	BY

Class 108 Driving Motor Brake

Built: British Railways, Derby Carriage Works 1960

Diagram	**Type**	**Weight**	**Seats**	**Note**
DQ2.13.1A	DMBS	29.5t	52	
DQ2.13.2B	DMBS	29.5t	52	Refurbished

For full details see series commencing No 51416.

Veh No	Dia	SC	Liv	Pool	Dep
51901	2B			PCH	CH
51902	2B			PCH	CH
51903	2B			PCH	CH
51904	2B			PCH	CH
51905	2B			PCH	CH
51906	2B			PCH	CH
51907	2B			PCH	CH
51908	2B			PCH	CH
51909	2B		N	NNL	BY
51911	2B			PCH	CH
51912	2B			NNL	BY
51913	2B			PCH	CH
51914	2B		N	NNL	BY
51916	1A			NNL	BY
51917	2B			PCH	CH
51919	1A	L		PLE	LE
51920	1A			PCH	CH
51922	1A	L		PLE	LE
51924	2B	L		PLE	LE
51925	2B			PHA	HA
51926	2B			PHA	HA
51927	1A			PCH	CH
51928	2B	L		PLE	LE
51930	2B	L		PLE	LE
51931	2B	L		PLE	LE
51932	2B			PLA	LA
51933	2B			PLA	LA
51935	2B			PBX	BX
51936	2B			PHA	HA
51937	2B			PTS	TS
51938	2B			PBX	BX
51939	2B			PLA	LA

Veh No	Dia	SC	Liv	Pool	Dep
51940	2B			PLA	LA
51941	2B			PBX	BX
51942	2B		N	NNL	BY
51943	2B			PBX	BX
51945	2B			PBX	BX
51947	1A	L		PBX	BX
51948	2B			PBX	BX
51950	2B			PBX	BX

Class 107 — Driving Motor Brake

Built: British Railways, Derby Carriage Works 1960

Diagram	Type	Weight	Seats	Note
DQ2.11.1C	DMBS	35t	52	Refurbished

Engines: Two Leyland 150bhp (112kW) 6-cyl horizontal
Transmission: Four speed epicyclic gearbox/ carden shaft
Dimensions: 18.49m L × 2.82m W × 3.87m H. Gangwayed within unit
Maximum speed: 70mph
Brakes: Vacuum
AWS: Fitted

Veh No	Dia	SC	Liv	Pool	Dep
51985	IC			PHA	HA
51986	IC		S	PED	ED
51987	IC		S	PED	ED
51988	IC			PHA	HA
51989	IC		S	PED	ED
51990	IC		S	PED	ED
51991	IC			PHA	HA
51992	IC			PHA	HA
51993	IC		S	PED	ED
51994	IC			PHA	HA
51996	IC		S	PED	ED
51997	IC		S	PED	ED
51998	IC		S	PED	ED
51999	IC		S	PED	ED
52000	IC		S	PHA	HA
52001	IC		S	PED	ED
52004	IC			PED	ED
52005	IC		S	PED	ED
52006	IC		S	PED	ED
52007	IC		S	PED	ED
52008	IC		S	PED	ED
52010	IC		S	PED	ED

Class 107 — Driving Motor

Built: British Railways, Derby Carriage Works 1960

Diagram	Type	Weight	Seats	Toilet	Note
DP2.15.1C	DMS(L)	35.5t	65	1	Refurbished

Engines: Two Leyland 150bhp (112kW) 6-cyl horizontal
Transmission: Four speed epicyclic gearbox/ carden shaft
Dimensions: 18.49m L × 2.82m W × 3.87m H. Gangwayed within unit
Maximum speed: 70mph
Brakes: Vacuum
AWS: Fitted

Veh No	Dia	SC	Liv	Pool	Dep
52011	IC			*PHA*	HA
52012	IC		S	*PED*	ED
52013	IC			*PHA*	HA
52015	IC		S	*PED*	ED
52016	IC			*PED*	ED
52018	IC		S	*PED*	ED
52019	IC		S	*PED*	ED
52020	IC		S	*PED*	ED
52021	IC		S	*PED*	ED
52023	IC		S	*PED*	ED
52024	IC		S	*PED*	ED
52025	IC		S	*PED*	ED
52026	IC			*PHA*	HA
52028	IC			*PHA*	HA
52029	IC		S	*PED*	ED
52030	IC			*PED*	ED
52031	IC		S	*PED*	ED
52033	IC		S	*PED*	ED
52034	IC		S	*PED*	ED
52035	IC			*PHA*	HA
52036	IC			*PHA*	HA

Class 108 — Driving Motor

Built: British Railways, Derby Carriage Works 1960

Diagram	Type	Weight	Seats	Toilet	Note
DP2.27.0A	DMS(L)	28.5t	65	1	Refurbished
DP2.27.1B*	DMS(L)	28.5t	65	1	*Unofficial code

For full details see series commencing No 51561.

Veh No	Dia	SC	Liv	Pool	Dep
52038	IB	L		*PLE*	LE
52039	IB			*PBX*	BX
52041	IB	L		*PLE*	LE
52042	IB			*PED*	ED
52043	IB			*PHA*	HA
52044	IB	L		*PLE*	LE
52045	IB	L		*PLE*	LE
52046	OA	L		*PLE*	LE
52047	IB			*PLA*	LA
52048	IB	L		*PLE*	LE
52049	IB			*PBX*	BX
52050	IB			*PBX*	BX
52051	IB			*PHA*	HA
52053	IB			*PHA*	HA
52054	IB			*PLA*	LA
52055	IB	L		*PLE*	LE
52056	IB			*PBX*	BX
52057	IB			*PLA*	LA
52058	IB			*PBX*	BX
52059	IB			*PHA*	HA
52060	IB			*PBX*	BX
52061	OA	L		*PLE*	LE
52062	OA	L		*PBX*	BX
52063	IB			*PLA*	LA
52064	IB			*PBX*	BX
52065	OA	L		*PBX*	BX

Class 110 — Driving Motor Brake

Built: Birmingham RC&W Co 1961

Diagram	Type	Weight	Seats	Note
DQ2—	DMBS	32.5t	45	Refurbished. Official code DQ3.01.0B

For full details see series commencing No 51809.

Veh No	Dia	SC	Liv	Pool	Dep
52066				PNL	NL
52067				PNL	NL
52069				PNL	NL
52071				PNL	NL
52072				PNL	NL
52075				PNL	NL

Class 110 — Driving Motor

Built: Birmingham RC&W Co 1960

Diagram	Type	Weight	Toilet	Seats	Note
DP2.—	DMS	32.5t	66	1	Refurbished Official code DP3.13.1B

For full details see series commencing No 51829.

Veh No	Dia	SC	Liv	Pool	Dep
52077				PNL	NL
52080				PNL	NL
52081				PNL	NL
52082				PNL	NL
52084				PNL	NL
52085				PNL	NL

Class 114 — Driving Motor Brake

Built: British Railways, Derby Carriage Works 1956

Diagram	Type	Weight	Seats	Note
DQ2.17.2B	DMBS	38t	62	Refurbished

Engines: Two Leyland Albion 230bhp (172kW) 6-cyl horizontal
Transmission: Four speed epicyclic gearbox/ carden shaft
Dimensions: 20.45m L × 2.82m W × 3.86m H. Gangwayed within unit
Maximum speed: 70mph
Brakes: Vacuum
AWS: Fitted

Veh No	Dia	SC	Liv	Pool	Dep
53002	2B			PTS	TS
53005	2B			PTS	TS
53006	2B			PTS	TS
53008	2B			PTS	TS
53015	2B			PTS	TS
53018	2B			PTS	TS
53019	2B			PTS	TS
53021	2B			PTS	TS
53026	2B			PTS	TS
53030	2B			PTS	TS
53036	2B			PTS	TS
53037	2B			PTS	TS
53039	2B			PTS	TS
53044	2B			PTS	TS

Parcels Sector vehicles in this series.

Class 116 — Driving Motor Brake

Built: British Railways, Derby Carriage Works 1957

Diagram	Type	Weight	Seats	Note
DQ2.30.1A	DMBS	36.5t	65	Gangway
DQ2.30.2B	DMBS	36.5t	65	Gangway, Refurbished

For full details see series commencing No 51128 page xx

Veh No	*Dia*	*SC*	*Liv*	*Pool*	*Dep*
53050	2B	G		*PTS*	TS
53053	2B	G		*PTS*	TS
53054	2B	G		*PTS*	TS
53055	2B	G		*PTS*	TS
53056	2B	G		*PTS*	TS
53058	2B	G		*PTS*	TS
53060	2B	G		*PTS*	TS
53061	2B	G		*PTS*	TS
53071	1A	G		*PTS*	TS
53073	2B	G		*PTS*	TS
53079	2B	G		*PTS*	TS
53080	2B	GL#		*PCF*	CF
53082	2B	G		*PTS*	TS
53083	2B	G	N	*NGB*	00
53086	2B	GL#		*PCF*	CF
53089	2B	GL#		*PCF*	CF
53090	2B	G		*PTS*	TS

Series continued with No 53818.

Class 116 — Driving Motor

Built: British Railways, Derby Carriage Works 1957

Diagram	Type	Weight	Seats	Note
DP2.20.2B	DMS	36.5t	89	Gangway and Refurbished

For full details see series commencing No 51141.

Veh No	*Dia*	*SC*	*Liv*	*Pool*	*Dep*
53092	2B	G		*PTS*	TS
53093	2B	G		*PTS*	TS
53101	2B	G		*PTS*	TS
53102	2B	G		*PTS*	TS
53106	2B	G		*PTS*	TS
53114	2B	G		*PTS*	TS
53116	2B	G		*PTS*	TS
53122	2B	GL#		*PCF*	CF
53124	2B	G		*PTS*	TS
53128	2B	GL#		*PCF*	CF
53131	2B	GL#		*PCF*	CF
53132	2B	G		*PTS*	TS

Class 101 — Driving Motor

Built: Metropolitan-Cammell 1956

Diagram	Type	Weight	Engine	Seats	Toilet	Note
DP2.12.2B	DMS(L)	32.5t	AEC	57	1	Refurbished. Mk 2 Bogies
DP2.12.2C	DMS(L)	32.5t	Leyland	57	1	Refurbished. Mk 2 Bogies

Engines: Two AEC or Leyland 150bhp (112kW) 6-cyl horizontal
Transmission: Four speed epicyclic gearbox/ carden shaft
Dimensions: 18.49m L × 2.82m W × 3.85m H.
Maximum speed: 70mph
Brakes: Vacuum
AWS: Fitted

Veh No	*Dia*	*SC*	*Liv*	*Pool*	*Dep*
53139	2B	LR		*PNC*	NC
53141	2B			*PNL*	NL
53146	2C		S	*PED*	ED
53149	2C	LR		*PNC*	NC
53150	2C	LR		*PNC*	NC

Class 101 — Driving Motor Brake

Built: Metropolitan-Cammell 1956

Diagram	Type	Weight	Seats 1st	Seats Std	Note	
DQ3.—.2B	DMBC	32.5t	16	33	Leyland	Refurbished. Mk 2 Bogies
DQ2.02.2E	DMBS	32.5t	—	52	Leyland	Refurbished. Mk Bogies

Engines: Two AEC or Leyland 150bhp (112kW) 6-cyl horizontal
Transmission: Four speed epicyclic gearbox/ carden shaft
Dimensions: 18.49m L × 2.82m W × 3.85m H.
Maximum speed: 70mph
Brakes: Vacuum
AWS: Fitted

Veh No	*Dia*	*SC*	*Liv*	*Pool*	*Dep*
53155	3—2B			*NWR*	OO
53157	2022E			*PLA*	LA

Series continued with No 53164.

Class 101 — Driving Motor

Built: Metropolitan-Cammell 1956

Diagram	Type	Weight	Engine	Seats	Toilet	Note
DP2.14.2B	DMS(L)	32.5t	AEC	65	1	Refurbished
DP2.14.2C	DMS(L)	32.5t	Leyland	65	1	Refurbished

Engines: Two AEC or Leyland 150bhp (112kW) 6-cyl horizontal
Transmission: Four speed epicyclic gearbox/ carden shaft
Dimensions: 18.49m L × 2.82m W × 3.85m H.
Maximum speed: 70mph
Brakes: Vacuum
AWS: Fitted

Veh No	*Dia*	*SC*	*Liv*	*Pool*	*Dep*
53158	2C		S	*PED*	ED
53159	2C			*PNL*	NL
53160	2C		S	*PED*	ED
53162	2C			*PNL*	NL
53163	2B			*PHA*	HA

Series continued with No 53168.

Class 101 — Driving Motor Brake

Built: Metropolitan-Cammell 1957

Diagram	Type	Weight	Seats	Note
DQ2.02.2E	DMBS	32.5t	52	Refurbished. Mk 2 Bogies

For full details see No 53157.

Veh No	*Dia*	*SC*	*Liv*	*Pool*	*Dep*
53164	2E			*PHA*	HA
53165	2E			*PLA*	LA

Class 101 — Driving Motor

Built: Metropolitan-Cammell 1957

Diagram	Type	Weight	Engine	Seats	Toilet	Note
DP2.14.1A	DMS(L)	32.5t	AEC	65	1	—
DP2.14.2B	DMS(L)	32.5t	AEC	65	1	Refurbished
DP2.14.2C	DMS(L)	32.5t	Leyland	65	1	Refurbished

For full details see No 53158.

Veh No	Dia	SC	Liv	Pool	Dep
53168	2C	LR		PNC	NC
53169	2C	#		PNH	NH
53170	2C	LR		PNC	NC
53171	2C			PHA	HA
53176	2C			PHA	HA
53177	2C	LR		PNC	NC
53180	2C	LR		PNC	NC
53181	2C	R		PNC	NC
53182	2C	#		PHT	HT
53185	2C			PED	ED
53186	2B	†		PHA	HA
53187	2B	†		PHA	HA
53188	2C	#		PHT	HT
53189	1A	†		PHA	HA
53193	2C	LR		PNC	NC
53194	2C			PED	ED
53195	2C	#		PHT	HT
53196	2C	#		PHT	HT
53197	2B	†		PHA	HA

Class 101 — Driving Motor Brake

Built: Metropolitan-Cammell 1957

Design Code	Type	Weight	Engine	Seats	Note
DQ2.02.2B	DMBS	32.5t	AEC	52	Refurbished
DQ2.02.2E	DMBS	32.5t	Leyland	52	Refurbished

For full details see No 53157.

Veh No	Dia	SC	Liv	Pool	Dep
53198	2E			PED	ED
53200	2E			PLA	LA
53201	2B	†		PNC	NC
53202	2E			PNC	NC
53203	2E			PNC	NC
53204	2E			PNC	NC
53207	2E		N	NGB	00
53208	2B	†		PNC	NC
53211	2E			PHA	HA
53212	2E			PLA	LA
53214	2B	†#		PNL	NL
53215	2B	†		PHA	HA
53216	2E			PHA	HA
53219	2B	†#		PNH	NH
53222	2E	#		PCH	CH
53223	2E			PLA	LA
53224	2E			PCF	CF
53228	2E			PNC	NC
53229	2B	†		PHT	HT
53231	2E			PNC	NC

Parcels Sector vehicles in this series..

Class 101 — Driving Motor

Built: Metropolitan-Cammell 1957

Diagram	Type	Weight	Seats	Note
DP2.13.1C	DMS	32t	52	Refurbished. Mk 2 Bogies

Engines: Two Leyland 150bhp (112kW) 6-cyl horizontal

Transmission: Four speed epicyclic gearbox/ carden shaft

Dimensions: 18.49m L × 2.82m W × 3.85m H.

Maximum speed: 70mph

Brakes: Vacuum

AWS: Fitted

Veh No	Dia	SC	Liv	Pool	Dep
53235	IC	#		PNH	NH
53237	IC	#		PNL	NL
53238	IC	R		PNC	NC
53239	IC			PHA	HA
53240	IC	#		PNH	NH
53241	IC			PED	ED
53242	IC			PHA	HA
53243	IC			PHA	HA
53244	IC			PHA	HA
53245	IC			PHA	HA

Class 101 Driving Motor Brake

Built: Metropolitan-Cammell 1957

Diagram	Type	Weight	Seats	Note
DQ2.03.2B	DMBS	32.5t	44	Refurbished

Engines: Two Leyland 150bhp (112kW) 6-cyl horizontal
Transmission: Four speed epicyclic gearbox/ carden shaft
Dimensions: 18.49m L × 2.82m W × 3.85m H
Maximum speed: 70mph
Brakes: Vacuum
AWS: Fitted

Veh No	Dia	SC	Liv	Pool	Dep
53247	2B			PLA	LA
53248	2B			PLA	LA

Class 101 Driving Motor Brake

Built: Metropolitan-Cammell 1957

Diagram	Type	Engine	Weight	Seats	Note
DQ2.02.2B	DMBS	AEC	32.5t	52	Refurbished, AWS
DQ2.02.2E	DMBS	Leyland	32.5t	52	Refurbished, AWS
DQ2.02.3E	DMBS	Leyland	32.5t	52	Refurbished

For full details see series commencing 53157.

Veh No	Dia	SC	Liv	Pool	Dep
53250	2E			PHA	HA
53251	2B	†#		PNH	NH
53253	2E	#		PHA	HA
53256	3E			PLA	LA
53257	2E	#		PHT	HT

Parcels Sector vehicles in this series.

Class 101 Driving Motor

Built: Metropolitan-Cammell 1957

Diagram	Type	Weight	Seats 1st	Seats Std	Toilets	Note
DP2.10.2H	DMS(L)	32.5t	—	65	1	Refurbished, Mk 2 bogies
DP3.17.0A	DMC(L)	32.5t	12	46	1	Refurbished

For full details see series commencing No 51495.

Veh No	*Dia*	*SC*	*Liv*	*Pool*	*Dep*
53260	2102H			*PHA*	HA
53263	2102H	#		*PHT*	HT
53264	2102H			*PNH*	NH
53265	3170A			*NSS*	RG
53266	2102H	LR		*PNC*	NC
53267	2102H	LR		*PNC*	NC
53268	2102H			*PHA*	HA
53269	2102H			*PHA*	HA

Class 101 Driving Motor Brake

Built: Metropolitan-Cammell 1957

Diagram	Type	Weight	Engine	Seats	Note
DQ2.02.2B	DMBS	32.5t	AEC	52	Refurbished Mk 2 bogies
DQ2.02.2E	DMBS	32.5t	Leyland	52	Refurbished Mk 2 bogies
DQ2.32.0B	DMBS	32.5t	Leyland	49	Refurbished Mk 2 bogies

For full details see series commencing No 53157.

Veh No	*Dia*	*SC*	*Liv*	*Pool*	*Dep*
53290	022B	†		*PHA*	HA
53291	022E			*PHA*	HA
53293	022E			*PNC*	NC
53294	022E			*PHA*	HA
53296	022E			*NGB*	OO
53303	022B	†#		*PCH*	CH
53305	022E	LR		*PNC*	NC
53306	022E	†		*PCH*	CH
53307	022E	†		*PCH*	CH
53308	320B			*NSS*	RG
53309	022B	†#		*PCH*	CH
53310	022E			*NSS*	RG
53311	022E			*NSS*	RG
53312	320B			*NSS*	RG
53314	320B			*NSS*	RG
53315	022E	L		*PLA*	LA
53317	022B	†#		*PCH*	CH
53318	022E	#		*PCH*	CH
53319	022E	L		*PCF*	CF

Class 101 Driving Motor

Built: Metropolitan-Cammell 1958

Diagram	Type	Weight	Seats 1st	Seats Std	Toilet	Note
DP2.10.1B	DMS(L)	32.5t	—	65	1	Mk 2 bogies
DP2.10.1D	DMS(L)	32.5t	—	65	1	Mk 3 bogies
DP2.10.2F	DMS(L)	32.5t	—	65	1	Refurbished, Mk 3 bogies
DP2.10.2H	DMS(L)	32.5t	—	65	1	Mk 2 bogies

DP3.04.2F	DMC(L)	32.5t	12	53	1	Refurbished
DP3.04.2H	DMC(L)	32.5t	12	53	1	Mk 3 bogies, Refurbished
DP3.17.0B	DMC(L)	32.5t	12	53	1	Mk 2 bogies, Refurbished

For full details see series commencing No 51495.

Veh No	*Dia*	*SC*	*Liv*	*Pool*	*Dep*
53321	2102H	LR		*PNC*	NC
53322	3042H			*NSS*	RG
53323	2102H			*PCH*	CH
53324	2102H	#		*PCH*	CH
53325	2101B			*PCH*	CH
53326	3170B			*NSS*	RG
53327	3170B			*NSS*	RG
53330	2102F	L		*PLA*	LA
53331	3170B			*NSS*	RG
53332	3170B			*NSS*	RG
53333	3042F			*NSS*	RG
53334	2101D			*PNH*	NH
53335	2102H	L		*PNL*	NL
53336	2102F			*PCH*	CH
53337	2101D	#		*PCH*	CH
53338	2102H	#		*PCH*	CH

Class 100 — Driving Motor Brake

Built: Gloucester RC&W Co 1957

Diagram	**Type**	**Weight**	**Seats**
DQ2.01.1A	DMBS	30.5t	52

Engines: Two AEC 150bhp (112kW) 6-cyl horizontal
Transmission: Four speed epicyclic gearbox/ carden shaft
Dimensions: 18.49m L × 2.82m W × 3.85m H
Maximum speed: 70mph
Brakes: Vacuum
AWS: Fitted

Veh No	*Dia*	*SC*	*Liv*	*Pool*	*Dep*
53355	1A			*PNH*	NH

Class 105 — Driving Motor Brake

Built: Cravens
Parcels Sector vehicles in this series Nos 53361-73.

Class 104 — Driving Motor Brake

Built: Birmingham RC&W Co 1957

Design Code	**Type**	**Weight**	**Seats**
DQ2.05.1A	DMBS	31.5t	52

Engines: Two Leyland 150bhp (112kW) 6-cyl horizontal
Transmission: Four speed epicyclic gearbox/ carden shaft

Dimensions: 18.49m L × 2.82m W × 3.84m H
Maximum speed: 70mph
Brakes: Vacuum
AWS: Fitted

Veh No	*Dia*	*SC*	*Liv*	*Pool*	*Dep*
53421	1A			*PNH*	NH

Series continued with No 53429 below.

Class 104 Driving Motor

Built: Gloucester RC&W Co 1957

Design Code	**Type**	**Weight**	**Seats**	**Toilet**
DP2.09.1A	DMS(L)	31.5t	66	1

Engines: Two Leyland 150bhp (112kW) 6-cyl horizontal
Transmission: Four speed epicyclic gearbox/ carden shaft
Dimensions: 18.49m L × 2.82m W × 3.84m H
Maximum speed: 70mph
Brakes: Vacuum
AWS: Fitted
Window bars fitted: 53425

Veh No	*Dia*	*SC*	*Liv*	*Pool*	*Dep*
53425	1A			*PNH*	NH
53427	IA			*PCP*	CP(s)

Series continued with No 53487.

Class 104 Driving Motor Brake

Built: Birmingham RC&W Co 1957

Design Code	**Type**	**Weight**	**Seats**	**AWS**
DQ2.05.0A	DMBS	31.5t	52	Not fitted
DQ2.05.1A	DMBS	31.5t	52	Fitted

For full details see No 53421 above.
Window bars fitted: 53431/42/43/54/65/66/68/70/72/76

Veh No	*Dia*	*SC*	*Liv*	*Pool*	*Dep*
53429	1A			*NGB*	00
53431	1A			*PNH*	NH
53437	1A			*NGB*	00
53439	1A			*PNH*	NH
53442	1A			*PNH*	NH
53443	1A			*PNH*	NH
53444	1A			*PNH*	NH
53447	1A			*PNH*	NH
53451	1A			*PNH*	NH
53454	0A			*PNH*	NH
53455	1A		N	*NGB*	00
53460	1A			*PCP*	CP(s)
53464	1A			*PNH*	NH
53465	1A			*PNH*	NH
53466	1A			*PNH*	NH
53468	1A			*PNH*	NH
53470	1A			*NGB*	00
53472	1A			*PED*	ED

Veh No	Dia	SC	Liv	Pool	Dep
53474	1A			*PCP*	CP(s)
53476	1A			*PNH*	NH
53477	1A			*NGB*	00
53478	1A			*DXXZ*	ED
53479	1A			*NGB*	00

Series continued with No 53532.

Class 104 Driving Motor

Built: Birmingham RC&W Co 1957

Design Code	Type	Weight	Seats	Toilet	AWS
DP2.09.0A	DMS(L)	31.5t	66	1	Not fitted
DP2.09.1A	DMS(L)	31.5t	66	1	Fitted

Window bars fitted: 53493/94/96/99, 53500/11/12/16/28/31
For full details see series commencing No 53425.

Veh No	Dia	SC	Liv	Pool	Dep
53487	1A			*PNH*	NH
53492	1A			*PNH*	NH
53493	1A			*PNH*	NH
53494	1A			*PNH*	NH
53496	1A			*PCP*	CP(s)
53499	0A			*PNH*	NH
53500	1A			*PNH*	NH
53501	1A			*PCP*	CP(s)
53504	1A			*PNH*	NH
53507	1A			*PNH*	NH
53511	1A			*PNH*	NH
53512	1A			*PNH*	NH
53516	1A			*PNH*	NH
53517	1A			*PNH*	NH
53518	1A			*PNH*	NH
53520	1A			*PNH*	NH
53522	1A			*PNH*	NH
53528	0A			*PNH*	NH
53529	1A			*PNH*	NH
53530	1A			*DXXZ*	ED
53531	1A			*PNH*	NH

Class 104 Driving Motor Brake

Built: Birmingham RC&W Co 1958

Design Code	Type	Weight	Seats	AWS
DQ2.05.0A	DMBS	31.5t	52	Not fitted
DQ2.05.1A	DMBS	31.5t	52	Fitted

For full details see No 53421.

Veh No	Dia	SC	Liv	Pool	Dep
53532	1A			*PNH*	NH
53534	1A			*PNH*	NH
53536	1A			*PNH*	NH
53539	1A			*NGB*	00
53540	1A			*NGB*	00
53541	0A			*PNH*	NH

Class 104 — Driving Motor

Built: Birmingham RC&W Co 1958

Diagram	Type	Weight	Seats
DP2.17.1A	DMS(L)	31.5t	63

For full details see series commencing No 53425

Veh No	*Dia*	*SC*	*Liv*	*Pool*	*Dep*
53556	1A			*PNH*	NH

Class 108 — Driving Motor Brake

Built: British Railways Derby Carriage Works 1958

Diagram	Type	Weight	Seats	Note
DQ2.12.2B	DMBS	29.5t	52	Refurbished

Engines: Two Leyland 150bhp (112kW) 6-cyl horizontal
Transmission: Four speed epicyclic gearbox/carden shaft
Dimensions: 18.49m L × 2.79m W × 3.87m H
Maximum speed: 70mph
Brakes: Vacuum
AWS: Fitted

Veh No	*Dia*	*SC*	*Liv*	*Pool*	*Dep*
53599	2B			*NNL*	BY
53601	2B	#		*PNL*	NL
53602	2B			*PBR*	BR
53606	2B	#		*PNH*	NH
53607	2B	#		*PNL*	NL
53608	2B			*PBR*	BR
53612	2B			*PBR*	BR
53614	2B			*PBR*	BR
53616	2B			*PBR*	BR
53617	2B			*PCF*	CF
53618	2B			*PBR*	BR
53619	2B			*PBR*	BR
53620	2B			*PBR*	BR
53621	2B			*PBR*	BR
53622	2B			*PBR*	BR
53624	2B			*PCF*	CF
53625	2B	L		*PLE*	LE
53626	2B			*PBX*	BX
53627	2B			*PCF*	CF
53628	2B		N	*NNL*	BY
53629	2B			*PCF*	CF

Series continued with No 53924.

Class 108 — Driving Motor

Built: British Railways, Derby Carriage Works 1958

Diagram	Type	Weight	Seats	Toilet	Note
DQ2.19.0A	DMS(L)	28.5t	62	1	
DQ2.19.1B	DMS(L)	28.5t	62	1	Refurbished

Engines: Two Leyland 150bhp (112kW) 6-cyl horizontal
Transmission: Four speed epicyclic gearbox/carden shaft
Dimensions: 18.49m L × 2.82m W × 3.85m H.
Maximum speed: 70mph
Brakes: Vacuum
AWS: Fitted

Veh No	*Dia*	*SC*	*Liv*	*Pool*	*Dep*
53630	1B			*PHA*	HA
53631	1B			*PHA*	HA
53632	1B			*PHA*	HA
53633	1B	L		*PLE*	LE
53634	0A			*PBX*	BX
53635	1B			*PCF*	CF
53636	1B			*PBX*	BX
53637	1B			*PLA*	LA
53638	1B			*PLA*	LA
53639	1B			*PLA*	LA
53641	1B			*PHA*	HA
53642	1B			*PHA*	HA
53643	1B			*PHA*	HA
53644	1B			*PHA*	HA
53645	1B			*PHA*	HA
53646	1B			*PLA*	LA

Class 120 Driving Motor

Built: British Railways, Swindon Works 1957

Diagram	**Type**	**Weight**	**Seats**	**Note**	
DP2.04.0A	DMS(L)	37t	68	2	—
DP2.04.1C	DMS(L)	37t	68	2	Refurbished

Engines: Two AEC 150bhp (112kW) 6-cyl horizontal
Transmission: Four speed epicyclic gearbox/carden shaft
Dimensions: 20.45m L × 2.82m W × 3.84m H.
Maximum speed: 70mph
Brakes: Vacuum
AWS: Fitted

Veh No	*Dia*	*SC*	*Liv*	*Pool*	*Dep*
53658	0A	†		*PHA*	HA
53682	IC	†		*PHA*	HA
53686	IC	†		*PHA*	HA

Class 120 Driving Motor Brake

Built: British Railways, Swindon Works 1957

Diagram	**Type**	**Weight**	**Seats**	**Note**	
DQ2.--.0A	DMBS	36.5t	34	—	DQ3.03.0A
DQ2.--.1B	DMBS	36.5t	34	Refurbished	DQ3.03.1B

Engines: Two AEC 150bhp (112kW) 6-cyl horizontal

Dimensions: 20.45m L × 2.82m W × 3.84m H.
Maximum speed: 70mph

Transmission: Four speed epicyclic gearbox/ carden shaft

Brakes: Vacuum
AWS: Fitted

Veh No	*Dia*	*SC*	*Liv*	*Pool*	*Dep*
53699	1B			PHA	HA
53700	0A			PHA	HA
53732	1B			PHA	HA
53733	1B			PHA	HA

Class 101 — Driving Motor

Built: Metropolitan-Cammell 1957

Diagram	**Type**	**Weight**	**Engine**	**Seats 1st**	**Seats Std**	**Toilet**	**Note**
DP2.10.2E	DMS	32.5t	AEC	—	65	1	Refurbished
DP3.04.2H	DMC	32.5t	Leyland	12	53	1	Refurbished

For full details see series commencing No 51495.

Veh No	*Dia*	*SC*	*Liv*	*Pool*	*Dep*
53746	2102E	†		PHA	HA
53751	3042H			NSS	RG

Class 105 — Driving Motor

Built: Cravens 1957

Diagram	**Type**	**Weight**	**Seats**	**Toilet**
DQ2.11.1B	DMS	30t	63	1

Engines: Two Leyland 150bhp (112kW) 6-cyl horizontal
Transmission: Four speed epicyclic gearbox/ carden shaft

Dimensions: 18.49m L × 2.82m W × 3.77m H.
Maximum speed: 70mph
Brakes: Vacuum
AWS: Not fitted

Veh No	*Dia*	*SC*	*Liv*	*Pool*	*Dep*
53812	1B			PNH	NH

Class 116 — Driving Motor Brake

Built: British Railways, Derby Carriage Works 1957

Diagram	**Type**	**Weight**	**Seats**	**Note**
DQ2.19.1A	DMBS	36.5t	65	
DQ2.30.1A	DMBS	36.5t	65	Gangwayed
DQ2.30.2B	DMBS	36.5t	65	Gangwayed and Refurbished

For full details see series commencing No 53050.

Veh No	Dia	SC	Liv	Pool	Dep
53818	302B	G		PTS	TS
53820	302B	G	N	NGB	00
53822	302B	G		PTS	TS
53826	302B	G		PTS	TS
53827	302B	G		PTS	TS
53837	302B	G		PTS	TS
53838	302B	G		PTS	TS
53843	302B	G#		PCF	CF
53844	302B	G		PTS	TS
53848	302B	G#		PCF	CF
53849	302B	G		PTS	TS
53850	302B	G		PTS	TS
53853	302B	G		PTS	TS
53854	302B	G		PTS	TS
53855	302B	G#		PCF	CF
53858	302B	G		PCF	CF
53863	301A	G		PTS	TS
53865	302B	G		PTS	TS
53866	302B	G#		PNH	NH
53869	302B	G#		PNH	NH

Class 116 Driving Motor

Built: British Railways, Derby Carriage Works 1957

Diagram	Type	Weight	Seats	Note
DP2.01.1A	DMS	36.5t	95	
DP2.20.1A	DMS	36.5t	89	Gangwayed
DP2.20.2B	DMS	36.5t	89	Ganwayed and Refurbished

For full details see series commencing No 53092.

Veh No	Dia	SC	Liv	Pool	Dep
53873	202B	G		PTS	TS
53878	202B	G		PTS	TS
53880	202B	G		PTS	TS
53881	202B	G		PTS	TS
53886	202B	G		PTS	TS
53887	202B	G#		PNH	NH
53890	202B	G#		PTS	TS
53891	202B	G		PTS	TS
53893	202B	G		PTS	TS
53894	202B	G		PTS	TS
53897	202B	G		PTS	TS
53902	202B	G		PTS	TS
53907	202B	G		PTS	TS
53908	202B	G#		PCF	CF
53911	202B	G#		PCF	CF
53916	201A	G		PTS	TS
53919	202B	G		PTS	TS
53921	202B	G		PTS	TS
53922	202B	G#		PNH	NH

Class 108 Driving Motor Brake

Built: British Railways, Derby Carriage Works 1959

Diagram	Type	Weight	Seats	Note
DQ2.12.1A	DMBS	29.5t	52	
DQ2.12.2B	DMBS	29.5t	52	Refurbished

For full details see series commencing No 53599.
Special livery: Green: 53964

Veh No	*Dia*	*SC*	*Liv*	*Pool*	*Dep*
53924	2B			*PCH*	CH
53925	1A			*PBX*	BX
53926	2B	L		*PLE*	LE
53927	2B			*PCH*	CH
53928	2B	L		*PLE*	LE
53929	2B			*PCH*	CH
53930	1A			*PBX*	BX
53931	1A			*PCH*	CH
53932	2B			*PBX*	BX
53933	1A	L		*PHA*	HA
53934	2B			*PNH*	NH
53935	2B	L		*PLE*	LE
53938	2B			*PCH*	CH
53939	2B	L		*PLE*	LE
53940	2B			*PCH*	CH
53941	2B			*PBR*	BR
53942	2B	L		*PLE*	LE
53943	2B			*PNH*	NH
53944	2B			*PNH*	NH
53945	2B	L		*PLE*	LE
53947	2B	L		*PLE*	LE
53948	2B			*PNH*	NH
53949	2B			*PNH*	NH
53950	2B			*PHT*	HT
53951	1A			*PHT*	HT
53952	1A			*PHT*	HT
53953	1A			*PHT*	HT
53954	1A			*PHT*	HT
53955	1A			*PHT*	HT
53956	1A			*PHT*	HT
53957	1A			*PHT*	HT
53958	1A			*PHT*	HT
53959	1A			*PHT*	HT
53960	1A			*PHT*	HT
53962	1A			*PHT*	HT
53963	1A			*PHT*	HT
53964	1A		★	*PCH*	CH
53965	1A			*PCH*	CH
53966	1A			*PCH*	CH
53968	1A			*PCH*	CH
53969	2B			*PCH*	CH
53970	2B			*PNH*	NH
53971	2B			*PNH*	NH
53973	2B			*PHT*	HT
53974	2B			*PNH*	NH
53975	2B			*PNH*	NH
53976	2B			*PNH*	NH
53977	2B			*PNH*	NH
53978	2B			*PNH*	NH
53980	1A			*PNH*	NH
53981	2B			*PNH*	NH
53982	2B			*PNH*	NH
53983	2B			*PNH*	NH
53986	2B			*PCH*	CH
53987	1A			*PCH*	CH

Class 114 — Driving Trailer

Built: British Railways, Derby Carriage Works 1956

Diagram	**Type**	**Weight**	**Seats**	**Toilet**	**Note**
DS2.--.0A	DTS	30t	74	1	Refurbished, Official Diagram DS3.13.3B

Dimensions: 20.45m L × 2.35m W × 3.86m H. Gangwayed within unit
Maximum speed: 70mph

Brakes: Vacuum
AWS: Fitted

Veh No	Dia	SC	Liv	Pool	Dep
54006	0A			PTS	TS
54008	0A			PTS	TS
54009	0A			PTS	TS
54010	0A			PTS	TS
54011	0A			PTS	TS
54012	0A			PTS	TS
54013	0A			PTS	TS
54015	0A			PTS	TS
54019	0A			PTS	TS
54024	0A			PTS	TS
54027	0A			PTS	TS
54039	0A			PTS	TS
54043	0A			PTS	TS
54047	0A		#	PTS	TS

Parcels Sector vehicles in this series.

Class 101 Driving Trailer

Built: Metropolitan-Cammell 1957

Diagram	Type	Weight	Seats 1st	Seats Std	Toilet	Note
DS2.06.2B	DTS	25.5t	—	65	1	Refurbished
DS3.02.2B	DTC	25.5t	12	53	1	Refurbished

Dimensions: 18.49m L × 2.35m W × 3.85m H. Gangwayed within unit
Maximum speed: 70mph
Brakes: Vacuum
AWS: Fitted

Veh No	Dia	SC	Liv	Pool	Dep
54050	2062B			PNC	NC
54054	2062B			PCP	CPs
54055	2062B			PNC	NC
54056	2062B			PNH	NH
54060	2062B			PNC	NC
54061	2062B			PNH	NH
54062	2062B			PNC	NC
54065	2062B			PNC	NC
54068	3022B		N	NNE	CA
54070	3022B			NWR	OO
54071	2062B			PCP	CP
54073	2062B			PNC	NC
54075	2062B			PNH	NH
54080	2062B			PNC	NC
54081	2062B			PNH	NH
54085	2062B			PNH	NH

Series continued with No 54332.

Class 111 Driving Trailer

Built: Metropolitan-Cammell 1957

Diagram	Type	Weight	Seats	Toilet	Note
DS2.--.0A	DTS	25.5t	65	1	Refurbished. Official code DS3.12.1B

Dimensions: 18.49m L × 2.35m W × 3.85m H. Gangwayed within unit
Maximum speed: 70mph
Brakes: Vacuum
AWS: Fitted

Veh No	Dia	SC	Liv	Pool	Dep
54091	0A			PCH	CH

Class 108 Driving Trailer

Built: British Railways, Derby Carriage Works 1958

Diagram	Type	Weight	Seats 1st	Seats Std	Toilet	Note
DS2.07.2B	DTS	21.5t	—	65	1	Refurbished
DS3.10.2B	DTC	21.5t	12	53	1	Refurbished

Dimensions: 18.49m L × 2.79m W × 3.87m H. Gangwayed within unit
Maximum speed: 70mph
Brakes: Vacuum
AWS: Fitted

Veh No	*Dia*	*SC*	*Liv*	*Pool*	*Dep*
54191	2072B			*PBR*	BR
54194	3102B			*NNL*	BY
54196	2072B			*PNH*	NH
54197	2072B			*PBR*	BR
54201	2072B			*PBR*	BR
54202	2072B			*PBR*	BR
54203	2072B			*PBR*	BR
54204	2072B			*PBR*	BR
54205	2072B			*PBR*	BR
54207	2072B			*PBR*	BR
54208	2072B			*PBR*	BR
54209	2072B			*PBR*	BR
54210	2027B			*PCF*	CF
54212	2072B			*PCH*	CH
54213	3102B		N	*NMY*	BY
54214	2072B			*PCH*	CH

Class 101 Driving Trailer

Built: Metropolitan-Cammell 1957

Diagram	Type	Weight	Seats	Toilet	AWS	Note
DS2.10.1B	DTS	25.5t	57	1	Not fitted	Refurbished
DS2.10.1C	DTS	25.5t	57	1	Fitted	

Dimensions: 18.49m L × 2.35m W × 3.85m H.
Maximum speed: 70mph
Brakes: Vacuum

Veh No	*Dia*	*SC*	*Liv*	*Pool*	*Dep*
54218	1C			*PNC*	NC
54219	1B			*PCP*	CPs
54220	1C			*PNH*	NH

Class 108 Driving Trailer

Built: British Railways, Derby Carriage Works 1959

Diagram	Type	Weight	Seats 1st	Seats Std	Toilet	Note
DS2.07.1A	DTS	21.5t	—	65	1	
DS2.07.2B	DTS	21.5t	—	65	1	Refurbished
DS2.—.1A*	DTS	22.5t	—	65	1	Official code DS3.11.1A
DS2.—.2B*	DTS	22.5t	—	65	1	Refurbished. Official code DS3.11.2B
DS3.10.1A	DTC	21.5t	12	53	1	
DS3.10.2B	DTC	21.5t	12	53	1	Refurbished
DS3.11.1A*	DTC	22.5t	12	53	1	
DS3.11.2B*	DTC	22.5t	12	53	1	Refurbished

Dimensions: 18.49m L × 2.79m or 2.82m* W × 3.87m H. Gangwayed within unit
Maximum speed: 70mph
Brakes: Vacuum
AWS: Fitted
Special livery: Green 54247

Veh No	*Dia*	*SC*	*Liv*	*Pool*	*Dep*
54221	2072B			*PCH*	CH
54222	3102B			*NMY*	BY
54223	3102B			*NMY*	BY
54224	3102B			*NMY*	BY
54225	2072B			*PNH*	NH
54227	2072B			*PHT*	HT
54228	3102B			*NMY*	BY
54230	2072B			*PBR*	BR
54231	2072B			*PCH*	CH
54232	2072B			*PCH*	CH
54235	2071A			*PHT*	HT
54236	2071A			*PHT*	HT
54238	2071A			*PHT*	HT
54239	2071A			*PHT*	HT
54240	2071A			*PHT*	HT
54241	2071A			*PHT*	HT
54242	2071A			*PHT*	HT
54243	2071A			*PHT*	HT
54244	2071A			*PHT*	HT
54245	2071A			*PHT*	HT
54246	2072B			*PNH*	NH
54247	2071A		★	*PCH*	CH
54248	2071A			*PCH*	CH
54249	2071A			*PCH*	CH
54251	2071A			*PCH*	CH
54252	2072B			*PCH*	CH
54253	2072B			*PNH*	NH
54256	2071A			*PNH*	NH
54257	3102B			*NMY*	BY
54258	2072B			*PNH*	NH
54259	3102B			*NMY*	BY
54260	2072B			*PCH*	CH
54261	2072B			*PNH*	NH
54262	2072B			*PHT*	HT
54263	2072B			*PHT*	HT
54264	2072B			*PNH*	NH
54265	2071A			*PHT*	HT
54266	2072B			*PNH*	NH
54267	2072B			*PCF*	CF
54268	2072B			*PNH*	NH
54269	2072B			*PCH*	CH
54270	2071A			*PCH*	CH
54271	3112B			*NNL*	BY
54272	2—1A			*PCH*	CH
54273	2—2B			*PCH*	CH
54274	3112B			*NMY*	BY
54275	2—1A			*PCH*	CH
54276	2—1A			*PCH*	CH
54277	2—2B			*PCH*	CH
54278	2—2B			*PCH*	CH
54279	3112B			*NNL*	BY

Series continued with No 54484.

Class 121 — Driving Trailer

Built: Pressed Steel Co 1960

Diagram	Type	Weight	Seats	Note
DS2.01.1B	DTS	30t	91	Refurbished, Non-Gangwayed
DS2.—.1A	DTS	30t	89	Refurbished, Gangwayed within unit

Dimensions: 20.45m L × 2.82m W × 3.86m H.
Maximum speed: 70mph
Brakes: Vacuum
AWS: Fitted

Veh No	*Dia*	*SC*	*Liv*	*Pool*	*Dep*
54280	2011B			*NWR*	OO
54283	2011B		N	*NWR*	OO
54284	2011B			*PLA*	LA
54287	2—1A		N	*NWR*	OO
54289	2—1A		N	*NWR*	OO

Class 101 Driving Trailer

Built: Metropolitan-Cammell 1958

Diagram	Type	Weight	Seats 1st	Seats Std	Toilet	Note
DS2.06.1A	DTS	25.5t	—	65	1	
DS2.06.2B	DTS	25.5t	—	65	1	Refurbished
DS2.02.2B	DTC	25.5t	12	53	1	Refurbished

For details see series commencing No 54050.
AWS: Fitted

Veh No	*Dia*	*SC*	*Liv*	*Pool*	*Dep*
54332	2062B			*PNC*	NC
54335	2062B			*PNC*	NC
54340	2062B			*PNC*	NC
54342	2062B			*PNC*	NC
54343	2062B			*PNC*	NC
54345	2062B			*PHT*	HTs
54346	2062B			*PNC*	NC
54347	2062B			*PNC*	NC
54348	2062B			*PNC*	NC
54350	2062B			*PCP*	CPs
54351	2062B			*PNC*	NC
54352	2062B			*PNC*	NC
54354	2062B			*PNC*	NC
54355	2061A			*PNC*	NC
54358	3022B			*NNL*	BY
54362	2062B			*PNH*	NH
54363	2062B			*PNC*	NC
54365	2062B			*PNL*	NL
54367	2062B			*PCP*	CPs
54368	2062B			*PNC*	NC
54369	2062B			*PNC*	NC
54370	2062B			*PHT*	HT
54371	3022B		N	*NWR*	OO
54372	3022B			*NWR*	OO
54375	2062B			*PNH*	NH
54379	2062B			*PNC*	NC
54380	2062B			*PNC*	NC
54381	2062B			*PCP*	CPs
54382	3022B		N	*NNE*	CA
54385	3022B		N	*NWR*	OO
54387	2062B			*PNC*	NC
54388	2062B			*PNC*	NC
54391	2062B			*PHT*	HTs
54393	2062B			*PNC*	NC
54396	3022B			*NWR*	OO
54398	2062B			*PCP*	CPs
54399	2062B			*PNC*	NC
54401	2062B			*PCP*	CPs
54402	3022B		N	*NNE*	CA
54405	3022B		N	*NNE*	CA
54408	2062B			*PNH*	NH

Class 108 — Driving Trailer

Built: British Railways, Derby Carriage Works 1960

Diagram	Type	Weight	Seats 1st	Seats Std	Toilet	Note
DS2.--.1A*	DTS	22.5t	—	65	1	
DS2.--.2B*	DTS	22.5t	—	65	1	Refurbished, Official Code DS3.11.2B
DS3.11.1A*	DTC	22.5t	12	53	1	
DS3.11.2B*	DTC	22.5t	12	53	1	Refurbished

For full details see series commencing No 54221.

Veh No	Dia	SC	Liv	Pool	Dep
54484	2—2B			*PCH*	CH
54485	2—2B			*PCH*	CH
54486	2—2B			*PCH*	CH
54487	2—2B			*PCH*	CH
54488	2—2B			*PCH*	CH
54489	2—2B			*PCH*	CH
54490	2—2B			*PCH*	CH
54491	3112B			*NMY*	BY
54492	2—2B			*PBR*	BR
54493	3111A		N	*NNL*	BY
54494	2—2B			*PCH*	CH
54495	3112B			*NMY*	BY
54496	2—2B			*PCH*	CH
54497	2—2B			*PCH*	CH
54498	2—2B			*PCH*	CH
54499	3112B			*NMY*	BY
54500	3112B			*NMY*	BY
54501	2—2B			*PCH*	CH
54503	2—2B			*PNH*	NH
54504	2—1A			*PNH*	NH

Class 122 — Driving Motor Brake

Built: Gloucester RC&W Co 1958

Diagram	Type	Weight	Seats	Note
DQ2.22.0A	DMBS	36.5t	65	AWS not fitted
DQ2.22.1B	DMBS	36.5t	65	AWS fitted

Engines: Two AEC 150bhp (112kW) 6-cyl horizontal
Transmission: Four speed epicyclic gearbox/ carden shaft
Dimensions: 20.45m L × 2.82m W × 3.86m H. Non-gangwayed, side doors to each seating bay, driving cab each end
Maximum speed: 70mph
Brakes: Vacuum

Veh No	Dia	SC	Liv	Pool	Dep
55000	1B			*PLA*	LA
55003	1B			*PLA*	LA
55004	0A	#		*NNL*	BY
55005	1B			*PLA*	LA
55006	1B			*PLA*	LA
55009	1B			*PLA*	LA
55011	0A	#		*NNL*	BY
55012	1B			*PLA*	LA

Class 121 — Driving Motor Brake

Built: Pressed Steel Co 1960

Diagram	Type	Weight	Seats	Note
DQ2.21.1C	DMBS	38t	65	Refurbished

Engines: Leyland 150bhp (112kW) 6-cyl horizontal
Transmission: Four speed epicyclic gearbox/ carden shaft
Dimensions: 20.45m L × 2.82m W × 3.86m H. Non-gangwayed, side doors to each seating bay, driving cab each end
Maximum speed: ??mph
Brakes: Vacuum
AWS: Fitted
Special livery: WMPTE (Midland): 55033

Veh No	*Dia*	*SC*	*Liv*	*Pool*	*Dep*
55020	IC		N	*NWR*	OO
55021	IC		N	*NWR*	OO
55022	IC		N	*NWR*	OO
55023	IC			*NWR*	OO
55024	IC			*NWR*	OO
55025	IC			*NWR*	OO
55026	IC			*PLA*	LA
55027	IC			*NWR*	OO
55028	IC		N	*NWR*	OO
55029	IC		N	*NWR*	OO
55030	IC			*NWR*	OO
55031	IC		N	*NWR*	OO
55032	IC			*PTS*	TS
55033	IC		★	*PTS*	TS
55034	IC			*PTS*	TS

Railbus and Sprinter vehicles commence on page 56.
Parcels Sector Vehicles in the 559xx series, see pages 72/73.

Class 116 — Trailer

Built: British Railways Derby Carriage Works 1957

Diagram	Type	Weight	Seats	Note
DT2.09.1B	TS	29.5t	98	Refurbished

Dimensions: 19.58m L × 2.82m W × 3.86m H. Gangwayed throughout
Maximum speed: 70mph
Brakes: Vacuum

Veh No	*Dia*	*SC*	*Liv*	*Pool*	*Dep*
59032	1B			*PTS*	TS
59040	1B			*PHT*	HTs

Class 101 — Trailer

Built: Metropolitan-Cammell 1956

Diagram	Type	Weight	Seats	Toilet	Note
DT2.01.1B	TS	25.5t	61	1	Refurbished

Dimensions: 18.49m L × 2.82m W × 3.85m H. Gangwayed throughout
Maximum speed: 70mph
Brakes: Vacuum

Veh No	*Dia*	*SC*	*Liv*	*Pool*	*Dep*
59042	1B			*PHA*	HA

Series continued with No 59061.

Class 101 — Trailer Brake

Built: Metropolitan-Cammell 1956

Diagram	Type	Weight	Seats	Toilet	Note
DU2.02.1B	TBS	25.5t	45	1	Refurbished

Dimensions: 18.49m L × 2.82m W × 3.85m H. Gangwayed throughout
Maximum speed: 70mph
Brakes: Vacuum

Veh No	*Dia*	*SC*	*Liv*	*Pool*	*Dep*
59049	1B		S	*PED*	ED
59050	1B			*PLE*	LE
59055	1B			*PNC*	NC

Series continued with No 59073.

Class 101 — Trailer

Built: Metropolitan-Cammell 1957

Diagram	Type	Weight	Seats	Toilet	Note
DT2.02.1B	TS	25.5t	71	1	Refurbished

For full details see No 59042.

Veh No	*Dia*	*SC*	*Liv*	*Pool*	*Dep*
59061	1B			*PHA*	HA
59065	1B			*PHA*	HA
59072	1B			*PHA*	HA

Series continued with No 59086.

Class 101 — Trailer Brake

Built: Metropolitan-Cammell 1956

Diagram	Type	Weight	Seats	Toilet	Note
DU2.03.1B	TBS	25.5t	53	1	Refurbished

For full details see series commencing No 59049.

Veh No	*Dia*	*SC*	*Liv*	*Pool*	*Dep*
59073	1B			*PHA*	HA
59074	1B		S	*PED*	ED
59077	1B			*PNC*	NC
59078	1B			*PNL*	NL
59079	1B			*PNC*	NC
59080	1B			*PHA*	HA
59084	1B			*PNC*	NC
59085	1B			*PNC*	NC

Series continued with No 59092.

Class 101 — Trailer

Built: Metropolitan-Cammell 1957

Diagram	Type	Weight	Seats	Toilet	Note
DT2.01.1B	TS	25.5t	61	1	Refurbished
DT2.28.0A	TS	25.5t	58	1	Refurbished

For full details see No 59042.

Veh No	*Dia*	*SC*	*Liv*	*Pool*	*Dep*
59086	011B			*PHA*	HA
59090	011B		S	*PED*	ED
59091	280A			*NSS*	RG

Series continued with No 59101.

Class 101 — Trailer Brake

Built: Metropolitan-Cammell 1957

Diagram	Type	Weight	Seats	Toilet	Note
DU2.02.1B	TBS	25.5t	45	1	Refurbished

For full details see series commencing No 59049.

Veh No	*Dia*	*SC*	*Liv*	*Pool*	*Dep*
59092	1B			*PNC*	NC
59093	1B			*PNL*	NL
59095	1B			*PNC*	NC
59096	1B			*PNL*	NL

Series continued with No 59113.

Class 101 Trailer

Built: Metropolitan-Cammell 1957

Diagram	Type	Weight	Seats	Toilet	Note
DT2.02.1B	TS	25.5t	71	1	Refurbished
DT2.28.0A	TS	25.5t	58	1	Refurbished

For full details see No 59042.

Veh No	*Dia*	*SC*	*Liv*	*Pool*	*Dep*
59101	280A			*NSS*	RG
59104	021B			*PHA*	HA
59105	021B			*NSB*	RG
59107	021B			*PHA*	HA

Series continued with No 59302.

Class 101 Trailer Brake

Built: Metropolitan-Cammell 1957

Diagram	Type	Weight	Seats	Toilet	Note
DU2.03.1B	TBS	25.5t	53	1	Refurbished

For full details see series commencing No 59049.

Veh No	*Dia*	*SC*	*Liv*	*Pool*	*Dep*
59113	1B	*#*		*PHA*	HA

Class 101 Trailer

Built: Metropolitan-Cammell 1958

Diagram	Type	Weight	Seats	Toilet	Note
DT2.20.1D	TS	25.5t	65	1	Refurbished, Mk 4 bogies
DT2.28.0A	TS	25.5t	58	1	Refurbished, Mk 1 bogies
DT2.28.0B	TS	25.5t	58	1	Refurbished, Mk 4 bogies

For full details see series commencing No 59034.

Veh No	*Dia*	*SC*	*Liv*	*Pool*	*Dep*
59115	280A			*NSS*	RG
59116	201D			*PHA*	HA
59117	201D			*NSS*	RG
59118	201D			*PLA*	LA
59124	201D			*PHA*	HA
59125	280B			*NSS*	RG
59128	201D			*NSS*	RG
59130	201D			*PLA*	LA

Series continued with No 59525.

Class 104 Trailer

Built: Birmingham RC&W Co 1957

Diagram	Type	Weight	Seats	Toilet
DT2.03.1A	DTS	24.5t	69	1
DT2.18.0A	DTS	24.5t	66	1

Dimensions: 18.49m L × 2.82m W × 3.81m H. Gangwayed throughout
Maximum speed: 70mph
Brakes: Vacuum

Veh No	*Dia*	*SC*	*Liv*	*Pool*	*Dep*
59137	180A			*PBX*	BX
59144	180A			*PBX*	BX
59148	180A			*PBX*	BX
59149	180A			*PBX*	BX
59152	180A			*PBX*	BX
59153	180A			*PHA*	HA
59155	180A			*PBX*	BX
59163	180A			*NNL*	BY
59168	180A			*PNL*	NL
59183	180A			*PBX*	BX
59187	180A			*PBX*	BX
59195	031A			*PCP*	CPs
59206	031A			*NNL*	BY
59207	031A			*PBX*	BX

Class 104 Trailer Brake

Built: Birmingham RC&W Co 1958

Diagram	Type	Weight	Seats	Toilet
DU2.04.0A	TBS	25.5t	51	1

Dimensions: 18.49m L × 2.82m W × 3.81m H. Gangwayed throughout
Maximum speed: 70mph
Brakes: Vacuum

Veh No	*Dia*	*SC*	*Liv*	*Pool*	*Dep*
59228	0A			*PNH*	NH

Class 108 Trailer Brake

Built: British Railways, Derby Carriage Works 1958

Diagram	Type	Weight	Seats	Toilet
DU2.01.1B	TBS	23.5T	50	1

Dimensions: 18.49m L × 2.79m W × 3.87m H. Gangwayed throughout
Maximum speed: 70mph
Brakes: Vacuum

Veh No	*Dia*	*SC*	*Liv*	*Pool*	*Dep*
59245	1B			*PHA*	HA
59246	1B			*PNL*	NL
59248	1B			*PHA*	HA
59249	1B			*PNL*	NL
59250	1B			*PNL*	NL

Class 101 — Trailer

Built: Metropolitan-Cammell 1957

Diagram	Type	Weight	Seats	Toilet	Note
DT2.02.1B	TS	25.5t	71	1	Refurbished

For full details see series commencing No 59042.

Veh No	*Dia*	*SC*	*Liv*	*Pool*	*Dep*
59302	1B			*PHA*	HA
59303	1B			*PHA*	HA
59304	1B			*PHA*	HA
59305	1B			*PHA*	HA
59306	1B			*NSS*	RG

Class 116 — Trailer

Built: British Railways, Derby Carriage Works 1957

Diagram	Type	Weight	Seats	Note
DT2.15.1B	TS	29t	102	Refurbished
DT2.19.0A	TS	29t	88	Gangwayed
DT2.19.1B	TS	29t	88	Refurbished, Gangwayed

Dimensions: 19.58m L × 2.82m W × 3.86m H. Some gangwayed throughout (G)

Maximum speed: 70mph

Brakes: Vacuum

Veh No	*Dia*	*SC*	*Liv*	*Pool*	*Dep*
59330	91B	G		*PCP*	CPs
59335	91B	G		*PTS*	TS
59344	90A	G		*PTS*	TS
59353	91B	G		*PTS*	TS
59367	51B			*PTS*	TS

Series continued with No 59442.

Class 108 — Trailer

Built: British Railways, Derby Carriage Works 1958

Diagram	Type	Weight	Seats	Toilet	Note
DT2.05.1B	TS	22.5t	68	1	Refurbished
DT2.06.0A*	TS	2.5t	68	1	
DT2.06.1B*	TS	2.5t	68	1	Refurbished

Dimensions: 15.41m L × 2.79m W × 3.87m H. Gangwayed throughout

Maximum speed: 70mph

Brakes: Vacuum

Veh No	*Dia*	*SC*	*Liv*	*Pool*	*Dep*
59380	51B			*PLE*	LE
59381	51B			*PLE*	LE
59382	51B			*PLE*	LE
59383	51B			*PLE*	LE

Veh No	Dia	SC	Liv	Pool	Dep
59384	51B			*PLE*	LE
59385	51B			*PLE*	LE
59386	61B			*PHA*	HA
59387	61B			*PHA*	HA
59388	60A			*PBX*	BX
59389	61B			*PBX*	BX
59390	61B			*PBX*	BX

Class 119 Trailer

Built: Gloucester RC&W Co 1958

Diagram	Type	Weight	Seats	Toilet
DT2.16.0A	TS	31.5t	60	2

Dimensions: 19.81m L × 2.82m W × 3.86m H. Originally fitted with miniature buffet at one end. Buffet area converted to provide luggage space

Maximum speed: 70mph
Brakes: Vacuum

Veh No	Dia	SC	Liv	Pool	Dep
59416	0A			*NWR*	RG
59419	0A			*NSS*	RG
59421	0A		N	*NWR*	RG
59424	0A			*NSB*	RG
59425	0A			*NSS*	RG
59430	0A			*NWR*	RG
59435	0A		N	*NWR*	RG
59437	0A		N	*NSS*	RG

Class 116 Trailer

Built: British Railways Derby Carriage Works 1958

Diagram	Type	Weight	Seats	Note
DT2.19.1B	TS	29t	88	Refurbished and Gangwayed

For full details see series commencing No 59330.

Veh No	Dia	SC	Liv	Pool	Dep
59442	91B	G		*PTS*	TS
59444	91B	G		*PTS*	TS
59445	91B	G		*PTS*	TS
59446	91B	G		*PTS*	TS
59448	91B	G		*PTS*	TS

Class 118 Trailer

Built: Birmingham RC&W Co 1960

Diagram	Type	Weight	Seats	Note	
DT2.—.0A	TS	30.5t	70	2	Official code DT3.05.0A
DT2.—.1B	TS	30.5t	70	2	Refurbished. Official code DT3.05.1B

Dimensions: 20.45m L × 2.82m W × 3.86m H. Gangwayed throughout

Maximum speed: 70mph
Brakes: Vacuum

Veh No	Dia	SC	Liv	Pool	Dep
59469	0A			*PCF*	CF
59473	1B			*PTS*	TS
59481	0A			*PTS*	TS
59482	0A			*PLA*	LA
59483	1B			*PTS*	TS

Class 117 Trailer

Built: Pressed Steel Co 1959

Diagram	Type	Weight	Seats 1st	Seats Std	Toilet	Note
DT2.—.1C	TS	30.5t	—	70	2	Refurbished. Official code DT3.05.1C
DT3.05.1C	TC	30.5t	22	48	2	Refurbished

Dimensions: 20.45m L × 2.82m W × 3.86m H. Gangwayed througout
Maximum speed: 70mph

Brakes: Vacuum
Special livery: GWR chocolate and cream: 59520

Veh No	Dia	SC	Liv	Pool	Dep
59484	3051C			*NWR*	RG
59485	3051C		N	*NWR*	RG
59486	2—1C			*PTS*	TS
59487	3051C		N	*NWR*	RG
59488	3051C		N	*NWR*	RG
59489	3051C			*NWR*	RG
59490	2—1C			*PTS*	TS
59491	3051C		N	*NWR*	RG
59492	2—1C			*PTS*	TS
59493	3051C		N	*NWR*	RG
59494	3051C		N	*NWR*	RG
59495	3051C		N	*NWR*	RG
59496	3051C		N	*NWR*	RG
59497	3051C			*NWR*	RG
59498	3051C		N	*NWR*	RG
59499	3051C		N	*NWR*	RG
59500	2—1C			*PTS*	TS
59501	3051C		N	*NWR*	RG
59502	3051C		N	*NWR*	RG
59503	3051C		N	*NWR*	RG
59504	2—1C			*PTS*	TS
59505	2—1C			*PTS*	TS
59506	3051C		N	*NWR*	RG
59507	3051C		N	*NWR*	RG
59508	3051C		N	*NWR*	RG
59509	2—1C			*PTS*	TS
59510	3051C		N	*NWR*	RG
59511	3051C		N	*NWR*	RG
59512	2—1C			*PTS*	TS
59513	3051C			*NWR*	RG
59514	3051C		N	*NWR*	RG
59515	3051C			*NWR*	RG
59516	2—1C			*PTS*	TS
59517	2—1C			*PTS*	TS
59518	3051C		N	*NWR*	RG
59519	3051C		N	*NWR*	RG
59520	2—1C		★	*PTS*	TS
59521	2—1C			*PTS*	TS
59522	2—1C			*PTS*	TS

Class 101 Trailer

Built: Metropolitan-Cammell 1959

Diagram	Type	Weight	Seats	Toilet	Note
DT2.02.1B	TS	25.5t	71	1	Refurbished. Mk 1 Bogies
DT2.20.1B	TS	25.5t	65	1	Refurbished. Mk 1 Bogies
DT2.20.1D	TS	25.5t	65	1	Refurbished. Mk 4 Bogies
DT2.28.1C	TS	25.5t	58	1	Refurbished. Mk 1 Bogies

For full details see series commencing No 59032.

Veh No	*Dia*	*SC*	*Liv*	*Pool*	*Dep*
59525	201B			*PHA*	HA
59526	201B			*NSS*	RG
59530	201D			*NSS*	RG
59532	201B			*PHA*	HA
59536	201D			*PNC*	NC
59539	201D			*PCF*	CF
59540	201B			*NSS*	RG
59542	201B		S	*PED*	ED
59543	201D			*NSS*	RG
59561	201D			*PLA*	LA
59565	201D			*PWY*	NL
59570	281C			*NSS*	RG
59571	021B			*PHA*	HA

Series continued with No 59688.

Class 127 Trailer

Built: British Railways, Derby Carriage Works 1959

Diagram	Type	Weight	Seats	Toilet	Note
DT2.26.0A	TS	30.5t	86	2	
DT2.26.1B	TS	30.5t	86	2	Refurbished

Dimensions: 20.45m L × 2.82m W × 3.86m H. Gangwayed throughout

Maximum speed: 70mph

Brakes: Vacuum

Veh No	*Dia*	*SC*	*Liv*	*Pool*	*Dep*
59589	1B			*PTS*	TS
59590	0A			*PTS*	TS
59591	1B			*PTS*	TS
59592	1B			*PTS*	TS
59593	1B			*PTS*	TS
59594	1B			*PTS*	TS
59595	0A			*PTS*	TS
59596	0A			*PTS*	TS
59597	1B			*PTS*	TS
59598	0A			*PTS*	TS
59600	0A			*PTS*	TS
59602	1B			*PTS*	TS
59603	1B			*PTS*	TS
59604	1B			*PTS*	TS
59606	0A			*PTS*	TS
59607	0A			*PTS*	TS
59608	1B			*PTS*	TS
59609	0A			*PTS*	TS
59610	0A			*PTS*	TS
59611	0A			*PTS*	TS
59612	0A			*PTS*	TS
59613	0A			*PTS*	TS
59614	0A			*PTS*	TS
59615	0A			*PTS*	TS
59616	1B			*PTS*	TS
59617	0A			*PTS*	TS

Class 127 Trailer

Built: British Railways, Derby Carriage Works 1959

Diagram	Type	Weight	Seats	Note
DT2.08.0A	TS	29.5t	106	
DT2.08.1D	TS	29.5t	106	Refurbished
DT2.29.1D	TS	30.5t	98	Refurbished, Gangwayed

Dimensions: 20.45m L × 2.82m W × 3.86m H. Some gangwayed throughout (G)

Maximum speed: 70mph
Brakes: Vacuum

Veh No	*Dia*	*SC*	*Liv*	*Pool*	*Dep*
59621	081D			*PCP*	CPs
59622	080A			*PCP*	CPs
59625	291D	G		*PTS*	TS
59627	080A			*PCP*	CPs
59629	291D	G		*PTS*	TS
59631	080A			*PCP*	CPs
59632	291D	G		*PTS*	TS
59641	291D	G		*PTS*	TS
59643	291D	G		*PTS*	TS
59648	291D	G		*PTS*	TS

Class 115 Trailer

Built: British Railways, Derby Carriage Works 1960

Diagram	Type	Weight	Seats 1st	Seats Std	Toilet	Note
DT2.08.0B	TS	29.5t	—	106		
DT2.08.1C	TS	29.5t	—	106		Refurbished
DT2.27.1B	TS	30.5t	—	70	2	Refurbished
DT2.29.1C	TS	30.5t	—	98		Refurbished, Gangwayed
DT2.—.0A	TS	30.5t	—	66	2	Gangwayed
DT2.—.1B	TS	30.5t	—	66	2	Refurbished, Gangwayed
DT3.03.1B	TC	30.5t	30	40	2	Refurbished

Dimensions: 20.45m L × 2.82m W × 3.86m H. Non-gangwayed, except where shown (G)

Maximum speed: 70mph
Brakes: Vacuum

Veh No	*Dia*	*SC*	*Liv*	*Pool*	*Dep*
59651	2081C			*NMY*	BY
59652	2081C			*NMY*	BY
59653	2080B			*PCP*	CPs
59654	2081C		N	*NMY*	BY
59655	2080B			*NMY*	BY
59656	2080B			*NMY*	BY
59657	2081C			*NMY*	BY
59658	2291C	G		*PTS*	TS
59659	2081C			*NMY*	BY
59660	2081C			*NMY*	BY
59661	2291C	G		*PTS*	TS
59662	2081C			*NMY*	BY
59663	2081C			*NMY*	BY
59664	3031B			*NMY*	BY
59665	3031B			*NMY*	BY
59666	2271B	D		*PCP*	CPs

Veh No	Dia	SC	Liv	Pool	Dep
59667	3031B			NMY	BY
59668	2—1B	G		PTS	TS
59669	3031B			NMY	BY
59670	2—0A	G		PTS	TS
59671	3031B			NMY	BY
59672	2—1B	G		PTS	TS
59673	2—0A	G		PTS	TS
59674	2—0A	G		PTS	TS
59675	3031B			NMY	BY
59676	3031B			NMY	BY
59677	2—0A	G		PTS	TS
59678	3031B			NMY	BY

Series continued with No 59713.

Class 101 Trailer

Built: Metropolitan-Cammell 1959

Diagram	Type	Weight	Seats	Toilet	Note
DT2.20.1D	TS	25.5t	65	1	Refurbished

For full details see series commencing No 59034.

Veh No	Dia	SC	Liv	Pool	Dep
59688	1D			PHA	HA
59690	1D			PNL	NL

Class 110 Trailer

Built: Birmingham RC&W Co 1961

Diagram	Type	Weight	Seats	Toilet	Note
DT2.07.1B	TS	24.5t	72	1	Refurbished

Dimensions: 18.48m L × 2.82m W × 3.88m H. Gangwayed throughout

Maximum speed: 70mph

Brakes: Vacuum

Veh No	Dia	SC	Liv	Pool	Dep
59694	1B			PNL	NL
59696	1B			PHA	HA
59697	1B			PHA	HA
59701	1B			PHA	HA
59709	1B			PCF	CF
59710	1B			PHA	HA

Series continued with No 59809.

Class 115 Trailer

Built: British Railways, Derby Carriage Works 1960

Diagram	Type	Weight	Seats 1st	Seats Std	Toilet	Note
DT2.08.0B	TS	29.5t	—	106		
DT2.08.1C	TS	29.5t	—	106		Refurbished
DT2.27.1B	TS	30.5t	—	70		Refurbished
DT2.29.1B	TS	30.5t	—	98		Gangwayed
DT2.—.0A	TS	30.5t	—	66	2	Gangwayed
DT2.—.1B	TS	30.5t	—	66	2	Refurbished, Gangwayed
DT3.03.0A	TC	30.5t	30	40	2	
DT3.03.1B	TC	30.5t	30	40	2	Refurbished

For details see series commencing No 59651.

Veh No	*Dia*	*SC*	*Liv*	*Pool*	*Dep*
59713	2291B	G		*PTS*	TS
59715	2081C			*PCP*	CPs
59716	2081C			*PCP*	CPs
59717	2080B			*PCP*	CPs
59719	2—1B	G		*PTS*	TS
59720	2—0A	G		*PTS*	TS
59721	2—0A	G		*PTS*	TS
59722	2—0A	G		*PTS*	TS
59723	2—0A	G		*PTS*	TS
59724	2—0A	G		*PTS*	TS
59725	2081C			*PCP*	CPs
59726	2291C	G		*PTS*	TS
59727	2081C		N	*NMY*	BY
59728	2081C			*NMY*	BY
59729	2081C		N	*NMY*	BY
59731	2081C			*NMY*	BY
59732	2081C		N	*NMY*	BY
59733	2081C			*NMY*	BY
59734	2291C	G		*NNL*	BY
59735	2291C	G		*NNL*	BY
59736	2081C			*NMY*	BY
59737	2081C			*NMY*	BY
59738	2081C			*NMY*	BY
59739	2081C			*NMY*	BY
59740	2081C			*NMY*	BY
59741	2291C	G		*PTS*	TS
59743	2291C	G		*PTS*	TS
59744	2080B			*PCP*	CPs
59745	2270A	G		*PTS*	TS
59746	3031B			*NMY*	BY
59747	3031B			*NMY*	BY
59748	2271B			*PCP*	CPs
59749	3031B			*NMY*	BY
59750	3031B			*NMY*	BY
59751	2270A	G		*PTS*	TS
59752	3030A			*NMY*	BY
59753	2—0A	G		*PTS*	TS
59754	3030A			*NMY*	BY
59755	3031B		N	*NMY*	BY
59756	2—0A	G		*PTS*	TS
59757	2—0A	G		*PTS*	TS
59758	3030A			*NMY*	BY
59759	3031B			*NMY*	BY
59760	2—1B	G		*PTS*	TS
59761	3031B			*NMY*	BY
59762	3031B		N	*NMY*	BY
59763	3031B			*NMY*	BY
59764	3031B			*NMY*	BY

Class 107 — Trailer

Built: British Railways, Derby Carriage Works 1960

Diagram	Type	Weight	Seats	Toilet	Note
DT2.04.0A	TS	28.5t	71	1	
DT2.04.1B	TS	28.5t	71	1	Refurbished

Dimensions: 18.49m L × 2.82m W × 3.87m H. Gangwayed throughout

Maximum speed: 70mph

Brakes: Vacuum

Veh No	Dia	SC	Liv	Pool	Dep
59782	1B		S	PED	ED
59783	1B		S	PED	ED
59784	1B		S	PED	ED
59785	1B		S	PHA	HA
59786	1B		S	PHA	HA
59789	1B			PHA	HA
59790	1B		S	PED	ED
59791	1B			PHA	HA
59792	1B		S	PED	ED
59793	1B		S	PED	ED
59794	0A			PHA	HA
59795	1B			PED	ED
59796	1B			PED	ED
59797	1B			PHA	HA
59798	1B		S	PED	ED
59800	1B			PHA	HA
59801	1B		S	PED	ED
59802	1B		S	PED	ED
59803	1B		S	PED	ED
59804	1B		S	PED	ED
59805	1B			PED	ED
59806	1B		S	PED	ED
59807	1B		S	PED	ED

Class 110 Trailer

Built: Birmingham RC&W Co 1961

Diagram	Type	Weight	Seats	Toilet	Note
DT2.07.1B	TS	24.5t	72	1	Refurbished

For full details see Series commencing No 59694.

Veh No	Dia	SC	Liv	Pool	Dep
59809	1B			PHA	HA
59810	1B			PHA	HA
59812	1B			PCP	CPs
59817	1B			PHA	HA

Class 111 Driving Motor

Built: Metropolitan-Cammell 1957-59 (Modified 1982)

Diagram	Type	Weight	Engine	Seats	Toilet	Note
DW2.01.1B	DHS	32t	RR138B	65	1	Refurbished Mk 2 Bogies, official diagram DW3.01.1B
DW2.02.1B	DHS	32t	RR138C	65	1	Refurbished Mk 3 Bogies, official diagram DW3.02.1B

Engine: One Rolls-Royce 180hp (134kW) 6-cyl horizontal
Transmission: Four speed epicyclic gearbox, cardan shaft
Dimensions: 18.49m L × 2.82m W × 3.88m H, Gangwayed within unit.

Maximum speed: 70mph
Brakes: Vacuum
AWS: Fitted

Veh No	Dia	SC	Liv	Pool	Dep
78709	11B			PNL	NL
78711	11B			PNL	NL
78712	11B			PNL	NL
78713	11B			PNL	NL
78714	11B			PNL	NL
78717	21B			PNL	NL
78718	21B			PNL	NL
78719	21B			PNL	NL
78722	21B			PNL	NL

Class 111 — Driving Motor Brake

Built: Metropolitan-Cammell 1957-59 (Modified 1982)

Diagram	Type	Weight	Engine	Seats	Note
DY2.02.1C	DHBS	31t	RR138B	52	Refurbished Mk 2 Bogies
DY2.02.1D	DHBS	31t	RR138B	52	Refurbished Mk 3 Bogies
DY2.03.0A	DHBS	32t	RR138C	52	Refurbished Mk 3 Bogies

Engine: One Rolls-Royce 180hp (134kW) 6-cyl horizontal
Transmission: Four speed epicyclic gearbox, cardan shaft
Dimensions: 18.49m L × 2.82m W × 3.88m H, Gangwayed within unit.
Maximum speed: 70mph
Brakes: Vacuum
AWS: Fitted

Veh No	Dia	SC	Liv	Pool	Dep
78959	21C			PNL	NL
78960	21D			PNL	NL
78961	21D			PNL	NL
78962	21C			PNL	NL
78964	21C			PNL	NL
78967	30A			PNL	NL
78968	30A			PNL	NL
78969	30A			PNL	NL
78971	30A			PNL	NL

RAIL BUSES

Class 140 — 2-CAR

Built: British Rail, Derby Carriage Works, 1981
Development of LEV railbus. Vehicles mounted on 4-wheel underframes, and fitted with folding doors

Diagram	Type	Toilet	Seats
DP2.22.0A	DMSA(L)	1	50
DP2.23.0A	DMSB	—	52

Driving Motor Standard: DMSB
Driving Motor Standard: DMSA(L)
Engine: Leyland TL11 of 200bhp (152kW)
Transmission: Mechanical. SCG 4-speed epicyclic reversable gearbox/cardan shaft
Body: 16.20m L × 2.75m W × 3.91m H. Gangwayed throughout
Weight: 23 tonnes
Brakes: Air
AWS: Fitted
Maximum speed: 70mph

Unit No	SC	Pool	Dep	DMS	DMS(L)
140 001	v	PNL	NL (s)	55500	55501

Classes 141/0 & 141/1 — 2-CAR

Built: Leyland National/BREL Derby Works 1983
Development of Class 140. Modified Leyland bus bodies, mounted on 4-wheel rail chassis — fitted with folding doors. Class 141/1 modified 1988 by Alexander Barclay to operate in multiple with Classes 142-144

Diagram	Class	Type	Gearbox	Seats	Toilet	SC
DP2.28.0A	141/0	DMSA	SCG	50		
DP2.28.—	141/0	DMSA	Voith	50		V
DP2.2-.—	141/1	DMSA	SCG	50		
DP2.29.0A	141/0	DMSB(L)	SGG	44	1	
DP2.29.—	141/0	DMSB(L)	Voith	44	1	V
DP2.2-.—	141/1	DMSB(L)	SGG	44	1	

Driving Motor Standard: DMS
Driving Motor Standard: DMS(L)
Engine: Leyland TL11 of 200bhp (152kW)
Transmission: Mechanical. SCG or Voith 4-speed epicyclic reversable gearbox/cardan shaft
Body: 15.45m L × 2.75m W × 3.91m H. Gangwayed within unit
Weight: 21 tonnes
Brakes: Air
AWS: Fitted
Maximum speed: 75mph
Driving Motor Standard: DMS(L)
Details as above except
Weight: 21.5 tonnes
Livery: *West Yorkshire PTE* Class 141/1: Red and cream; Class 141/0: Green and cream

Class 141/1 Unit No	*Class 141/0* Unit No	SC	Pool	Dep	DMS	DMS(L)
141 101	(141 020)		PNL	NL	55521	55541
141 102	(141 001)		PNL	NL	55502	55522
141 103	(141 002)		PNL	NL	55503	55523
141 104	141 003		PNL	NL	55504	55524
141 105	(141 004)		PNL	NL	55505	55525
141 106	(141 005)		PNL	NL	55506	55526
141 107	(141 006)		PNL	NL	55507	55527
141 108	141 007		PNL	NL	55508	55528
141 109	(141 008)		PNL	NL	55509	55529
141 110	(141 009)		PNL	NL	55510	55530
141 111	(141 010)		PNL	NL	55511	55531
141 112	(141 011)		PNL	NL	55512	55532
141 113	(141 012)	v	PNL	NL	55513	55533
141 114	141 013		PNL	NL	55514	55534
141 115	(141 014)		PNL	NL	55515	55535
141 116	(141 015)		PNL	NL	55516	55536

Unit No	Unit No	SC	Pool	Dep	DMS	DMS(L)
141 117	(141 016)		*PNL*	NL	55517	55537
141 118	141 017		*PNL*	NL	55518	55538
141 119	(141 018)		*PNL*	NL	55519	55539
141 120	(141 019)		*PNL*	NL	55520	55540

Class 141/0 units not shown in parenthesis not so modified.

Class 142 2 CAR Pacers

Built: Associated Rail Technologies (Leyland/BREL Derby) 1985

Diagram	Type	Gearbox	Weight	Seats	Toilet	SC
DP2.34.0A	DMS	SCG	24.5t	62		
DP2.34.—	DMS	Voith	24.5t	62		V
DP2.35.0A	DMS(L)	SCG	25t	59	1	
DP2.35.—	DMS(L)	Voith	25t	59	1	V

Driving Motor Standard: DMS
Engine: Leyland TL11 of 200bhp (152kW)
Transmission: Mechanical. SCG or Voith 4-speed epicyclic reversable gearbox/cardan shaft
Body: 15.55m L × 2.80m W × 3.86m H. Gangwayed within unit
Brakes: Air
AWS: Fitted
Maximum speed: 75mph
Livery: *Standard* Provincial Blue
Special: Greater Manchester PTE (Orange); 142 001-14
Western England (Brown and Cream): 142 015-27

Unit No	SC	Pool	Dep	DMS	DMS(L)
142 001		*PNH*	NH	55542	55592
142 002		*PNH*	NH	55543	55593
142 003		*PNH*	NH	55544	55594
142 004		*PNH*	NH	55545	55595
142 005		*PNH*	NH	55546	55596
142 006		*PNH*	NH	55547	55597
142 007		*PNH*	NH	55548	55598
142 008		*PNH*	NH	55549	55599
142 009		*PNH*	NH	55550	55600
142 010		*PNH*	NH	55551	55601
142 011		*PNH*	NH	55552	55602
142 012		*PNH*	NH	55553	55603
142 013		*PNH*	NH	55554	55604
142 014		*PNH*	NH	55555	55605
142 015		*PNH*	NH	55556	55606
142 016		*PHT*	HT	55557	55607
142 017		*PNH*	NH	55558	55608
142 018		*PHT*	HT	55559	55609
142 019		*PHT*	HT	55560	55610
142 020		*PHT*	HT	55561	55611
142 021		*PHT*	HT	55562	55612
142 022		*PHT*	HT	55563	55613
142 023	v	*PNH*	NH	55564	55614
142 024		*PNH*	NH	55565	55615
142 025		*PHT*	HT	55566	55616
142 026	v	*PNH*	NH	55567	55617
142 027		*PNH*	NH	55568	55618
142 028		*PNH*	NH	55569	55619
142 029		*PNH*	NH	55570	55620
142 030		*PNH*	NH	55571	55621
142 031		*PNH*	NH	55572	55622
142 032		*PNH*	NH	55573	55623
142 033		*PNH*	NH	55574	55624
142 034		*PNH*	NH	55575	55625
142 035		*PNH*	NH	55576	55626
142 036		*PNH*	NH	55577	55759
142 037		*PNH*	NH	55578	55628
142 038	v	*PNH*	NH	55579	55629
142 039	v	*PNH*	NH	55580	55630
142 040		*PNH*	NH	55581	55631

Unit No	SC	Pool	Dep	DMS	DMS(L)
142 041	v	PNH	NH	55582	55632
142 042		PNH	NH	55583	55633
142 043	v	PNH	NH	55584	55634
142 044		PNH	NH	55585	55635
142 045	v	PNH	NH	55586	55636
142 046		PNH	NH	55587	55637
142 047		PNH	NH	55588	55752
142 048		PNH	NH	55589	55639
142 049		PNH	NH	55590	55640
142 050	v	PNH	NH	55591	55641
142 051		PNH	NH	55701	55747
142 052		PNH	NH	55702	55748
142 053		PNH	NH	55703	55749
142 054		PNH	NH	55704	55750
142 055		PNH	NH	55705	55751
142 056		PNH	NH	55706	55638
142 057		PNH	NH	55707	55753
142 058		PNH	NH	55708	55754
142 059		PNH	NH	55709	55755
142 060		PNH	NH	55710	55756
142 061		PNH	NH	55711	55757
142 062		PNH	NH	55712	55758
142 063		PNH	NH	55713	55627
142 064		PNH	NH	55714	55760
142 065		PNH	NH	55715	55761
142 066		PNH	NH	55716	55762
142 067		PNH	NH	55717	55763
142 068		PNH	NH	55718	55764
142 069		PNH	NH	55719	55765
142 070		PNL	NL	55720	55766
142 071		PNL	NL	55721	55767
142 072		PNL	NL	55722	55768
142 073		PNL	NL	55723	55769
142 074		PNL	NL	55724	55770
142 075		PNL	NL	55725	55771
142 076		PNL	NL	55726	55772
142 077		PNL	NL	55727	55773
142 078		PNL	NL	55728	55774
142 079		PNL	NL	55729	55775
142 080		PNL	NL	55730	55776
142 081		PNL	NL	55731	55777
142 082		PNL	NL	55732	55778
142 083		PNL	NL	55733	55779
142 084		PNL	NL	55734	55780
142 085		PNL	NL	55735	55781
142 086		PNL	NL	55736	55782
142 087		PNL	NL	55737	55783
142 088		PNL	NL	55738	55784
142 089		PNL	NL	55739	55785
142 090		PNL	NL	55740	55786
142 091		PNL	NL	55741	55787
142 092		PNL	NL	55742	55788
142 093		PNL	NL	55743	55789
142 094		PNL	NL	55744	55790
142 095		PNL	NL	55745	55791
142 096		PNL	NL	55746	55792

Class 143 — 2-CAR — Pacers

Built: Walter Alexander/Andrew Barclay 1985

Diagram	Type	Gearbox	Weight	Seats	Toilet	SC
DP2.36.0A	DMSA	SGC	24t	62	—	
DP2.36.—	DMSA	Voith	24t	62	—	v
DP2.37.0A	DMSB(L)	SGC	24.5t	60	1	
DP2.37.—	DMSB(L)	Voith	24.5t	60	1	v

Driving Motor Standard: DMS
Engine: Leyland TL11 of 200bhp (152kW)
Transmission: Mechanical, SCG or Voith 4-speed epicyclic reversable gearbox/cardan shaft

Body: 15.55m L × 2.70m W × 3.62m H. Gangwayed within unit
Maximum speed: 75mph
Livery: *Standard*: Provincial Sector (Blue); *Special:* Tyne & Wear PTE (Yellow): 143020-25

Unit No	New Unit No	SC	Pool	Dep	DMS	DMS(L)
143 001		v	PHT	HT	55642	55667
143 002		v	PHT	HT	55643	55668
143 003			PHT	HT	55644v	55669
143 004		v	PHT	HT	55645	55670
143 005		v	PHT	HT	55646	55671
143 006		v	PHT	HT	55647	55672
143 007		v	PHT	HT	55648	55673
143 008		v	PHT	HT	55649	55674
143 009		v	PHT	HT	55650	55675
143 010		v	PHT	HT	55651	55676
143 011		v	PHT	HT	55652	55677
143 012		v	PHT	HT	55653	55678
143 013		v	PHT	HT	55654	55679
143 014		v	PHT	HT	55655	55680
143 015		v	PHT	HT	55656	55681
143 016		v	PHT	HT	55657	55682
143 017		v	PHT	HT	55658	55683
143 018		v	PHT	HT	55659	55684
143 019		v	PHT	HT	55660	55685
143 020			PHT	HT	55661	55686
143 021			PHT	HT	55662	55687
143 022			PHT	HT	55663	55688
143 023			PHT	HT	55664	55689
143 024			PHT	HT	55665	55690
143 025			PHT	HT	55666	55691

Class 144 — 2 or 3-CAR — Pacers

Built: Walter Alexander/BREL Derby 1986-88

Diagram	Type	Gearbox	Weight	Seats	Toilet	SC
DP2.40.0A	DMSA	SGC	24t	62		
DP2.40.--	DMSA	Voith	24t	62		v
DP2.41.0A	DMSB(L)	SGC	24.5t	60	1	
DP2.41.--	DMSB(L)	Voith	24.5t	60	1	v
DR2.05.0A	MS	SGC	23.5t	73		

Driving Motor Standard: DMS
Motor Standard: MS
Engine: Leyland TL11 of 200bhp (152kW)
Transmission: Mechanical. SCG or Voith 4-speed epicyclic reversable gearbox/cardan shaft
Body: 16.60m L × 2.70m W × 3.73m H. Gangwayed within unit
Maximum speed: 75mph
Livery: West Yorkshire PTE (red and cream)

Unit No	New Unit No	SC	Pool	Dep	DMS	MS	DMS(L)
144 001			PNL	NL	55801		55824
144 002			PNL	NL	55802		55825
144 003			PNL	NL	55803		55826
144 004			PNL	NL	55804		55827
144 005			PNL	NL	55805		55828
144 006			PNL	NL	55806		55829
144 007			PNL	NL	55807		55830
144 008			PNL	NL	55808		55831
144 009		v	PNL	NL	55809		55832
144 010		v	PNL	NL	55810		55833

Unit No	New Unit No	SC	Pool	Dep	DMS	MS	DMS(L)
144 011		V	PNL	NL	55811		55834
144 012		V	PNL	NL	55812		55835
144 013		V	PNL	NL	55813		55836
144 014			PNL	NL	55814	55850	55837
144 015			PNL	NL	55815	55851	55838
144 016			PNL	NL	55816	55852	55839
144 017			PNL	NL	55817	55853	55840
144 018			PNL	NL	55818	55854	55841
144 019			PNL	NL	55819	55855	55842
144 020			PNL	NL	55820	55856	55843
144 021			PNL	NL	55821	55857	55844
144 022			PNL	NL	55822	55858	55845
144 023			PNL	NL	55823	55859	55846

20 METRE SPRINTER

Class 150/0 — 3-CAR

Built: BREL York Works 1984

Three-car prototype suburban unit

Diagram	Type	Weight	Seats	Toilet
DP2.30.0A	DMSA(L)	35.8t	75	1
DP2.31.1A	DMSB	35.6t	79	—
DR2.02.0A	MS	34.4t	84	—

Engine: Cummins NT 855R4 of 285hp (312kW)
Transmission: Voith-Gemeinder
Maximum speed: 75mph
Public address, driver/guard communication, air brakes and AWS fitted
Driving Motor Standard: DMSA(L)
Driving Motor Standard: DMS
Body: 20.06m L × 2.73m W × 3.77m H.
Gangwayed within unit
Motor Standard: MS
Body: 20.18m L × 2.73m W × 3.77m H.
Gangwayed throughout
Livery: Provincial Sector (Blue)

Unit No	SC	Pool	Dep	DMS(L)	MS	DMS
150 001		PDY	DY	55200	55400	55300

Class 150/1 — 2 or 3-CAR

Built: BREL York Works 1985

Diagram	Type	Weight	Seats	Toilet	SC
DP2.38.0A	DMSA(L)	36.5t	68	1	
DP2.38.--	DMSA(L)	36.5t	68	1	RETB Socket
DP2.39.0A	DMSB	36.5t	70		

DP2.39.--	DMSB	36.5t	70		RETB Socket
DP2.42.0A	DMSA(L)*	37.5t	73	1	See Class 150/2
DP2.43.0A	DMSB†	36.5t	76		for full details

Engines: Cumins NT 855R5 of 285hp (213kW)
Transmission: Voith-Gemeinder
Body: 20.06m L × 2.73m W × 3.77m H.
Gangwayed within unit
Maximum speed: 75mph

Public address, driver-guard communication, air brakes and AWS fitted
Driving Motor Standard: DMS(L)
Driving Motor Standard: DMS
Livery: Provincial Sector (Blue)

Unit No	*SC*	*Pool*	*Dep*	*DMS(L)*	*DMS(L)** *DMS†*	*DMS*
150 101		*PDY*	DY	52101		57101
150 102		*PDY*	DY	52102		57102
150 103		*PDY*	DY	52103		57103
150 104		*PDY*	DY	52104		57104
150 105		*PDY*	DY	52105		57105
150 106		*PDY*	DY	52106		57106
150 107		*PDY*	DY	52107		57107
150 108		*PDY*	DY	52108		57108
150 109		*PDY*	DY	52109		57109
150 110		*PDY*	DY	52110		57110
150 111		*PDY*	DY	52111		57111
150 112		*PDY*	DY	52112		57112
150 113		*PDY*	DY	52113		57113
150 114		*PDY*	DY	52114		57114
150 115		*PDY*	DY	52115		57115
150 116	R	*PDY*	DY	52116		57116
150 117	R	*PDY*	DY	52117		57117
150 118	R	*PDY*	DY	52118		57118
150 119	R	*PDY*	DY	52119		57119
150 120	R	*PDY*	DY	52120		57120
150 121	R	*PDY*	DY	52121		57121
150 122	R	*PDY*	DY	52122		57122
150 123		*PDY*	DY	52123		57123
150 124		*PDY*	DY	52124		57124
150 125	R	*PDY*	DY	52125		57125
150 126	R	*PDY*	DY	52126		57126
150 127	R	*PDY*	DY	52127		57127
150 128		*PDY*	DY	52128		57128
150 129	R	*PDY*	DY	52129		57129
150 130		*PDY*	DY	52130		57130
150 131	R	*PDY*	DY	52131		57131
150 132	R	*PDY*	DY	52132		57132
150 133	R	*PDY*	DY	52133		57133
150 134		*PDY*	DY	52134		57134
150 135	R	*PDY*	DY	52135		57135
150 136	R	*PDY*	DY	52136		57136
150 137	R	*PDY*	DY	52137		57137

Unit No	SC	Pool	Dep	DMS(L)	DMS(L)* DMS†	DMS
150 138	R	*PDY*	DY	52138		57138
150 139	R	*PDY*	DY	52139		57139
150 140	R	*PDY*	DY	52140		57140
150 141	R	*PDY*	DY	52141	57253†	57141
150 142	R	*PDY*	DY	52142	57212†	57142
150 143	R	*PDY*	DY	52143	52205*	57143
150 144	R	*PDY*	DY	52144	52212†	57144
150 145	R	*PDY*	DY	52145		57145
150 146	R	*PDY*	DY	52146	52253*	57146
150 147	R	*PDY*	DY	52147		57147
150 148	R	*PDY*	DY	52148		57148
150 149	R	*PDY*	DY	52149		57149
150 150	R	*PDY*	DY	52150		57150

Class 150/2 — 2-CAR

Built: BREL York Works 1987

Diagram	Type	Weight	Seats	SC
DP2.42.0A	DMSA(L)	37.5t	73	
DP2.42.--	DMSA(L)	37.5t	70	†
DP2.43.0A	DMS	36.5t	76	

Engine: Cummins NT 855R5 of 285bhp (213kW)
Transmission: Voith-Gemeinder
Maximum speed: 75mph
Public address and driver-guard communication fitted

Driving Motor Standard: DMS(L)
Driving Motor Standard: DMS
Dimensions: 20.06m L × 2.73m W × 3.77m H. Gangwayed throughout

Unit No	SC	Pool	Dep	DMS(L)	DMS
150 201		*PNH*	NH	52201	57201
150 202		*PNL*	NL	52202†	57202
150 203		*PNH*	NH	52203	57203
150 204		*PNL*	NL	52204†	57204
150 205		Not formed			
150 206		*PNL*	NL	52206†	57206
150 207		*PNH*	NH	52207	57207
150 208		*PHA*	HA	52208	57208
150 209		*PNH*	NH	52209	57209
150 210		*PNL*	NL	52210†	57210
150 211		*PNH*	NH	52211	57211
150 212		*PNL*	NL (at ZD)	52212†	
150 213		*PNH*	NH	52213	57213
150 214		*PNL*	NL	52214†	57214
150 215		*PNH*	NH	52215	57215
150 216		*PNL*	NL	52216†	57216
150 217		*PNH*	NH	52217	57217
150 218		*PNL*	NL	52218†	57218
150 219		*PNH*	NH	52219	57219
150 220		*PNL*	NL	52220†	57220
150 221		*PNH*	NH	52221	57221
150 222		*PNL*	NL	52222†	57222
150 223		*PNH*	NH	52223	57223
150 224		*PNL*	NL	52224†	57224
150 225		*PNH*	NH	52225	57225
150 226		*PNL*	NL	52226†	57226
150 227		*PNH*	NH	52227	57227
150 228		*PNL*	NL	52228†	57228
150 229		*PNH*	NH	52229	57229
150 230		*PNL*	NL	52230†	57230

150 231	*PNH*	NH	52231	57231
150 232	*PNL*	NL	52232†	57232
150 233	*PNH*	NH	52233	57233
150 234	*PNL*	NL	52234†	57234
150 235	*PNH*	NH	52235	57235
150 236	*PNL*	NL	52236†	57236
150 237	*PNH*	NH	52237	57237
150 238	*PNL*	NL	52238†	57238
150 239	*PNH*	NH	52239	57239
150 240	*PNL*	NL	52240†	57240
150 241	*PNH*	NH	52241	57241
150 242	*PNL*	NL	52242†	57242
150 243	*PNH*	NH	52243	57243
150 244	*PNL*	NL	52244†	57244
150 245	*PHA*	HA	52245	57245
150 246	*PNL*	NL	52246†	57246
150 247	*PCF*	CF	52247	57247
150 248	*PNL*	NL	52248†	57248
150 249	*PCF*	CF	52249	57249
150 250	*PNL*	NL	52250†	57250
150 251	*PCF*	CF	52251	57251
150 252	*PNL*	NL	52252†	57252
150 253	Not formed			
150 254	*PNL*	NL	52254†	57254
150 255	*PHA*	HA	52255	57255
150 256	*PNL*	NL	52256†	57256
150 257	*PHA*	HA	52257	57257
150 258	*PNL*	NL	52258†	57258
150 259	*PHA*	HA	52259	57259
150 260	*PNL*	NL	52260†	57260
150 261	*PCF*	CF	52261	57261
150 262	*PNL*	NL	52262†	57262
150 263	*PCF*	CF	52263	57263
150 264	*PHA*	HA	52264	57264
150 265	*PCF*	CF	52265	57265
150 266	*PCF*	CF	52266	57266
150 267	*PCF*	CF	52267	57267
150 268	*PCF*	CF	52268	57268
150 269	*PCF*	CF	52269	57269
150 270	*PCF*	CF	52270	57270
150 271	*PCF*	CF	52271	57271
150 272	*PCF*	CF	52272	57272
150 273	*PCF*	CF	52273	57273
150 274	*PCF*	CF	52274	57274
150 275	*PCF*	CF	52275	57275
150 276	*PCF*	CF	52276	57276
150 277	*PCF*	CF	52277	57277
150 278	*PCF*	CF	52278	57278
150 279	*PCF*	CF	52279	57279
150 280	*PCF*	CF	52280	57280
150 281	*PCF*	CF	52281	57281
150 282	*PCF*	CF	52282	57282
150 283	*PHA*	HA	52283	57283
150 284	*PHA*	HA	52284	57284
150 285	*PHA*	HA	52285	57285

Class 151 — 3-CAR

Built: Metro-Cammell 1985

Diagram	Type	Weight	Seats	Toilet
DP2.32.0A	DMSA(L)	32.4t	68	1
DP2.33.0A	DMSB	32.4t	80	
DR2.04.0A	MS	32.1t	84	

Engines: Cummins NT 855 R4 of 285hp (213kW)
Transmission: Mechanical
Maximum speed: 75mph
Public address, driver-guard communication, air brakes and AWS fitted
Driving Motor Standard: DMSA(L)
Driving Motor Standard: DMSB
Dimensions: 19.98m L × 2.81m W × 3.89m H. Gangwayed within unit.
Motor Second: MS
Dimensions: 19.60m L × 2.81m W × 3.89m H. Gangwayed throughout

Class 101 DTS No 54089 leads the 11.10 Peterborough-Cambridge at Manea on 4 March 1988. *Bryan Philpott*

Carrying the distinctive Strathclyde PTE livery, Class 107 DMU set No 107444 pauses at Holytown with the 13.26 Glasgow-Edinburgh Waverley on 24 August 1987. *Douglas Young*

The green-liveried Class 108 unit, comprising DMBS vehicle No 53964 and DTS vehicle No 54247, near Carlisle on 22 October 1987. *D. McAlone*

Ten West Yorkshire PTE Class 144 Pacer DMUs have been fitted with centre cars to relieve overcrowding. Here, three-car unit No 144020 leaves Guiseley with the 13.40 Ilkley-Leeds on 23 April 1988. *John E. Oxley*

Class 150/1 'Sprinter' DMU No 150148 leaves Charlbury with the 17.36 Oxford-Moreton-in-Marsh on 14 June 1988.
Colin Underhill

The first 'Sprinter' to Bournemouth was Class 155 No 155319 seen here in the New Forest near Beaulieu Road on 25 March 1988. *David Warwick*

Class 156 'Sprinter' DMU No 156402 at Sheffield on 24 May 1988. *Graham Hudson*

On 14 August 1987, Class 205 DEMU No 205020, still in blue and grey livery, passes Dunbridge with the 15.33 Portsmouth-Salisbury. *David Warwick*

Departmental route-learning saloon No ADB 975659 trundles eastbound through Cardiff Central station on 16 February 1988.
Hugh Ballantyne

Class 310 EMU No 310068, in Network SouthEast livery, approaches Watford Junction with the 10.36 Birmingham-Euston.
John E. Oxley

A morning commuter service from Watford Junction arrives at Euston formed of Class 313 unit No 313006 on 5 July 1988.
Hugh Ballantyne

The 13.56 Luton-Farringdon service, formed of Class 319 'Thameslink' EMU No 319022, calls at Elstree & Borehamwood on Bank Holiday Monday 30 May 1988. *John E. Oxley*

Class 419 MLV No 9004 in Royal Mail red livery, forms part of a parcels service for Redhill at London Bridge on 10 November 1988. *Brian Morrison*

Class 421/3 (4-CIG) unit No 1704 leads the 14.47 Victoria-Hastings at Clapham Junction on 1 April 1988. *John E. Oxley*

Class 442 unit Nos 2421/19 form the 11.45 Waterloo-Poole at Southampton on 5/11/88. *Brian Morrison*

Class 455/8 unit No 5818 leaves Clapham Junction on 1 April 1988. *John E. Oxley*

Unit No	Former Unit No	SC	Pool	Dep	DMS	MS	DMS(L)
151 003	(151 001)		PDY	DY	55202	55402	55302
151 004	(151 002)		PDY	DY	55203	55403	55303

Class 154 3-CAR

Built: BREL York Works 1985
Modified at BR EDU, Railway Technical Centre, Derby, 1986, from Class 150 prototype unit No 150002. Public address and driver guard communication fitted. Air conditioning on DMS vehicles

Design Codes	Type	Weight	Seats	Toilet
DP2.46.0A	DMSA(L)	37.9t	58	1
DP2.47.0A	DMSB	37.9t	60	
DR2.03.0A	MS	34.4t	97	

Driving Motor Standard: DMS(L)
Engine: Cummins NTA 855RI of 350hp (275kW)
Transmission: Voith
Body: 20.06m L × 2.73m W × 3.77m H. Gangwayed within unit
Driving Motor Standard: DMS
Transmission: Twin Disc

Motor Standard: MS
Engine: Rolls-Royce Eagle C6 305R of 350hp (275kW)
Dimensions: 20.18m L × 2.81m W × 3.77m H
Maximum speed: 75mph
Livery: Provincial Sector (Blue)

Unit No	Former Unit No	SC	Pool	Dep	DMS	MS	DMS(L)
154 002	(154 001)		PDY	DY	55201	55401	55301

23 METRE SUPER SPRINTER UNITS

Classes 155/0 & 155/1 2-CAR

Built: Leyland National Bus 1987-88
Public address, driver-guard communication, air brakes and AWS fitted

Design Codes	Class	Type	Weight	Seats	Toilet	
DP2.48.0A	155/0	DMS(L)	38.8t	80	1	Wheelchair provision
DP2.48.1B	155/1	DMS(L)	39.4t	80	1	Wheelchair provision
DP2.49.0A	155/0	DMS	37.9t	80		
DP2.49.1B	155/1	DMS	38.6t	80		

Driving Motor Standard: DMSA(L)
Driving Motor Standard: DMSB
Engine: Cummins NT855 R5 of 285hp (213kW)
Transmission: Voith/Gemeinder
Dimensions: 23.21m L × 2.69m W × 3.81m H. Gangwayed throughout

Maximum speed: 75mph
Livery: Class 155/0 *Provincial Sector*: 155301-35
Class 155/1 *Metro Red* (West Yorks PTE): 155341-47

Unit No	*SC*	*Pool*	*Dep*	*DMS*	*DMS(L)*
Class 155/0					
155 301		*PCF*	CF	52301	57301
155 302		*PCF*	CF	52302	57302
155 303		*PCF*	CF	52303	57303
155 304		*PCF*	CF	52304	57304
155 305		*PCF*	CF	52305	57305
155 306		*PCF*	CF	52306	57306
155 307		*PCF*	CF	52307	57307
155 308		*PCF*	CF	52308	57308
155 309		*PCF*	CF	52309	57309
155 310		*PCF*	CF	52310	57310
155 311		*PCF*	CF	52311	57311
155 312		*PCF*	CF	52312	57312
155 313		*PCF*	CF	52313	57313
155 314		*PCF*	CF	52314	57314
155 315		*PCF*	CF	52315	57315
155 316		*PCF*	CF	52316	57316
155 317		*PCF*	CF	52317	57317
155 318		*PCF*	CF	52318	57318
155 319		*PCF*	CF	52319	57319
155 320		*PCF*	CF	52320	57320
155 321		*PCF*	CF	52321	57321
155 322		*PCF*	CF	52322	57322
155 323		*PCF*	CF	52323	57323
155 324		*PCF*	CF	52324	57324
155 325		*PCF*	CF	52325	57325
155 326		*PCF*	CF	52326	57326
155 327		*PCF*	CF	52327	57327
155 328		*PCF*	CF	52328	57328
155 329		*PCF*	CF	52329	57329
155 330		*PCF*	CF	52330	57330
155 331		*PCF*	CF	52331	57331
155 332		*PCF*	CF	52332	57332
155 333		*PCF*	CF	52333	57333
155 334		*PCF*	CF	52334	57334
155 335		*PCF*	CF	52335	57335
Class 155/1					
155 341		*PNL*	NL	52341	57341
155 342		*PNL*	NL	52342	57342
155 343		*PNL*	NL	52343	57343
155 344		*PNL*	NL	52344	57344
155 345		*PNL*	NL	52345	57345
155 346		*PNL*	NL	52346	57346
155 347		*PNL*	NL	52347	57347

Class 156 — 2-CAR

Built: Metropolitan-Cammell 1987-89

Design Codes	**Type**	**Weight**	**Seats**	**Toilet**	**SC**
DP2.44.0A	DMSA(L)	38.6t	79	1	
DP2.44.—	DMSA(L)	38.6t	79	1	RP
DP2.45.0A	DMSB	37.9t	84		
DP2.45	DMSB	37.9t	84		RP

Driving Motor Standard: DMS(L)
Driving Motor Standard: DMS
Engines: Cummins NT 855R5 of 285hp (213kW)
Transmission: Voith/Gemeinder
Dimensions: 23.05m L × 2.73m W × 3.81m H. Gangwayed throughout
Maximum speed: 75mph
Standard livery: *Provincial Sector* (Blue) 156401-
Special livery: *Strathclyde PTE* (Orange) 156——

Unit No	*SC*	*Pool*	*Dep*	*DMS(L)*	*DMS*
156 401		*PNC*	NC	52401	57401
156 402		*PNC*	NC	52402	57402
156 403		*PNC*	NC	52403	57403
156 404		*PNC*	NC	52404	57404
156 405		*PNC*	NC	52405	57405
156 406		*PNC*	NC	52406	57406
156 407		*PNC*	NC	52407	57407
156 408		*PNC*	NC	52408	57408
156 409		*PNC*	NC	52409	57409
156 410		*PNC*	NC	52410	57410
156 411		*PNC*	NC	52411	57411
156 412		*PNC*	NC	52412	57412
156 413		*PNC*	NC	52413	57413
156 414		*PNC*	NC	52414	57414
156 415		*PNC*	NC	52415	57415
156 416		*PNC*	NC	52416	57416
156 417		*PNC*	NC	52417	57417
156 418		*PNC*	NC	52418	57418
156 419		*PNC*	NC	52419	57419
156 420		*PNC*	NC	52420	57420
156 421		*PNC*	NC	52421	57421
156 422		*PNC*	NC	52422	57422
156 423		*PNC*	NC	52423	57423
156 424		*PNC*	NC	52424	57424
156 425		*PNC*	NC	52425	57425
156 426		*PNC*	NC	52426	57426
156 427		*PNC*	NC	52427	57427
156 428		*PNC*	NC	52428	57428
156 429		*PNC*	NC	52429	57429
156 430		*PCK*	CK	52430	57430
156 431		*PCK*	CK	52431	57431
156 432		*PCK*	CK	52432	57432
156 433		*PCK*	CK	52433	57433
156 434		*PCK*	CK	52434	57434
156 435		*PCK*	CK	52435	57435
156 436		*PCK*	CK	52436	57436
156 437		*PCK*	CK	52437	57437
156 438		*PNC*	NC	52438	57438
156 439		*PCK*	CK	52439	57439
156 440		*PNC*	NC	52440	57440
156 441		*PNL*	NL	52441	57441
156 442		*PCK*	CK	52442	57442
156 443		*PNL*	NL	52443	57443
156 444		*PNL*	NL	52444	57444
156 445		*PIS*	IS	52445	57445
156 446		*PIS*	IS	52446	57446
156 447		*PHA*	HA	52447	57447
156 448		*PIS*	IS	52448	57448
156 449		*PIS*	IS	52449	57449
156 450		*PHA*	HA	52450	57450
156 451		*PIS*	IS	52451	57451
156 452		*PIS*	IS	52452	57452
156 453		*PIS*	IS	52453	57453
156 454		*PIS*	IS	52454	57454
156 455		*PIS*	IS	52455	57455
156 456		*PHA*	HA	52456	57456
156 457		*PIS*	IS	52457	57457
156 458		*PIS*	IS	52458	57458
156 459		*PHA*	HA	52459	57459
156 460		*PIS*	IS	52460	57460
156 461		*PHA*	HA	52461	57461
156 462		*P*		52462	57462
156 463		*P*		52463	57463
156 464		*P*		52464	57464
156 465		*P*		52465	57465
156 466		*P*		52466	57466
156 467		*P*		52467	57467
156 468		*P*		52468	57468
156 469		*P*		52469	57469
156 470		*P*		52470	57470
156 471		*P*		52471	57471
156 472		*P*		52472	57472
156 473		*P*		52473	57473
156 474		*P*		52474	57474
156 475		*P*		52475	57475
156 476		*P*		52476	57476
156 477		*P*		52477	57477
156 478		*P*		52478	57478

Unit No	SC	Pool	Dep	DMS(L)	DMS
156 479		P		52479	57479
156 480		P		52480	57480
156 481		P		52481	57481
156 482		P		52482	57482
156 483		P		52483	57483
156 484		P		52484	57484
156 485		P		52485	57485
156 486		P		52486	57486
156 487		P		52487	57487
156 488		P		52488	57488
156 489		P		52489	57489
156 490		P		52490	57490
156 491		P		52491	57491
156 492		P		52492	57492
156 493		P		52493	57493
156 494		P		52494	57494
156 495		P		52495	57495
156 496		P		52496	57496
156 497		P		52497	57497
156 498		P		52498	57498
156 499		P		52499	57499
156 500		P		52500	57500
156 501		P		52501	57501
156 502		P		52502	57502
156 503		P		52503	57503
156 504		P		52504	57504
156 505		P		52505	57505
156 506		P		52506	57506
156 507		P		52507	57507
156 508		P		52508	57508
156 509		P		52509	57509
156 510		P		52510	57510
156 511		P		52511	57511
156 512		P		52512	57512
156 513		P		52513	57513
156 514		P		52514	57514

23 METRE EXPRESS SPRINTER UNITS

Class 158 — 2 or 3-CAR

Built: BREL Derby Carriage Works 1989-90
Air conditioning, public address, driver-guard communication, air brakes and AWS fitted

Design Codes	Type	Weight	Seats	Toilet
DP2.51.0A	DMSA	38t	74	1
DP2.52.0A	DMSB	38t	72	1
DR2.07.0A	MS	38t	74	2

All seating is officially classified 'Standard'. Sections may be given embellishments appropriate to areas of operation for a higher category.

Driving Motor Standard: DMSA(L)
Driving Motor Standard: DMSB(L)
Motor Standard: MS(L)
Engines: Cummins NT855R5 of 350hp (275kW)
Transmission: Voith-Gemeinder
Dimensions: 22.16m L × 2.70m W × 3.81m H. Gangwayed throughout
Maximum speed: 90mph

Unit No	SC	Pool	Dep	DMS	MS	DMS(L)
158 601		P		52701		57701
158 602		P		52702		57702
158 603		P		52703		57703
158 604		P		52704		57704
158 605		P		52705		57705
158 606		P		52706		57706
158 607		P		52707		57707
158 608		P		52708		57708
158 609		P		52709		57709
158 610		P		52710		57710

Unit No	SC	Pool	Dep	DMS	DMS(L)
158 611		P		52711	57711
158 612		P		52712	57712
158 613		P		52713	57713
158 614		P		52714	57714
158 615		P		52715	57715
158 616		P		52716	57716
158 617		P		52717	57717
158 618		P		52718	57718
158 619		P		52719	57719
158 620		P		52720	57720
158 621		P		52721	57721
158 622		P		52722	57722
158 623		P		52723	57723
158 624		P		52724	57724
158 625		P		52725	57725
158 626		P		52726	57726
158 627		P		52727	57727
158 628		P		52728	57728
158 629		P		52729	57729
158 630		P		52730	57730
158 631		P		52731	57731
158 632		P		52732	57732
158 633		P		52733	57733
158 634		P		52734	57734
158 635		P		52735	57735
158 636		P		52736	57736
158 637		P		52737	57737
158 638		P		52738	57738
158 639		P		52739	57739
158 640		P		52740	57740
158 641		P		52741	57741
158 642		P		52742	57742
158 643		P		52743	57743
158 644		P		52744	57744
158 645		P		52745	57745
158 646		P		52746	57746
158 647		P		52747	57747
158 648		P		52748	57748
158 649		P		52749	57749
158 650		P		52750	57750
158 651		P		52751	57751
158 652		P		52752	57752
158 653		P		52753	57753
158 654		P		52754	57754
158 655		P		52755	57755
158 656		P		52756	57756
158 657		P		52757	57757
158 658		P		52758	57758
158 659		P		52759	57759
158 660		P		52760	57760
158 661		P		52761	57761
158 662		P		52762	57762
158 663		P		52763	57763
158 664		P		52764	57764
158 665		P		52765	57765
158 666		P		52766	57766
158 667		P		52767	57767
158 668		P		52768	57768
158 669		P		52769	57769
158 670		P		52770	57770
158 671		P		52771	57771
158 672		P		52772	57772
158 673		P		52773	57773
158 674		P		52774	57774
158 675		P		52775	57775
158 676		P		52776	57776
158 677		P		52777	57777
158 678		P		52778	57778
158 679		P		52779	57779
158 680		P		52780	57780
158 681		P		52781	57781
158 682		P		52782	57782
158 683		P		52783	57783
158 684		P		52784	57784
158 685		P		52785	57785
158 686		P		52786	57786
158 687		P		52787	57787
158 688		P		52788	57788
158 689		P		52789	57789
158 690		P		52790	57790
158 691		P		52791	57791
158 692		P		52792	57792
158 693		P		52793	57793
158 694		P		52794	57794
158 695		P		52795	57795
158 696		P		52796	57796
158 697		P		52797	57797
158 698		P		52798	57798
158 699		P		52799	57799
158 700		P		52800	57800
158 701		P		52801	57801
158 702		P		52802	57802
158 703		P		52803	57803
158 704		P		52804	57804

Unit No	SC	Pool	Dep	DMS(L)	DMS
158 705		P		52805	57805
158 706		P		52806	57806

Note: MS Vehicle numbers 58701-15. Allocation to units to be advised.

PARCELS SECTOR UNITS

Vehicles listed in this section are those reported allocated to the Director of Parcels Sector. Former passenger stock vehicles are having most, if not all, seating removed.

Some single-car units were purpose-built, others are having major modifications including roller-shutter doors.

Class 101 — Driving Motor

Built: Metropolitan-Cammell 1957, to Parcels stock from 1985

Diagram	Type	Weight	Engine	Note
DX5.--.2B	DMLV	32.5t	AEC	Refurbished, Official Diagram DQ2.02.2B
DX5.--.2E	DMLV	32.5t	Leyland	Refurbished, Official Diagram DQ2.02.2E

Engines: Two AEC or Leyland 150bhp (112kW) 6-cyl horizontal
Transmission: Four-speed epicyclic gearbox/carden shaft
Dimensions: 18.49m L × 2.82m W × 3.85m H. Gangwayed within unit
Maximum speed: 70mph
Brakes: Vacuum

Veh No	Dia	SC	Liv	Pool	Dep
51430	2E			RXXN	CA
51439	2E			RXXN	CA
51441	2E			RXXN	CA
53218	2B			RXXN	CA
53221	2E			RXXN	CA
53230	2B			RXXN	CA
53233	2E			RXXN	CA
53255	2E			RXXN	CA

Classes 114 and 114/1 — Driving Motor

Built: British Railways, Derby Carriage Works 1956, conversions from passenger stock

Diagram	Type	Weight	Engines	Note
DX5.--.2B	DMLV	38t	Albion	Refurbished, Officially Diagram DQ2.17.2B
DX5.13.0A	DMLV	38t	Albion	Roller Shutter Doors
DX5.13.0B	DMLV	38t	TL11	

Engines: Two Leyland Albion 230hp (172kW) 6-cyl horizontal or Leyland TL11 200hp (152kW)
Dimensions: 20.45m L × 2.35m W × 3.86m H
Maximum speed: 70mph
Brakes: Vacuum
AWS: Fitted

Veh No	*Former Veh No*	*Dia*	*SC*	*Liv*	*Pool*	*Dep*
53004		DX5.--.2B	#		*RXXN*	CA
53020		DX5.--.2B	#		*RXXN*	CA
53027		DX5.--.2B	#		*RXXN*	CA
53035		DX5.--.2B			*RXXN*	CA
53038		DX5.--.2B			*RXXN*	CA
53040		DX5.--.2B			*RXXN*	CA
53046		DX5.--.2B			*RXXN*	CA

Class 114/1

55930	(53010)	DX5.13.0B		RR	*RXXN*	CA
55931	(53040)	DX5.13.0A		RR	*RXXN*	CA
55932	(53032)	DX5.13.0B			*RXXN*	CA

Class 105 — Driving Motor

Built: Cravens 1956, to Parcels stock from 1985

Diagram	**Type**	**Weight**	**AWS**	**Official Diagram**
DX5.--.0B	DMLV	29.5t	Not fitted	DQ2.07.0B
DX5.--.1B	DMLV	29.5t	Fitted	DQ2.07.1B

Engines: Two Leyland 150bhp (112kW) 6-cyl horizontal
Transmission: Four-speed epicyclic gearbox/ carden shaft
Dimensions: 18.50m L × 2.82m W × 3.84m H. Gangwayed within unit
Maximum speed: 70mph
Brakes: Vacuum

Veh No	*Dia*	*SC*	*Liv*	*Pool*	*Dep*
53361	1B			*RXXN*	CA
53364	0B			*RXXN*	CA
53365	0B			*RXXN*	CA
53367	1B			*RXXN*	CA
53368	1B			*RXXN*	CA
53373	1B			*RXXN*	CA

Classes 114 and 114/1 — Driving Trailer

Built: British Railways, Derby Carriage Works 1956, conversions from passenger stock commenced 1986

Parcels Units

Class	Diagram	Type	Weight	Toilet	Note
114	DX5.—.3B	DTLV	30t	1	Refurbished, Official Diagram DS3.13.3B
114/1	DX5.14.0A	DTLV	30t	1	Roller Shutter Doors

Dimensions: 20.45m L × 2.35m W × 3.86m H

Maximum speed: 70mph
Brakes: Vacuum

Veh No	*Former Veh No*	*Dia*	*SC*	*Liv*	*Pool*	*Dep*
54028		5.—.3B			*RXXN*	CA
54041		5.—.3B			*RXXN*	CA
54042		5.—.3B			*RXXN*	CA
54900	(54034, 55933)	5.14.0A			*RXXN*	CA
54901	(54016)	5.14.0A		RR	*RXXN*	CA
54902	(54036)	5.14.0A			*RXXN*	CA

Class 127 Driving Motor

Built: British Railways, Derby Carriage Works 1959 as DMBS, converted for parcels and newspaper traffic in 1985

Diagram	Type	Weight
DX5.06.0A	DMLV	40t

Engines: Two Rolls-Royce 238bhp (178kW) 8-cyl horizontal
Transmission: Hydro-Torque convertor
Dimensions: 20.45m L × 2.82m W × 3.87m H. Non-gangwayed, side doors. Shutter blind in place of former brake section doors
AWS: Fitted
Livery: Parcels (Blue with red band)
Special Livery: *Green*: 55966/67

Veh No	*Dia*	*SC*	*Liv*	*Pool*	*Dep*
55966	0A		*	*RXXN*	LO
55967	0A		*	*RXXN*	LO
55968	0A			*RXXN*	LO
55969	0A			*RXXN*	LO
55970	0A			*RXXN*	LO
55971	0A			*RXXN*	LO
55972	0A			*RXXN*	LO
55973	0A			*RXXN*	LO
55975	0A			*RXXN*	LO
55976	0A			*RXXN*	LO
55977	0A			*RXXN*	LO
55978	0A			*RXXN*	LO
55979	0A			*RXXN*	LO
55980	0A			*RXXN*	LO
55981	0A			*RXXN*	LO
55982	0A			*RXXN*	LO
55983	0A			*RXXN*	LO
55984	0A			*RXXN*	LO
55985	0A			*RXXN*	LO
55986	0A			*RXXN*	LO
55987	0A			*RXXN*	LO

Class 128 — Driving Motor Luggage Van

Built: Gloucester RC&W Co 1959

Diagram	Type	Weight
DX5.01.0A	DMLV	41.5t
DX5.02.0B	DMLV	40.5t

Engines: Two Leyland Albion 230hp (172kW) 6-cyl horizontal
Transmission: Four-speed epicyclic gearbox/ carden shaft
Dimensions: 20.45m L × 2.82m W × 3.87m H. Driving cab each end
Maximum speed: 70mph
Brakes: Vacuum
AWS: Fitted
Single car can haul a tail load. 55991/92 only gangwayed throughout blanked off
Livery: Post Office Red

Veh No	*Dia*	*SC*	*Liv*	*Pool*	*Dep*
55991	1.0A		RR	*RXXN*	CA
55992	1.0A		RR	*RXXN*	CA
55993	2.0B		RR	*RXXN*	CA
55994	2.0B		RR	*RXXN*	CA
55995	2.0B		RR	*RXXN*	CA

DIESEL-ELECTRIC MULTIPLE-UNITS

Class 203 (SR 4L)

Built: British Rail, Eastleigh Works, 1957 as six-car units. Present formation introduced in 1986

DMEE Diagram	SR Code	Type	Weight	Seats	Toilet
DB2.02.0A	MAIA	DMBS	56t	30	
DH2.02.0A	SBIA	TS(L)	30.5t	60	2

Driving Motor Brake Standard Saloon: DMBS
Engine: English Electric 4-cyl type 4SRKT Mk II of 500bhp
Dimensions: 20.35m L × 2.82m W × 3.86m H. Gangwayed within unit
Brakes: Electro-Pneumatic
AWS: Fitted
Power/Control equipment: Two nose-suspended, axle-hung, traction motors, main generator English Electric Type 824
Livery: Green

Unit No	*Pool*	*Dep*	*DMBS*	*TS*	*TS*	*DMBS*
203 001	*NKC*	SU	60014	60522	60523	60015

NB: 60014 named *St Leonards*

Class 205 (SR 3H)

Built: British Rail Eastleigh Works 1957 as two-car units, trailer added in 1959

Diagram	SR Code	Type	Weight	Seats 1st	Seats Std	Toilet	SC
DB2.03.0A	NA	DMBS	57t	52			
DB2.04.0A	NA1A	DMBS	57t	42			*
DE3.01.0A	VA/VA1A	DTC(L)	32.5t	13	50	2	
DE3.02.0A	VA1C/VA3C	DTC(L)	32.5t	19	50	2	†
DE3.03.0A	VA2B	DTC(L)	34.5t	13	62	2	*
DH2.03.0A	TA/TA1A	TS	30.5t		104		

Motor Brake Standard: DMBS
Engine: English Electric 4-cyl type 4SRKT Mk II of 600hp
Power/Control equipment: Two nose suspended axle hung traction motors, main generator English Electric Type 824
Dimensions: 20.35m L × 2.82m W × 3.86m H. Non gangwayed

Maximum speed: 75mph
Driving Trailer Composite: DTC(L)
Dimensions: as DMBS
Trailer Standard Semi-Open: TS
Dimensions: 20.82m L × 2.82m W × 3.86m H. Non gangwayed

Unit No	Liv	Pool	Dep	DMBS	TS	DTC
205 001	N	*NKC*	SU	60100	60650	60800
205 002		*NKC*	SU	60101	60651	60801
205 008		*NKC*	SU	60120	60657	60820†
205 009		*NKC*	SU	60108	60658	60808†
205 012		*NKC*	SU	60111	60661	60811†
205 015		*NKC*	SU	60114	60664	60814†
205 016		*NKC*	SU	60115	60665	60815†
205 018		*NKC*	SU	60117	60667	60817†
205 023		*NKC*	SU	60122	60668	60822†
205 024		*NKC*	SU	60123	60669	60823
205 025		*NSS*	EH	60124	60670	60824
205 026		*NSS*	EH	60125	60671	60825
205 027		*NSS*	EH	60145*	60672	60826*
205 028		*NSS*	EH	60146*	60673	60827*
205 029	N	*NSS*	EH	60147*	60674	60828*
205 030		*NSS*	EH	60148*	60675	60829*
205 031		*NSS*	EH	60149*	60676	60830*
205 032		*NSS*	EH	60150*	60677	60831*
205 033		*NSS*	EH	60151*	60678	60832*

Class 205/1 (SR 3H (M))

Built: British Railways Eastleigh Works 1957
Refurbished, gangwayed version of Class 205 (3H).
Details as Class 205 except as follows:

Diagram	SR Code	Type	Weight	Seats	Toilet
DB2.03.1C	MB	DMBS	57t	52	
DE2.04.0A	VA	DTS(L)	32.5t	76	2
DH2.03.1B	SE	TS	30.5t	104	

Driving Motor Brake Standard: DMBS
Trailer Standard Open: TS
Driving Trailer Standard: DTS(L)

Unit No	Liv	Pool	Dep	DMBS	TS	DTC
205 101		*NKC*	SU	60110	60660	60810

Class 207 (SR 3D)

Built: British Railways Eastleigh Works, 1962

Diagram	SR Code	Type	Weight	Seats 1st	Seats Std	Toilet
DB2.05.0A	NB	DMBS	57t	42		
DE2.01.0A	VB	DTS	31.5t	76		
DH3.01.0A	TB	TC	31.5t	24	42	1

Motor Brake Standard Open: DMBS
Power/Control equipment: Two nose-suspended axle-hung traction motors, main generator English Electric type 824

Dimensions: 20.35m L × 2.82m W × 3.86m H. Non gangwayed
Brakes: Electro-Pneumatic
AWS: Fitted

Unit No	Liv	Pool	Dep	DMBS	TS	DTC
207 001		*NSX*	SU	60126	60600	60900
207 002	N	*NSX*	SU	60127	60601	60901
207 004		*NSX*	SU	60129	60603	60903
207 005		*NSS*	EH	60130	60604	60904
207 010		*NSS*	EH	60135	60609	60909
207 011		*NSX*	SU	60139	60610	60910
207 013		*NSS*	EH	60138	60612	60912
207 017		*NSS*	EH	60142	60616	60916

AC ELECTRIC MULTIPLE-UNITS

Class 302 4-Car

Built: British Railways Doncaster and York 1958
Design: BR non-gangwayed
Some units refurbished and fitted with gangways within unit, public address and driver/guard communication 1984/85 (R); some other units modified to open saloon accommodation (O)
Supply: 6.25 and 25kV ac overhead

Traction Motors (MBS): Four 192hp (140kW) dc English Electric
Maximum speed: 75mph
Dimensions: *Driving coaches:* 20.36m L × 2.82m W × 3.86m H. *Trailer coaches:* 20.18m L × 2.82m W × 3.86m H; 3.98m H Pantograph housed on MBS
AWS: Driving coaches fitted

Diagram	*Type*	*Weight*	*Seats 1st*	*Seats Std*	*Toilet*
Motor Brake Standard:					
ED2.05.0A	MBS. Compartment	55t	—	96	—
ED2.16.2C	MBS. Refurbished	55t	—	76	—
ED2.17.0A	MBS. Open	55t	—	82	—

Driving Trailer Standard:					
ED2.05.0A	DTS. Compartment	32.5t	—	108	—
EE2.19.0C	DTS. Refurbished	32.5t	—	88	—
EE2.23.0A	DTS. Open	32.5t	—	92	—
Battery Driving Trailer Standard/Composite:					
EF2.01.0A	BDTS. Open	36.5t	—	80	2
EF2.01.0B	BDTS. Open (o units)	36.5t	—	80	2
EF3.03.0C	BDTC. Refurbished	36t	24	52	1
Trailer Standard/Composite:					
EH2.23.0B	TS. Open	30t	—	86	1
EH2.23.0D	TS. Refurbished	30t	—	86	1
EH3.02.0A	TC. Semi-Open	30.5t	19	60	2

Special Livery: *Dark Green:* 302200

Unit No	(old No)	SC	Liv	Pool	Dep	BDTS	MBS	TC	DTS
						EF201	*ED205*	*EM302*	*EE205*
302200	(302207)		★	*NTS*	EM	75091#	61066	70066	75039
						BDTC	**MBS**	**TS**	**DTS**
						EF303	*ED216*	*EH223*	*EE219*
302201		R		*NTS*	EM	75085	61060	70060	75033
302202		R		*NTS*	EM	75086	61061	70061	75034
302203	(302263)	R		*NTS*	EM	75311	61122	70122	75236
302204		R		*NTS*	EM	75088	61063	70063	75036
302205		R		*NTS*	EM	75089	61064	70064	75037
302206		R		*NTS*	EM	75090	61065	70065	75038
302207	(302310)	R		*NTS*	EM	75358	61226	70226	75283
302208	(302308)	R		*NTS*	EM	75356	61224	70224	75281
302209		R		*NTS*	EM	75093	61068	70068	75041
302210		R		*NTS*	EM	75094	61069	70069	75042
302211		R		*NTS*	EM	75095	61070	70070	75043
302212		R		*NTS*	EM	75096	61071	70071	75044
302213		R		*NTS*	EM	75097	61072	70072	75060
302214	(302304)	R		*NTS*	EM	75352	61220	70220	75277
302215		R		*NTS*	EM	75099	61074	70074	75062
302216		R		*NTS*	EM	75100	61075	70075	75063
302217		R	N	*NTS*	EM	75190	61076	70076	75064
302218		R		*NTS*	EM	75191	61077	70077	75065
302219		R		*NTS*	EM	75192	61078	70078	75066
302220		R		*NTS*	EM	75193	61079	70079	75067
302221		R		*NTS*	EM	75194	61080	70080	75068
302222		R		*NTS*	EM	75195	61081	70081	75069
302223	(302293)	R		*NTS*	EM	75341	61209	70209	75266
302224		R		*NTS*	EM	75197	61083	70083	75071
302225		R		*NTS*	EM	75198	61084	70084	75072
302226		R		*NTS*	EM	75199	61085	70085	75073
302227	(302277)	R		*NTS*	EM	75325	61193	70193	75250
302228		R		*NTS*	EM	75201	61087	70087	75075
302229		R		*NTS*	EM	75202	61088	70088	75076

Unit No	(old No)	SC	Liv	Pool	Dep	BDTC	MBS	TS	DTS
302230	(302232)	R		*NTS*	EM	75205	61091	70091	75079

Unit No	(old No)	SC	Liv	Pool	Dep	BDTC	MBS	TS	DTS
						EF201	*ED205*	*EH302*	*EE205*
		0				*EF201*	*ED217*	*EH302*	*EE223*
302231				*NGE*	IL	75204#	61090	70090	75078
302234		0		*NGE*	IL	75207#	61093#	70120	75081
302235				*NSP*	ILs	75208#	61100#	70094	75082
302237				*NSP*	ILs	75333#	61096#	70096	75084
302238				*NSP*	PQs	75360	61097#	70112	75226
302239		0		*NGE*	IL	75287	61098#	70125	75272#
302241				*NGE*	IL	75289#	61094#	70100	75214
302243				*NSP*	PQs	75291#	61102#	70102	75216
302244				*NGE*	IL	75298#	61103#	70103	75217
302245		0		*NTS*	IL	75293#	61104#	70104	75218
302246				*NTS*	IL	75294#	61105#	70105	75219
302247				*NSP*	PQs	75295#	61106#	70106	75220
302248				*NSP*	PQs	75296#	61107#	70107	75221
302249				*NGE*	EM	75297#	61108#	70108	75222
302250	(302300)	0		*NTS*	EM	75348#	61216#	70216	75273#
302251		0		*NTS*	EM	75299#	61110#	70110	75224#
302252		0		*NTS*	IL	75300#	61111#	70111	75225#
302253	(302301)	0		*NTS*	EM	75349#	61217#	70217	75274#
302254		0		*NTS*	EM	75302#	61113#	70113	75227#
302255	(302303)	0		*NTS*	EM	75351#	61219#	70219	75276#
302256		0		*NGE*	IL	75304#	61115#	70115	75229#
302257				*NGE*	IL	75305#	61116#	70116	75230#
302258				*NGE*	IL	75326#	61117#	70117	75231#
302259		0		*NGE*	IL	75307#	61118#	70195#	75232#
302260	(302302)			*NTS*	EM	75321#	61218#	70132#	75246#
302261		0		*NTS*	EM	75309#	61120#	70073	75234#
302262		0		*NTS*	EM	75310	61121#	70131	75235#
302264				*NTS*	EM	75312#	61123#	70123	75254
302265				*NGE*	IL	75313#	61124#	70124	75238#
302267	(302307)			*NTS*	EM	75355#	61223	70223	75280#
302268				*NGE*	IL	75315#	61127#	70127#	75241#
302269				*NGE*	IL	75342#	61128#	70128#	75242#
302270				*NTS*	EM	75318#	61129#	70129#	75243#
302272		0		*NTS*	EM	75320#	61131#	70086#	75245#
302273	(302306)	0		*NTS*	EM	75354#	61222	70202	75279#
302274		0		*NTS*	EM	75322#	61190#	70190#	75247#
302275	(302311)	0		*NTS*	EM	75359#	61227	70227	75284#
302276	(302208)			*NGE*	IL	75092#	61067	70067	75040
302278				*NTS*	EM	75306#	61194#	70194#	75251#
302280		0		*NTS*	EM	75328#	61196#	70196#	75253#
302282				*NTS*	EM	75329#	61198#	70198	75255#
302283		0		*NGE*	IL	75331#	61199#	70130#	75256#

Unit No	(old No)	SC	Liv	Pool	Dep	BDTC	MBS	TS	DTS
302284		0		*NTS*	EM	75332#	61200#	70200	75257#
302285		0		*NGE*	IL	75210#	61201#	70201	75258#
302286				*NTS*	EM	75334#	61202#	70222	75259#
302289				*NGE*	IL	75337#	61205#	70205	75262#
302290				*NGE*	IL	75338#	61206#	70206	75263#
302291				*NSP*	PQs	75339#	61207#	70207	75264#
302292		0		*NTS*	EM	75340	61208	70208	75265
302295				*NSP*	PQs	75343#	61211#	70211	75268#
302296		0		*NTS*	EM	75344#	61212#	70212	75269#
302298		0		*NTS*	EM	75346#	61214#	70214	75271#

Class 302/1 3-Car (PCLS)

To be introduced 1989 using non-asbestos insulated coaches converted for conveyance of mail and parcels traffic.

Unit No	Liv	Pool	Dep	BDTV	MBV	DTV
302 ---		*REMA*	IL	—	—	—
302 ---		*REMA*	IL	—	—	—
302 ---		*REMA*	IL	—	—	—

Class 303 3-Car

Built: Pressed Steel 1959
Design: BR saloons with sliding doors. Non-gangwayed, unless shown (G). Gangwayed units equipped with public address equipment
Supply: 25kV ac overhead
Traction motors (MBS): Four 207hp (155kW) dc AEI (MV)
Maximum speed: 75mph
Dimensions: 20.18m L × 2.82m W × 3.86m H; 3.98m H Pantograph housed
AWS: Driving coaches fitted

Diagram	*Type*	*Weight*	*Seats*
Motor Brake Standard:			
ED2.01.0A	MBS	56t	70
ED2.--.--	MBS (G)	56t	48
Driving Trailer Standard:			
EE2.06.0A	DTS	34.5t	83
EE2.--.--	DTS (G)	34.5t	56
Battery Driving Trailer Standard:			
EF2.02.0A	BDTS	38t	83
EF2.--.--	BDTS (G)	38t	56

(No Diagram officially issued for Gangwayed units).

Unit No	SC	Liv	Pool	Dep	DTS *EE2*	MBS *ED2*	BDTS *EF2*
303 001	MG	S	*PGW*	GW	75566	61481	75601
303 003	MG	S	*PGW*	GW	75568	61483	75603
303 004	MG	S	*PGW*	GW	75569	61484	75604
303 005	M		*PGW*	GW	75570	61485	75605
303 006	MG	S	*PGW*	GW	75571	61486	75606

Unit No	SC	Liv	Pool	Dep	DTS	MBS	BDTS
303 008	MG	S	*PGW*	GW	75573	61488	75608
303 009	MG	S	*PGW*	GW	75574	61489	75609
303 010	MG	S	*PGW*	GW	75575	61490	75610
303 011	MG	S	*PGW*	GW	75576	61491	75611
303 012	MG	S	*PGW*	GW	75577	61492	75612
303 013	MG	S	*PGW*	GW	75578	61493	75613
303 014	MG	S	*PGW*	GW	75579	61494	75614
303 016	MG	S	*PGW*	GW	75581	61496	75616
303 019	MG	S	*PGW*	GW	75584	61499	75619
303 020	MG	S	*PGW*	GW	75585	61500	75620
303 021	MG	S	*PGW*	GW	75586	61501	75621
303 023	MG	S	*PGW*	GW	75588	61503	75623
303 024	MG	S	*PGW*	GW	75589	61504	75624
303 025	MG	S	*PGW*	GW	75590	61505	75625
303 027	MG	S	*PGW*	GW	75592	61507	75627
303 028	MG	S	*PGW*	GW	75600	61508	75635
303 029	M	S	*PGW*	GW	75594	61509	75629
303 032	MG	S	*PGW*	GW	75597	61512	75632
303 033	MG	S	*PGW*	GW	75595	61860	75817
303 034	MG	S	*PGW*	GW	75599	61514	75634
303 036		M	*PLG*	LG	75746	61812	75802
303 037	MG	S	*PGW*	GW	75747	61813	75803
303 038	MG	S	*PGW*	GW	75748	61814	75804
303 039	M	S	*PGW*	GW	75749	61815#	75805
303 040	MG	S	*PGW*	GW	75750	61816	75806
303 041		M	*PLG*	LG	75751	61817	75807
303 042	M	S	*PGW*	GW	75752	61818	75808
303 043	MG	S	*PGW*	GW	75572	61819	75809
303 045	MG	S	*PGW*	GW	75755	61821	75811
303 046	MG	S	*PGW*	GW	75756	61822	75812
303 047	MG	S	*PGW*	GW	75757	61823	75813
303 048		M	*PLG*	LG	75758	61824	75814
303 049		M	*PLG*	LG	75759	61825	75815
303 050		M	*PLG*	LG	75760	61826	75816
303 052		S	*PGW*	GW	75762	61828	75818
303 053		M	*PLG*	LG	75763	61829	75819
303 054	MG	S	*PGW*	GW	75764	61830	75820
303 055	MG	S	*PGW*	GW	75765	61831	75821
303 056	MG	S	*PGW*	GW	75766	61832	75822
303 057		M	*PLG*	LG	75767	61833	75823
303 058	MG	S	*PGW*	GW	75768	61834	75824
303 060		M	*PLG*	LG	75770	61836	75826
303 061	MG	S	*PGW*	GW	75771	61837	75827
303 062	M		*PGW*	GW	75772	61838	75828
303 063	M	S	*PGW*	GW	75773	61839	75829
303 065	MG	S	*PGW*	GW	75775	61841	75831
303 066		M	*PLG*	LG	75776	61842	75832

Unit No	SC	Liv	Pool	Dep	DTS	MBS	BDTS
303 067		M	*PLG*	LG	75777	61843	75833
303 068		S	*PGW*	GW	75596	61844#	75834
303 069	M	S	*PGW*	GW	75779	61845	75607
303 070	MG	S	*PGW*	GW	75780	61846	75836
303 071	MG	S	*PGW*	GW	75781	61847	75837
303 072		S	*PGW*	GW	75782	61848	75838
303 073	MG	S	*PGW*	GW	75783	61849	75839
303 075	M	S	*PGW*	GW	75785	61851	75841
303 076	M	S	*PGW*	GW	75786	61852	75842
303 077	MG	S	*PGW*	GW	75787	61853	75843
303 078		M	*PLG*	LG	75788	61854	75844
303 079	MG	S	*PGW*	GW	75789	61855	75845
303 080	MG	S	*PGW*	GW	75790	61856	75846
303 082		M	*PLG*	LG	75792	61858	75848
303 083	MG	S	*PGW*	GW	75793	61859	75849
303 085	MG	S	*PGW*	GW	75795	61861	75851
303 086		S	*PGW*	GW	75796	61862#	75852
303 087	MG	S	*PGW*	GW	75797	61863	75853
303 088	MG	S	*PGW*	GW	75798	61864	75854
303 089	MG	S	*PGW*	GW	75799	61865	75855
303 090	MG	S	*PGW*	GW	75800	61866	75856
303 091	MG	S	*PGW*	GW	75801	61867	75857

Class 304 — 3-Car

Built: British Railways Wolverton 1960/61
Design: BR, non-gangwayed saloons
Supply: 25kV ac overhead
Traction motors (MBS): Four 207hp (155kW) dc AEI (BTH)
Maximum speed: 75mph
Dimensions: *Driving coaches:* 20.31m L × 2.82m W × 3.88m H; *MBS:* 20.17m L × 2.82m W × 3.98m H Pantograph housed
AWS: Driving coaches fitted

Diagram	*Type*	*Weight*	*Seats*	*Toilets*
Motor Brake Standard:				
ED2.03.0A	MBS	56t	72	—
ED2.15.0A	MBS	54.5t	82	—
Battery Driving Trailer Standard:				
EF2.03.0A	BDTS	36t	80	2
EF2.04.0A	BDTS	37t	80	2
Driving Trailer Brake Standard:				
EG2.02.0A	DTBS	32t	82	—
EG2.03.0A	DTBS	32.5t	82	—

Unit No	Pool	Dep	DTBS *EG202*	MBS *ED215*	BDTS *EF223*
304 001	*PLG*	LG	75645	61045	75045
304 002	*PLG*	LG	75646	61046	75046
304 003	*PLG*	LG	75647	61047	75047
304 004	*PLG*	LG	75648	61048	75048
304 005	*PLG*	LG	75649	61049	75049
304 006	*PLG*	LG	75650	61050	75050
304 007	*PLG*	LG	75651	61051	75051
304 008	*PLG*	LG	75652	61052	75052
304 009	*PLG*	LG	75653	61053	75053
304 010	*PLG*	LG	75654	61054	75054
304 011	*PLG*	LG	75655	61055	75055
304 012	*PLG*	LG	75656	61056	75056

Unit No	Pool	Dep	DTBS	MBS	BDTS
304 013	*PLG*	LG	75657	61057	75057
304 014	*PLG*	LG	75658	61058	75058
304 015	*PLG*	LG	75659	61059	75059
			EG203	*ED203*	*EF204*
304 016	*PLG*	LG	75660	61628	75680
304 017	*PLG*	LG	75661	61629	75681
304 019	*PLG*	LG	75663	61631	75683
304 020	*PLG*	LG	75664	61632	75684
304 021	*PLG*	LG	75665	61633	75685
304 023	*PLG*	LG	75667	61635	75687
304 024	*PLG*	LG	75668	61636	75688
304 027	*PLG*	LG	75671	61639	75691
304 028	*PLG*	LG	75672	61640	75692
304 029	*PLG*	LG	75673	61641	75693
304 030	*PLG*	LG	75674	61642	75694
304 032	*PLG*	LG	75676	61644	75696
304 033	*PLG*	LG	75677	61645	75697
304 034	*PLG*	LG	75678	61646	75698
304 035	*PLG*	LG	75679	61647	75699
304 036	*PLG*	LG	75858	61873	75868
304 037	*PLG*	LG	75859	61874	75869
304 039	*PLG*	LG	75861	61876	75871
304 040	*PLG*	LG	75862	61877	75872
304 041	*PLG*	LG	75863	61878	75873
304 042	*PLG*	LG	75864	61879	75874
304 043	*PLG*	LG	75865	61880	75875
304 045	*PLG*	LG	75867	61882	75877

Class 305/1 — 3-Car

Built: British Railways, York 1960
Design: BR, non-gangwayed saloons
Supply: 6.25 and 25kV ac overhead
Traction motors (MBS): Four 200p (150kW) dc GEC
Maximum speed: 75mph
Dimensions: *Driving coaches:* 20.36m L × 2.82m W × 3.84m H; *MBS:* 20.27m L × 2.82m W × 3.98m H Pantograph housed
AWS: Driving coaches fitted

Diagram	*Type*	*Weight*	*Seats*
Motor Brake Standard:			
ED2.04.0B	MBS	55t	82
Driving Trailer Standard:			
EE2.09.0B	DTS	31.5t	92
Battery Driving Trailer Standard:			
EF2.05.0A	BDTS	35t	92

Unit No	SC	Pool	Dep	BDTS	MBS	DTS
				EF205	*ED204*	*EE209*
305 401	F	*NNE*	IL	75462	61429	75514
305 402	F	*NNE*	IL	75463	61430	75515
305 403	F	*NNE*	IL	75506	61473	75558
305 404	F	*NNE*	IL	75508	61475	75560
305 405	F	*NNE*	IL	75466	61433	75518
305 406	F	*NNE*	IL	75467	61434	75519
305 407	F	*NNE*	IL	75468	61435	75520
305 408	F	*NNE*	IL	75469	61436	75521
305 409	F	*NNE*	IL	75470	61437	75522
305 410	F	*NNE*	IL	75471	61438	75523
305 411	F	*NNE*	IL	75509	61476	75561
305 412	F	*NNE*	IL	75473	61440	75525
305 413	F	*NNE*	IL	75474	61441	75526
305 414	F	*NNE*	IL	75510	61477	75562
305 415	F	*NNE*	IL	75476	61443	75528
305 416	F	*NNE*	IL	75477	61444	75529
305 417	F	*NNE*	IL	75478	61445	75530
305 418		*NNE*	IL	75479	61446	75531
305 419	F	*NNE*	IL	75511	61478	75563
305 420	F	*NNE*	IL	75481	61448	75533
305 421	F	*NNE*	IL	75482	61449	75534
305 422	F	*NNE*	IL	75513	61480	75565

Class 305/2 — 4-Car

Built: British Railways, Doncaster 1960
Design: BR Saloons, gangwayed within set
Supply: 6.25 and 25kV ac
Traction Motors: Four 205hp (154kW) dc GEC
Maximum speed: 75mph
AWS: All driving coaches fitted
All units refurbished and fitted with public address system and driver/guard communications
Dimensions: *Driving coaches:* 19.88m L × 2.82m W × 3.86m H; *Trailer coaches:* 20.18m L × 2.82m W × 3.86m H; 3.98m H Pantograph housed

Diagram	*Type*	*Weight*	*Seats 1st*	*Seats Std*	*Toilet*
Motor Brake Standard:					
ED2.16.0A	MBS	55t	—	76	—
Driving Trailer Standard:					
EE2.20.0A	DTS	33t	—	88	—
Battery Driving Trailer Composite:					
EF3.04.0A	BDTC	36t	24	52	1
Trailer Standard:					
EH2.23.0A	TS	30t	—	86	1

Unit No	SC	Pool	Dep	DTS *EE220*	TS *EH223*	MBS *ED216*	BDTC *EF304*
305 501		*NNE*	IL	75443	70356	61410	75424
305 502		*NTS*	EM	75444	70357	61421	75425
305 503		*NTS*	EM	75445	70358	61412	75426
305 504		*NTS*	EM	75446	70359	61413	75427
305 505		*NTS*	EM	75447	70360	61414	75435
305 506		*NTS*	EM	75448	70361	61415	75429
305 507		*NTS*	EM	75449	70362	61416	75430
305 508		*NTS*	EM	75450	70363	61417	75431
305 509		*NTS*	EM	75451	70364	61418	75432
305 510		*NTS*	EM	75452	70365	61419	75433
305 511		*NTS*	EM	75453	70366	61420	75434
305 513		*NNE*	IL	75455	70368	61422	75436
305 514		*NNE*	IL	75456	70369	61423	75437
305 515		*NNE*	IL	75457	70370	61424	75438
305 516		*NNE*	IL	75458	70371	61425	75439
305 517		*NNE*	IL	75459	70372	61426	75440
305 518		*NNE*	IL	75460	70373	61427	75441
305 519		*NNE*	IL	75461	70374	61428	75442

Class 305/3 — 4-Car

Built: British Railways, York 1960. This sub-Class introduced 1988, formed from Class 305/1 units plus TC from Class 302 units (see above for full details). All units facelifted

Diagram	*Type*	*Weight*	*Seats 1st*	*Seats Std*	*Toilet*
Motor Brake Standard:					
ED2.04.0B	MBS	55t	—	82	—
Driving Trailer Standard:					
EE2.09.0B	DTS	33.5t	—	92	—
Battery Driving Trailer Standard:					
EF2.05.0A	BDTS	35t	—	92	—
Trailer Composite:					
EH3.--.--	TC	30.5t	19	59	1

(No Diagram issued)

Unit No	Pool	Dep	BDTS	MBS	TC	DTS
			EF205	*ED204*	*EH3--*	*EE209*
305 521	*NTS*	EM	75464	61431	70098	75516
305 522	*NTS*	EM	75465	61432	70099	75517
305 523	*NTS*	EM	75472	61439	70221	75524
305 524	*NTS*	EM	75475	61442	70118	75527
305 525	*NTS*	EM	75480	61447	70213	75532
305 526	*NTS*	EM	75483	61450	70093	75535
305 527	*NTS*	EM	75507	61474	70204	75559
305 528	*NTS*	EM	75512	61479	70210	75564

Class 306 — 3-Car

Built: Metro-Cammell/BRCW 1949
Design: LNER, Sliding doors, non-gangwayed
Supply: 6.25 and 25kV ac overhead
Traction motors (DMS): Four 207hp (155kW) dc Crompton Parkinson
Maximum speed: 70mph
Special Livery: BR Green

Diagram	*Type*	*Weight*	*Seats*
Driving Motor Standard: *Dimensions:* 19.24m L × 2.82m W × 3.84m H			
EA2.03.0A	DMS	52t	62
Trailer Brake Standard: *Dimensions:* 17.40m L × 2.95m W × 3.98m H Pantograph housed			
EJ2.01.0A	TBS	27t	46
Driving Trailer Standard: *Dimensions:* 19.24m L × 2.82m W × 3.84m H			
EE2.11.0A	DTS	28t	60

Unit No	Pool	Dep	DMS	TBS	DTS
306 017	*NCH*	IL	65217	65417	65617

Note: Unit is available for special hire work only. At all other times it is securely housed at Ilford ETMD.

Class 307 — 4-Car

Built: British Railways, Eastleigh 1956, rebuilt for ac 1960. Refurbished 1981
Design: BR, gangwayed within unit. All units fitted with public address system and driver-guard communication
Supply: 6.25 and 25kV ac overhead
Traction Motors: Four 174hp (130kW) dc GEC
Maximum speed: 75mph
AWS: All driving coaches fitted
Dimensions: *Driving coaches:* 20.31m L × 2.82m W × 3.86m H; *Trailer coaches:* 20.18m L × 2.82m W × 3.86m H 3.98m H Pantograph housed

Diagram	*Type*	*Weight*	*Seats 1st*	*Seats Std*	*Toilet*
Motor Standard:					
EC2.04.0B	MS	47.5t	—	98	—
Driving Trailer Composite:					
EE3.07.0B	DTC	33t	24	52	1
Trailer Standard:					
EH2.22.0B	TS	31t	—	86	1
Battery Driving Trailer Brake Standard:					
EO2.02.0B	BDBS	43t	—	66	—

Unit No	Liv	Pool	Dep	BDBS *EO202*	MS *EC204*	TS *EH222*	DTC *EE307*
307 101		*NGE*	IL	75001	61001	70001	75101
307 102	N	*NGE*	IL	75002	61002	70002	75102
307 103		*NGE*	IL	75003	61003	70003	75103
307 104		*NGE*	IL	75004	61004	70004	75104
307 105	N	*NGE*	IL	75005	61005	70005	75105
307 106	N	*NGE*	IL	75006	61006	70006	75106
307 107		*NGE*	IL	75007	61007	70007	75107
307 108		*NGE*	IL	75008	61008	70008	75108
307 109		*NGE*	IL	75009	61009	70009	75109
307 110		*NGE*	IL	75010	61010	70010	75110
307 111		*NGE*	IL	75011	61011	70011	75111
307 112		*NGE*	IL	75012	61012	70012	75112
307 113		*NGE*	IL	75013	61013	70013	75113
307 114		*NGE*	IL	75014	61014	70014	75114
307 115		*NGE*	IL	75015	61015	70015	75115
307 116		*NGE*	IL	75016	61016	70016	75116
307 117	N	*NGE*	IL	75017	61017	70017	75117
307 118		*NGE*	IL	75018	61018	70018	75118
307 119		*NGE*	IL	75019	61019	70019	75119
307 120		*NGE*	IL	75020	61020	70020	75120
307 121		*NGE*	IL	75021	61021	70021	75121
307 122	N	*NGE*	IL	75022	61022	70022	75122
307 123		*NGE*	IL	75023	61023	70023	75123
307 124		*NGE*	IL	75024	61024	70024	75124
307 125		*NGE*	IL	75025	61025	70025	75125
307 126	N	*NGE*	IL	75026	61026	70026	75126
307 127		*NGE*	IL	75027	61027	70027	75127
307 128		*NGE*	IL	75028	61028	70028	75128
307 129		*NGE*	IL	75029	61029	70029	75129
307 130	N	*NGE*	IL	75030	61030	70030	75130
307 131		*NGE*	IL	75031	61031	70031	75131
307 132	N	*NGE*	IL	75032	61032	70032	75132

Class 308/1 — 4-Car

Built: British Railways, 1961
Design: BR gangwayed within set. All units refurbished. (See Class 305/2 for full details.)

Diagram	*Type*	*Weight*	*Seats 1st*	*Seats Std*	*Toilet*
Motor Brake Standard:					
ED2.16.1B	MBS	55t	—	76	—
Driving Trailer Standard:					
EE2.20.0B	DTS	33t	—	88	—
Battery Driving Trailer Composite:					
EF3.04.0B	BDTC	36t	24	52	1
Trailer Standard:					
EH2.23.0A	TS	30t	—	86	1†
EH2.23.0B	TS	30t	—	86	1

† Class 305/2 vehicle

Unit No	Pool	Dep	BDTC *EF304*	MBS *ED216*	TS *EH223*	DTS *EE220*
308 133	*NGE*	IL	75878	61883	70611	75887
308 134	*NGE*	IL	75879	61884	70612	75888
308 135	*NGE*	IL	75880	61885	70613	75889
308 136	*NGE*	IL	75881	61886	70614	75890
308 137	*NGE*	IL	75882	61887	70615	75891
308 138	*NGE*	IL	75883	61888	70367†	75892
308 139	*NGE*	IL	75884	61889	70617	75893
308 140	*NTS*	EM	75885	61890	70618	75894
308 141	*NTS*	EM	75886	61891	70619	75895
308 142	*NTS*	EM	75896	61892	70620	75929
308 143	*NTS*	EM	75897	61893	70621	75930
308 144	*NTS*	EM	75898	61894	70622	75931
308 145	*NTS*	EM	75899	61895	70623	75932
308 146	*NTS*	EM	75900	61896	70624	75933
308 147	*NTS*	EM	75901	61897	70625	75934
308 148	*NTS*	EM	75902	61898	70626	75935
308 149	*NTS*	EM	75903	61899	70627	75936
308 150	*NTS*	EM	75904	61900	70628	75937

Unit No	Pool	Dep	BDTC	MBS	TS	DTS
308 151	*NTS*	EM	75905	61901	70629	75938
308 152	*NTS*	EM	75906	61902	70630	75939
308 153	*NTS*	EM	75907	61903	70631	75940
308 154	*NTS*	EM	75908	61904	70632	75941
308 155	*NTS*	EM	75909	61905	70633	75942
308 156	*NTS*	EM	75910	61906	70634	75943
308 157	*NTS*	EM	75911	61907	70635	75944
308 158	*NTS*	EM	75912	61908	70636	75945
308 159	*NTS*	EM	75913	61909	70637	75946
308 160	*NTS*	EM	75914	61910	70638	75947
308 161	*NTS*	EM	75915	61911	70639	75948
308 162	*NTS*	EM	75916	61912	70640	75949
308 163	*NTS*	EM	75917	61913	70641	75950
308 164	*NTS*	EM	75918	61914	70642	75951
308 165	*NTS*	EM	75919	61915	70643	75952

Class 308/2 — 3-Car (PLCS)

Built: British Railways, 1961. To parcels stock use in 1984 by conversion of DTS to DTLV. Seating not for public use
Design: BR non-gangwayed
Power Supply: 6.25 and 25kV ac
Traction Motors (MLV): Four 192hp (144kW) dc English Electric
Maximum speed: 75mph
AWS: Driving vehicles fitted

Diagram	Type	Weight	Seats	Toilets	Dimensions: L × W × H (m)
Battery Driving Trailer Standard					
EF2.01.0A	BDTS	36.5t	80	2	20.36 × 2.82 × 3.86
EF2.08.0A	BDTS	36.5t	80	2	20.18 × 2.82 × 3.86
Driving Trailer Luggage Van					
EW5.01.0A	DTLV	32t	—		20.36 × 2.82 × 3.86
Motor Luggage Van					
EY5.01.0A	MLV	53t	—		20.18 × 2.82 × 3.98 Pantograph housed

Unit No	Pool	Dep	DTLV	MLV	BDTS
			EW501	*EY501*	*EF208*
308 993	*REMA*	IL	75959	68017	75926
308 994	*REMA*	IL	75960	68018	—
			EW501	*EY501*	*EF201*
308 995	*REMA*	IL	75961	68012	75347

Class 309 — Essex Express 4-Car

Built: British Railways York, 1962
Design: BR, gangwayed throughout. All units refurbished and fitted with public address system
Supply: 6.25 and 25kV ac
Traction Motors: Four 282hp (210kW) dc GEC
Maximum speed: 100mph
AWS: All driving vehicles fitted
Dimensions: 20.18m L × 2.82m W × 3.90m H

Diagram	*Type*	*Weight*	*Seats 1st*	*Seats Std*	*Toilet*	
Driving Motor Brake Standard:						
EB2.07.0A	DMBS	60.5t	—	48	—	Catering Trolley point
Motor Brake Standard:						
ED2.18.0A	MBS	57t	—	48	—	Catering Trolley point
Driving Trailer Standard:						
EE2.29.0A	DTS	32t	—	56	2	
Battery Driving Trailer Standard:						
EF2.16.0A	BDTS	41t	—	60	2	
Battery Driving Trailer Composite:						
EF3.05.0A	BDTC	37.5t	18	32	2	
Trailer Standard/Composite:						
EH2.27.0A	TS	35t	—	64	2	
EH2.28.0A	TS	35t	—	68	—	
EH2.29.0A	TS	35t	—	68	—	
EH3.09.0A	TC	36t	24	28	1	

Class 309/1

Unit No	**Liv**	**Pool**	**Dep**	**DMBS**	**TC**	**TS**	**BDTS**
				EB207	*EH309*	*EH227*	*EF216*
309 601	N	*NGE*	CC	61940	71573	71569	75984
309 602	N	*NGE*	CC	61941	71574	71570	75985
309 603	N	*NGE*	CC	61942	71575	71571	75986
309 604	N	*NGE*	CC	61943	71576	71572	75987
309 605	N	*NGE*	CC	61944	71111	71107	75988
309 606	N	*NGE*	CC	61945	71112	71108	75989
309 607	N	*NGE*	CC	61946	71113	71109	75990
309 608	N	*NGE*	CC	61947	71114	71110	75991

Class 309/3

Unit No	**Liv**	**Pool**	**Dep**	**BDTC**	**MBS**	**TS**	**DTS**
				EF305	*ED218*	*EH228*	*EE229*
309 611	N	*NGE*	CC	75637	61932	71754	75976
309 612	E	*NGE*	CC	75638	61933	71755	75977
309 613	N	*NGE*	CC	75639	61934∅	71756	75978
309 614	N	*NGE*	CC	75640	61935	71757	75979
309 615	N	*NGE*	CC	75641	61936	71758	75980
309 616	N	*NGE*	CC	75642	61937∅	71759	75981
309 617	N	*NGE*	CC	75643	61938∅	71760	75982
309 618	N	*NGE*	CC	75644	61939∅	71761	75983
				EF305	*ED218*	*EH229*	*EE229*
309 621	N	*NGE*	CC	75962	61925	70253	75969
309 622	N	*NGE*	CC	75963	61926	70254	75970
309 623	N	*NGE*	CC	75964	61927	70255	75971
309 624	N	*NGE*	CC	75965	61928	70256	75972

Unit No	Liv	Pool	Dep	BDTC	MBS	TS	DTS
309 625	N	*NGE*	CC	75966	61929	70257	75973
309 626	N	*NGE*	CC	75967	61930	70258	75974
309 627	N	*NGE*	CC	75968	61931	70259	75975

Class 310 4-Car

Built: British Railways Derby, 1965
Design: BR, driving trailers are gangwayed to adjacent vehicle. G=gangwayed within unit, F=Facelifted, interior restyled and public address system fitted as shown
Supply: 25kV ac overhead
Traction Motors: Four 270hp (202kW) dc English Electric

Maximum speed: 75mph
AWS: Fitted to driving vehicles
Dimensions: 20.18m L × 2.82m W *Height:* EF2.14 & all TS: 3.83m; EF2.10, EF2.11, DTS & DTC: 3.86m; MBS: 3.98m Pantograph housed

Diagram	*Type*	*Weight*	*Seats 1st*	*Seats Std*	*Toilet*	
Motor Brake Standard:						
ED2.10.0A	MBS	57t	—	70		
ED2.10.--*	MBS	57t	—	70	—	Facelifted
ED2.19.0A	MBS	57t	—	70	—	Through Gangway
ED2.19.1B	MBS	57t	—	70	—	Through Gangway
Driving Trailer Standard/Composite:						
EE2.37.0A	DTS	34.5t	—	75	2	Facelifted
EE3.06.0A	DTC	34.5t	25	43	2	
EE3.06.1B	DTC	34.5t	25	43	2	Facelifted
Battery Driving Trailer Standard:						
EF2.10.1B	BDTS	34.5t	—	68	2	Facelifted
EF2.11.0A	BDTS	37.5t	—	80	2	
EF2.11.1B	BDTS	37.5t	—	80	2	Facelifted
EF2.11.2C	BDTS	37.5t	—	80	2	
EF2.14.1B	BDTS	35t	—	75	2	Facelifted
Trailer Standard:						
EH2.08.0A	TS	31.5t	—	100	—	
EH2.08.--*	TS	31.5t	—	100	—	Facelifted
EH2.32.0A	TS	31.5t	—	98	—	Through Gangway
EH2.32.1B	TS	31.5t	—	98	—	Through Gangway

*Official diagrams not issued

Class 310/0

Unit No	SC	Liv	Pool	Dep	BDTS *EF21*	MBS *ED21*	TS *EH2*	DTC *EE306*
310 046	GF	N	*NGE*	EM	76130 *11B*	62071 *90A*	70731 *320A*	76180 *1B*
310 047	GF	N	*NGE*	EM	76131 *11B*	62072 *90A*	70732 *320A*	76181 *1B*

Unit No	SC	Liv	Pool	Dep	BDTS		MBS		TS		DTC	
310 048†			*PBY*	BY	76132	*10A*	62073	*00A*	70733	*080A*	76182	*0A*
310 049		N	*NGE*	EM	76133	*10A*	62074	*00A*	70734	*080A*	76183	*0A*
310 050	GF	N	*NNE*	EM	76134	*11B*	62075	*90A*	70735	*320A*	76184	*1B*
310 051			*NNW*	BY	76135	*10A*	62076	*00A*	70736	*080A*	76185	*0A*
310 052	GF	N	*NNE*	EM	76136	*11B*	62077	*90A*	70737	*320A*	76186	*1B*
310 053†			*PBY*	BY	76137	*10A*	62078	*00A*	70738	*080A*	76187	*0A*
310 054†			*PBY*	BY	76138	*10A*	62079	*00A*	70739	*080A*	76188	*0A*
310 056	GF	N	*NGE*	EM	76140	*11B*	62081	*00A*	70741	*080A*	76190	*1B*
310 057		N	*NGE*	EM	76141	*10A*	62082	*00A*	70742	*080A*	76191	*0A*
310 058	GF	N	*NGE*	EM	76142	*11B*	62083	*90A*	70743	*320A*	76192	*1B*
310 059	GF	N	*NGE*	EM	76143	*11B*	62084	*0--*	70744	*08--*	76205	*1B*
310 060			*NGE*	EM	76144	*10A*	62085	*00A*	70745	*080A*	76194	*0A*
310 061	GF	N	*NGE*	EM	76145	*11B*	62086	*90A*	70746	*320A*	76195	*1B*
310 062†			*PBY*	BY	76146	*10A*	62087	*00A*	70747	*080A*	76196	*0A*
310 063†			*PBY*	BY	76147	*10A*	62088	*00A*	70748	*080A*	76197	*0A*
310 064	GF	N	*NNE*	EM	76148	*11B*	62089	*90A*	70749	*320A*	76198	*1B*
310 065	GF	N	*NNE*	EM	76149	*11B*	62090	*90A*	70750	*320A*	76199	*1B*
310 066	GF	N	*NNE*	EM	76228	*01B*	62091	*90A*	70751	*320A*	76200	*1B*
310 067	GF	N	*NNE*	EM	76151	*11B*	62092	*90A*	70752	*320A*	76201	*1B*
310 068	GF	N	*NGE*	EM	76152	*11B*	62093	*90A*	70753	*320A*	76202	*1B*
310 069	GF	N	*NGE*	EM	76153	*11B*	62094	*90A*	70754	*320A*	76203	*1B*
310 070	GF	N	*NGE*	EM	76154	*11B*	62095	*90A*	70755	*320A*	76204	*1B*
310 074			*NGE*	EM	76158	*10A*	62099	*00A*	70759	*080A*	76208	*0A*
310 075	GF	N	*NNE*	EM	76159	*11B*	62100	*90A*	70760	*320A*	76209	*1B*
310 077	GF	N	*NNE*	EM	76161	*11B*	62102	*90A*	70762	*320A*	76211	*1B*
310 079		N	*NNE*	EM	76163	*10A*	62104	*00A*	70764	*080A*	76213	*0A*
310 080	GF	N	*NNE*	EM	76164	*11B*	62105	*90A*	70765	*320A*	76214	*1B*
310 081			*NGE*	EM	76165	*10A*	62106	*00A*	70766	*080A*	76215	*0A*
310 082	GF	N	*NNE*	EM	76166	*11B*	62107	*90A*	70767	*320A*	76216	*1B*
310 083		N	*NGE*	EM	76167	*10A*	62108	*00A*	70768	*080A*	76217	*0A*
310 084	GF	N	*NNE*	EM	76168	*11B*	62109	*90A*	70769	*320A*	76218	*1B*
310 085	GF	N	*NNE*	EM	76169	*11B*	62110	*90A*	70770	*320A*	76219	*1B*
310 086	F		*NNW*	BY	76170	*11B*	62111	*0--*	70771	*08--*	76220	*1B*
310 087	GF	N	*NNE*	EM	76171	*11B*	62112	*90A*	70772	*320A*	76221	*1B*
310 088		N	*NNE*	EM	76172	*10A*	62113	*00A*	70773	*080A*	76222	*0A*
310 089		N	*NNE*	EM	76173	*10A*	62114	*00A*	70774	*080A*	76223	*0A*
310 091	GF	N	*NNE*	EM	76175	*11B*	62116	*90A*	70776	*320A*	76225	*1B*
310 092	GF	N	*NNE*	EM	76176	*11B*	62117	*90A*	70777	*320A*	76226	*1B*
310 093	F		*NGE*	EM	76177	*11B*	62118	*0--*	70778	*08--*	76227	*1B*
310 094	GF	N	*NNE*	EM	76998	*41B*	62119	*90A*	70780	*320A*	76193	*1B*
310 095		N	*NNE*	EM	76179	*10A*	62120	*00A*	70779	*080A*	76229	*0A*

† Class 310/0 units for conversion to Class 310/1 during 1989/90.

Class 310/1

Unit No	Old No	SC	Liv	Pool	Dep	BDTS	MBS	TS	DTS
						EF2112C	*ED2191B*	*EH2321B*	*EE2370A*
310 101	(310 073)	GF	P	*PBY*	BY	76157	62098	70758	76207
310 102	(310 055)	GF	P	*PBY*	BY	76139	62080	70740	76189
310 103	(310 076)	GF	P	*PBY*	BY	76160	62101	70761	76210
310 104	(310 078)	GF	P	*PBY*	BY	76162	62103	70763	76212
310 105	(310 090)	GF	P	*PBY*	BY	76174	62115	70775	76224
310 106	(310 072)	GF	P	*PBY*	BY	76156	62097	70757	76206
310 107	(310)	GF	P	*PBY*					
310 108	(310)	GF	P	*PBY*					
310 109	(310)	GF	P	*PBY*					
310 110	(310)	GF	P	*PBY*					
310 111	(310)	GF	P	*PBY*					

Class 311 3-Car

Built: Cravens 1967
Design: BR, saloons with sliding doors, non-gangwayed
Supply: 25kV ac overhead (built also for 6.25kV ac)
Traction motors (MBS): Four 222hp dc AEI
Maximum speed: 75mph
Dimensons: 20.18m L × 2.82m W × 3.86m H; *MBS:* 3,98m H, pantograph housed

AWS: Fitted to driving vehicles

Diagram	*Type*	*Weight*	*Seats*
Motor Brake Standard			
ED2.11.0A	MBS	58t	70
Driving Trailer Standard:			
EE2.14.0A	DTS	34.5t	83
Battery Driving Trailer Standard:			
EF2.12.0A	BDTS	37.5t	83

Unit No	SC	Liv	Pool	Dep	DTS	MBS	BDTS
					EE2.14	*ED2.11*	*EF2.12*
311 092		S	*PGW*	GW	76403	62163	76422
311 097			*PGW*	GW	76408	62168	76427
311 098	M	S	*PGW*	GW	76409	62169	76428
311 099	M		*PGW*	GW	76410	62170	76429
311 102	M		*PGW*	GW	76413	62173	76432
311 103	M		*PGW*	GW	76414	62174	76433
311 104	M		*PGW*	GW	76415	62175	76434
311 105	M	S	*PGW*	GW	76416	62176	76435
311 107	M		*PGW*	GW	76418	62178	76437
311 108	M		*PGW*	GW	76419	62179	76438
311 109	M	S	*PGW*	GW	76420	62180	76439
311 110	M		*PGW*	GW	76421	62181	76440

Class 312 — 4-Car

Built: BREL York 1975
Design: BR, saloons, gangwayed within units. Public address system fitted.
Supply: 25kV ac overhead (Class 312/1 originally also fitted 6.25kV ac)
Traction motors: Four 270hp (202kW) dc GEC
Maximum speed: 90mph
Dimensons: 20.18m L × 2.82m W × 3.86m H; *MBS:* 3.98m H, pantograph housed
Headlight and AWS: Fitted to driving vehicles

Diagram	*Type*	*Weight*	*Seats 1st*	*Seats Std*	*Toilet*
Motor Brake Standard					
ED2.12.0B	MBS	56t	—	68	
ED2.13.0A	MBS	55.5t	—	68	
ED2.13.0B*	MBS	55.5t	—	68	
ED2.14.0B	MBS	55.5t	—	68	
Driving Trailer Composite					
EE3.05.1D	DTC	33t	25	47	
EE3.05.2B	DTC	33t	25	47	
EE3.05.2C*	DTC	33t	25	47	
Battery Driving Trailer Standard					
EF2.13.0C	BDTS	35t	—	84	1
EF2.13.1A	BDTS	35t	—	84	1
EF2.13.1B*	BDTS	35t	—	84	1
Trailer Second					
EH2.09.0C	TS	30.5t	—	98	
EH2.19.1A	TS	30.5t	—	98	
EH2.19.1B*	TS	30.5t	—	98	

*Unofficial codes, not yet issued

Class 312/0

Unit No	SC	Liv	Pool	Dep	BDTS *EF2130C*	MBS *ED2120B*	TS *EH2090C*	DTC *EE3051D*
312 701	F	N	*NGE*	CC	76949	62484	71168	78000
312 702	F	N	*NGE*	CC	76950	62485	71169	78001
312 703	F	N	*NGE*	CC	76951	62486	71170	78002
312 704	F		*NGE*	CC	76952	62487	71171	78003
312 705	F		*NGE*	CC	76953	62488	71172	78004
312 706	F	N	*NGE*	CC	76954	62489	71173	78005
312 707	F	N	*NGE*	CC	76955	62490	71174	78006
312 708	F	N	*NGE*	CC	76956	62491	71175	78007
312 709	F	N	*NGE*	CC	76957	62492	71176	78008
312 710	F	N	*NGE*	CC	76958	62493	71177	78009
312 711	F	N	*NGE*	CC	76959	62494	71178	78010
312 712	F	N	*NGE*	CC	76960	62495	71179	78011
312 713	F	N	*NGE*	CC	76961	62496	71180	78012
312 714	F	N	*NGE*	CC	76962	62497	71181	78013
312 715	F	N	*NGE*	CC	76963	62498	71182	78014
312 716	F	N	*NGE*	CC	76964	62499	71183	78015
312 717	F	N	*NGE*	CC	76965	62500	71184	78016
312 718	F	N	*NGE*	CC	76966	62501	71185	78017

Unit No	SC	Liv	Pool	Dep	BDTS	MBS	TS	DTC
312 719	F	N	*NGE*	CC	76967	62502	71186	78018
312 720	F	N	*NGE*	CC	76968	62503	71187	78019
312 721	F	N	*NGE*	CC	76969	62504	71188	78020
312 722	F	N	*NGE*	CC	76970	62505	71189	78021
312 723	F	N	*NGE*	CC	76971	62506	71190	78022
312 724	F	N	*NGE*	CC	76972	62507	71191	78023
312 725	F	N	*NGE*	CC	76973	62508	71192	78024
312 726	F	N	*NGE*	CC	76974	62509	71193	78025
					EF2130C	*ED2140B*	*EH2090C*	*EE3051D*
312 727	F	N	*NGE*	CC	76994	62657	71277	78045
312 728	F	N	*NGE*	CC	76995	62658	71278	78046
312 729	F		*NGE*	CC	76996	62659	71279	78047
312 730	F	N	*NGE*	CC	76997	62660	71280	78048

Unit Nos 312727-30 modified from Class 312/2 and renumbered from Unit Nos 312201-04 during 1988

CLASS 312/1

Unit No	SC	Liv	Pool	Dep	BDTS		MBS		TS		DTC	
					EF213		*ED213*		*EH219*		*EE305*	
312 781	F	N	*NGE*	CC	76975	*1B*	62510	*0B*	71194	*1B*	78026	*2C*
312 782			*NGE*	CC	76976	*1A*	62511	*0A*	71195	*1A*	78027	*2B*
312 783			*NGE*	CC	76977	*1A*	62512	*0A*	71196	*1A*	78028	*2B*
312 784	F	N	*NGE*	CC	76978	*1B*	62513	*0B*	71197	*1B*	78029	*2C*
312 785	F	N	*NGE*	CC	76979	*1B*	62514	*0B*	71198	*1B*	78030	*2C*
312 786			*NGE*	CC	76980	*1A*	62515	*0A*	71199	*1A*	78031	*2B*
312 787			*NGE*	CC	76981	*1A*	62516	*0A*	71200	*1A*	78032	*2B*
312 788	F	N	*NGE*	CC	76982	*1B*	62517	*0B*	71201	*1B*	78033	*2C*
312 789	F	N	*NGE*	CC	76983	*1B*	62518	*0B*	71202	*1B*	78034	*2C*
312 790			*NGE*	CC	76984	*1A*	62519	*0A*	71203	*1A*	78035	*2B*
312 791	F	N	*NGE*	CC	76985	*1B*	62520	*0B*	71204	*1B*	78036	*2C*
312 792	F	N	*NGE*	CC	76986	*1A*	62521	*0A*	71205	*1A*	78037	*2B*
312 793	F	N	*NGE*	CC	76987	*1B*	62522	*0B*	71206	*1B*	78038	*2C*
312 794	F	N	*NGE*	CC	76988	*1B*	62523	*0B*	71207	*1B*	78039	*2B*
312 795	F	N	*NGE*	CC	76989	*1B*	62524	*0B*	71208	*1B*	78040	*2C*
312 796			*NGE*	CC	76990	*1A*	62525	*0A*	71209	*1A*	78041	*2B*
312 797			*NGE*	CC	76991	*1A*	62526	*0A*	71210	*1A*	78042	*2B*
312 798	F	N	*NGE*	CC	76992	*1B*	62527	*0B*	71211	*1B*	78043	*2C*
312 799			*NGE*	CC	76993	*1B*	62528	*0A*	71212	*1A*	78044	*2B*

Class 313 — 3-Car

Built: BREL York 1976
Design: BR with sliding doors, gangwayed withing units and end doors. Driver/guard and public address systems fitted. Pressure and heating ventilation
Supply: 25kV ac overhead and 750V dc third rail
Traction motors (DMS & BDMS): Four 110hp (82.5kW) GEC G310AZ
Maximum speed: On 25kV: 70mph; on 750V (third rail) 30mph

Dimensons: *Driving coaches:* 19.80m L × 2.82m W × 3.58m H; *Trailer coach:* 19.92m L × 2.82m W ×3.98m H, pantograph housed
AWS: Fitted to driving vehicles

Diagram	*Type*	*Weight*	*Seats*
Driving Motor Standard			
EA2.04.0A	DMS	36t	74
EA2.04.0B	DMS	36t	74†
†Steel body, others aluminium			
Trailer Second, Pantograph			
EH2.10.0A	TS(P)	31t	84
Battery Driving Motor Second			
EI2.01.0A	BDMS	37.5t	74

Unit No	SC	Liv	Pool	Dep	DMS	TS(P)	BDMS
Class 313/1							
					EA2040A	*EH2100A*	*EI2010A*
313 001	D	N	*NNW*	BY	62529	71213	62593
313 002	D	N	*NNL*	BY	62530	71214	62594
313 003	D	N	*NNW*	BY	62531	71215	62595
313 004	D	N	*NNW*	BY	62532	71216	62596
313 005	D	N	*NNW*	BY	62533	71217	62597
313 006	D	N	*NNW*	BY	62534	71218	62598
313 007	D	N	*NNW*	BY	62535	71219	62599
313 008	D	N	*NNW*	BY	62536	71220	62600
313 009	D	N	*NNW*	BY	62537	71221	62601
313 010	D	N	*NNW*	BY	62538	71222	62602
313 011	D	N	*NNW*	BY	62539	71223	62603
313 012	D	N	*NNW*	BY	62540	71224	62604
313 013	D	N	*NNW*	BY	62541	71225	62605
313 014	D	N	*NNW*	BY	62542	71226	62606
313 015	DM	N	*NGN*	HE	62543	71227	62607
313 016	DM	N	*NGN*	HE	62544	71228	62608
313 017	DM	N	*NGN*	HE	62545	71229	62609
Class 313/0							
313 018	M	N	*NGN*	HE	62546	71230	62610
313 019	M		*NGN*	HE	62547	71231	62611
313 020	M		*NGN*	HE	62548	71232	62612
313 021	M		*NGN*	HE	62549	71233	62613
313 022	M	N	*NGN*	HE	62550	71234	62614
313 023	M		*NGN*	HE	62551	71235	62615
313 024	M	N	*NGN*	HE	62552	71236	62616
313 025	M		*NGN*	HE	62553	71237	62617

Unit No	SC	Liv	Pool	Dep	DMS	TS(P)	BDMS
313 026	M		*NGN*	HE	62554	71238	62618
313 027	M	N	*NGN*	HE	62555	71239	62619
313 028	M	N	*NGN*	HE	62556	71240	62620
313 029	M	N	*NGN*	HE	62557	71241	62621
313 030	M		*NGN*	HE	62558	71242	62622
313 031	M		*NGN*	HE	62559	71243	62623
313 032	M		*NGN*	HE	62560	71244	62624
313 033	M	N	*NGN*	HE	62561	71245	62625
313 034	M		*NGN*	HE	62562	71246	62626
313 035	M	N	*NGN*	HE	62563	71247	62627
313 036	M	N	*NGN*	HE	62564	71248	62628
313 037	M		*NGN*	HE	62565	71249	62629
					EA2040B	*EH2100A*	*EI2010A*
313 038	M	N	*NGN*	HE	62566	71250	62630
					EA2040A	*EH2100A*	*EI2010A*
313 039	M	N	*NGN*	HE	62567	71251	62631
313 040	M		*NGN*	HE	62568	71252	62632
313 041	M		*NGN*	HE	62569	71253	62633
313 042	M		*NGN*	HE	62570	71254	62634
313 043	M		*NGN*	HE	62571	71255	62635
313 044	M		*NGN*	HE	62572	71256	62636
313 045	M		*NGN*	HE	62573	71257	62637
313 046	M		*NGN*	HE	62574	71258	62638
313 047	M		*NGN*	HE	62575	71259	62639
313 048	M	N	*NGN*	HE	62576	71260	62640
313 049	M		*NGN*	HE	62577	71261	62641
313 050	M		*NGN*	HE	62578	71262	62642
313 051	M		*NGN*	HE	62579	71263	62643
313 052	M		*NGN*	HE	62580	71264	62644
313 053	M		*NGN*	HE	62581	71265	62645
313 054	M		*NGN*	HE	62582	71266	62646
313 055	M		*NGN*	HE	62583	71267	62647
313 056	M		*NGN*	HE	62584	71268	62648
313 057	M		*NGN*	HE	62585	71269	62649
313 058	M		*NGN*	HE	62586	71270	62650
313 059	M		*NGN*	HE	62587	71271	62651
313 060	M		*NGN*	HE	62588	71272	62652
313 096			*NGE*	CC	62589	71273	62653
313 097			*NGE*	CC	62590	71274	62654
313 098			*NGE*	CC	62591	71275	62655
313 099			*NGE*	CC	62592	71276	62656

Class 314 — 3-Car

Built: BREL York 1979
Design: BR, saloons with sliding doors gangwayed within unit and end doors. Public address system fitted. Pressure and heating ventilation
Supply: 25kV ac overhead
Traction motors: (DMS) Four 110hp (82.5kW) GEC 6310AZ or Brush TM61-53, interchangeable
Maximum speed: 75mph

Dimensons: *Driving coaches:* 19.80m L × 2.82m W × 3.58m H; *Trailer vehicle:* 19.92m L × 2.82m W ×3.98m H pantograph housed
AWS: Driving vehicles fitted

Diagram	*Type*	*Weight*	*Seats*	
Driving Motor Standard				
EA2.06.0A	DMS	34.5t	68	
EA2.06.0B	DMS	34.5t	68	Emergency tool box
Trailer Second, Pantograph				
EH2.11.0A	TS	33t	76	

Unit No	SC	Liv	Pool	Dep	DMS *EA2060A*	TS(P) *EH2110A*	DMS *EA2060B*
314 201		S	*PGW*	GW	64583	71450	64584
314 202	M	S	*PGW*	GW	64585	71451	64586
314 203		S	*PGW*	GW	64587	71452	64588
314 204		S	*PGW*	GW	64589	71453	64590
314 205	M	S	*PGW*	GW	64591	71454	64592
314 206		S	*PGW*	GW	64593	71455	64594
314 207	M	S	*PGW*	GW	64595	71456	64596
314 208	M	S	*PGW*	GW	64597	71457	64598
314 209	M	S	*PGW*	GW	64599	71458	64600
314 210		S	*PGW*	GW	64601	71459	64602
314 211	M	S	*PGW*	GW	64603	71460	64604
314 212	M	S	*PGW*	GW	64605	71461	64606
314 213	M	S	*PGW*	GW	64607	71462	64608
314 214	M	S	*PGW*	GW	64609	71463	64610
314 215	M	S	*PGW*	GW	64611	71464	64612
314 216	M	S	*PGW*	GW	64613	71465	64614

Class 315 — 4-Car

Built: BREL York 1980
Design: BR, saloons with sliding doors, gangwayed within units and end doors. Driver/guard communication and public address system fitted. Pressure and heating ventilation
Supply: 25kV ac

Traction motors: (DMS) Four 110hp (82.5kW) GEC 310AZ or Brush TM61-53, interchangeable
Maximum speed: 75mph
Dimensons: *Driving coaches:* 19.80m L × 2.82m W × 3.58m H; *Trailer coaches:* 20.18m L × 2.82m W ×3.58m H, pantograph housed

AWS: Driving vehicles fitted

Diagram	*Type*	*Weight*	*Seats*	
Driving Motor Standard				
EA2.07.0A	DMS	35t	74	
EA2.07.0B	DMS	35t	74	Emergency tool box
Trailer Standard				
EH2.16.0A	TS	25.5t	86	
EH2.17.0A	TS	32t	84	Pantograph

NSE Classification: *Class 315/0:* Units 315842-61 (GEC equipment); *Class 315/1:* Units 315801-41 (Brush equipment)

Unit No	SC	Liv	Pool	Dep	DMS *EA2070A*	TS *EH2160A*	TS(P) *EH2170A*	DMS *EA2070B*
315 801	M		*NGE*	IL	64461	71281	71389	64462
315 802	M		*NGE*	IL	64463	71282	71390	64464
315 803	M		*NGE*	IL	64465	71283	71391	64466
315 804	M		*NGE*	IL	64467	71284	71392	64468
315 805	M		*NGE*	IL	64469	71285	71393	64470
315 806			*NGE*	IL	64471	71286	71394	64472
315 807			*NGE*	IL	64473	71287	71395	64474
315 808			*NGE*	IL	64475	71288	71396	64476
315 809			*NGE*	IL	64477	71289	71397	64478
315 810			*NGE*	IL	64479	71290	71398	64480
315 811			*NGE*	IL	64481	71291	71399	64482
315 812		N	*NGE*	IL	64483	71292	71400	64484
315 813			*NGE*	IL	64485	71293	71401	64486
315 814			*NGE*	IL	64487	71294	71402	64488
315 815			*NGE*	IL	64489	71295	71403	64490
315 816		N	*NGE*	IL	64491	71296	71404	64492
315 817		N	*NGE*	IL	64493	71297	71405	64494
315 818		N	*NGE*	IL	64495	71298	71406	64496
315 819		N	*NGE*	IL	64497	71299	71407	64498
315 820		N	*NGE*	IL	64499	71300	71408	64500
315 821		N	*NGE*	IL	64501	71301	71409	64502
315 822			*NGE*	IL	64503	71302	71410	64504
315 823		N	*NGE*	IL	64505	71303	71411	64506
315 824		N	*NGE*	IL	64507	71304	71412	64508
315 825		N	*NGE*	IL	64509	71305	71413	64510
315 826			*NGE*	IL	64511	71306	71414	64512
315 827			*NGE*	IL	64513	71307	71415	64514
315 828		N	*NGE*	IL	64515	71308	71416	64516
315 829		N	*NGE*	IL	64517	71309	71417	64518
315 830		N	*NGE*	IL	64519	71310	71418	64520
315 831		N	*NGE*	IL	64521	71311	71419	64522
315 832		N	*NGE*	IL	64523	71312	71420	64524
315 833		N	*NGE*	IL	64525	71313	71421	64526
315 834		N	*NGE*	IL	64527	71314	71422	64528
315 835			*NGE*	IL	64529	71315	71423	64530
315 836		N	*NGE*	IL	64531	71316	71424	64532
315 837		N	*NGE*	IL	64533	71317	71425	64534
315 838		N	*NGE*	IL	64535	71318	71426	64536
315 839		N	*NGE*	IL	64537	71319	71427	64538

Unit No	SC	Liv	Pool	Dep	DMS	TS	TS(P)	DMS
315 840		N	*NGE*	IL	64539	71320	71428	64540
315 841		N	*NGE*	IL	64541	71321	71429	64542
315 842		N	*NGE*	IL	64543	71322	71430	64544
315 843		N	*NGE*	IL	64545	71323	71431	64546
315 844		N	*NGE*	IL	64547	71324	71432	64548
315 845		N	*NGE*	IL	64549	71325	71433	64550
315 846		N	*NGE*	IL	64551	71326	71434	64552
315 847		N	*NGE*	IL	64553	71327	71435	64554
315 848		N	*NGE*	IL	64555	71328	71436	64556
315 849		N	*NGE*	IL	64557	71329	71437	64558
315 850		N	*NGE*	IL	64559	71330	71438	64560
315 851		N	*NGE*	IL	64561	71331	71439	64562
315 852		N	*NGE*	IL	64563	71332	71440	64564
315 853		N	*NGE*	IL	64565	71333	71441	64566
315 854		N	*NGE*	IL	64567	71334	71442	64568
315 855		N	*NGE*	IL	64569	71335	71443	64570
315 856		N	*NGE*	IL	64571	71336	71444	64572
315 857		N	*NGE*	IL	64573	71337	71445	64574
315 858		N	*NGE*	IL	64575	71338	71446	64576
315 859		N	*NGE*	IL	64577	71339	71447	64578
315 860		N	*NGE*	IL	64579	71340	71448	64580
315 861		N	*NGE*	IL	64581	71341	71449	64582

Class 317 — 4-Car

Built: BREL Derby and York 1981
Design: BR, saloons with sliding doors, gangwayed throughout. Public address and Driver/guard communication system fitted. Pressure and heating ventilation. Equipped for driver-only operation
Supply: 25kV ac overhead
Traction motors: (**MS**) Four 332hp (249kW) GEC G315BZ
Maximum speed: 90mph
Dimensions: *Driving coaches:* 20.13m L × 2.82m W × 3.77m H; *Trailer coaches:* 20.18m L × 2.82m W ×3.77m H, pantograph housed
Toilets: Class 317/0 units are fitted with gravity toilets due to tunnel use

			Seats		
Diagram	*Type*	*Weight*	*1st*	*Std*	*Toilets*
Motor Standard					
EC2.02.0A	MS	49t	—	79	
EC2.05.0A	MS	49t	—	79	
EC2.08.0A	MS	49t	—	79	
Driving Trailer Standard					
EE2.16.0A	DTS(A)	29.5t	—	74	
EE2.17.0A	DTS(B)	29.5t	—	74	
EE2.24.0A	DTS(A)	29.5t	—	74	
EE2.25.0A	DTS(B)	29.5t	—	74	
EE2.32.0A	DTS(B)	29.5t	—	71	
EE2.35.0A	DTS(B)	29.5t	—	70	
Trailer Composite					
EH3.07.0A	TC	29t	22	46	2
EH3.08.0A	TC	28.3t	22	46	2

CLASS 317/0

Unit No	SC	Liv	Pool	Dep	DTS *EE2160A*	MS *EC2020A*	TC *EH3070A*	DTS *EE2350A*
317 301		N	*NNW*	BY	77024	62661	71577	77048
317 302		N	*NNW*	BY	77001	62662	71578	77049
317 303		N	*NNW*	BY	77002	62663	71579	77050
317 304		N	*NNW*	BY	77003	62664	71580	77051
317 305		N	*NNW*	BY	77004	62665	71581	77052
317 306		N	*NNW*	BY	77005	62666	71582	77053
317 307		N	*NNW*	BY	77006	62667	71583	77054
317 308		N	*NNW*	BY	77007	62668	71584	77055
317 309		N	*NNW*	BY	77008	62669	71585	77056
317 310		N	*NNW*	BY	77009	62670	71586	77057
317 311		N	*NNW*	BY	77010	62671	71587	77058
317 312		N	*NNW*	BY	77011	62672	71588	77059
317 313		N	*NNW*	BY	77012	62673	71589	77060
317 314		N	*NNW*	BY	77013	62674	71590	77061
317 315		N	*NNW*	BY	77014	62675	71591	77062
317 316		N	*NNW*	BY	77015	62676	71592	77063
317 317		N	*NNW*	BY	77016	62677	71593	77064
317 318		N	*NNW*	BY	77017	62678	71594	77065
317 319		N	*NNW*	BY	77018	62679	71595	77066
317 320		N	*NNW*	BY	77019	62680	71596	77067
317 321		N	*NNW*	BY	77020	62681	71597	77068
317 322		N	*NNW*	BY	77021	62682	71598	77069
317 323		N	*NNW*	BY	77022	62683	71599	77070
317 324		N	*NNW*	BY	77023	62684	71600	77071
317 325		N	*NNW*	BY	77000	62685	71601	77072
317 326		N	*NNW*	BY	77025	62686	71602	77073
317 327		N	*NNW*	BY	77026	62687	71603	77074
317 328		N	*NNW*	BY	77027	62688	71604	77075
317 329		N	*NNW*	BY	77028	62689	71605	77076
317 330		N	*NNW*	BY	77029	62690	71606	77077
317 331		N	*NNW*	BY	77030	62691	71607	77078
317 332		N	*NNW*	BY	77031	62692	71608	77079
317 333		N	*NNW*	BY	77032	62693	71609	77080
317 334		N	*NNW*	BY	77033	62694	71610	77081

CLASS 317/1

Unit No	SC	Liv	Pool	Dep	DTS	MS	TC	DTS
					EE2160A	*EC2080A*	*EH3080A*	*EE2350A*
317 335		N	*NGN*	HE	77034	62695	71611	77082
317 336		N	*NGN*	HE	77035	62696	71612	77083
					EE2160A	*EC2080A*	*EH3080A*	*EE2320A*
317 337		N	*NGN*	HE	77036	62697	71613	77084
317 338		N	*NGN*	HE	77037	62698	71614	77085
317 339		N	*NGN*	HE	77038	62699	71615	77086

Unit No	SC	Liv	Pool	Dep	DTS	MS	TC	DTS
317 340		N	*NGN*	HE	77039	62700	71616	77087
317 341		N	*NGN*	HE	77040	62701	71617	77088
317 342		N	*NGN*	HE	77041	62702	71618	77089
317 343		N	*NGN*	HE	77042	62703	71619	77090
317 344		N	*NGN*	HE	77043	62704	71620	77091
317 345			*NGN*	HE	77044	62705	71621	77092
					EE2160A	*EC2020A*	*EH3080A*	*EE2170A*
317 346		N	*NGN*	HE	77045	62706	71622	77093
317 347		N	*NGN*	HE	77046	62707	71623	77094
					EE2160A	*EC2080A*	*EH3080A*	*EE2320A*
317 348		N	*NGN*	HE	77047	62708	71624	77095

CLASS 317/2

Unit No	SC	Liv	Pool	Dep	DTS	MS	TC	DTS
					EE2240A	*EC2050A*	*EH3080A*	*EE2250A*
317 349		N	*NGN*	HE	77200	62846	71734	77220
317 350			*NGN*	HE	77201	62847	71735	77221
317 351		N	*NGN*	HE	77202	62848	71736	77222
317 352			*NGN*	HE	77203	62849	71739	77223
317 353			*NGN*	HE	77204	62850	71738	77224
317 354		N	*NGN*	HE	77205	62851	71737	77225
317 355			*NGN*	HE	77206	62852	71740	77226
317 356			*NGN*	HE	77207	62853	71742	77227
317 357			*NGN*	HE	77208	62854	71741	77228
317 358			*NGN*	HE	77209	62855	71743	77229
317 359		N	*NGN*	HE	77210	62856	71744	77230
317 360		N	*NGN*	HE	77211	62857	71745	77231
317 361			*NGN*	HE	77212	62858	71746	77232
317 362			*NGN*	HE	77213	62859	71747	77233
317 363			*NGN*	HE	77214	62860	71748	77234
317 364			*NGN*	HE	77215	62861	71749	77235
317 365		N	*NGN*	HE	77216	62862	71750	77236
317 366		N	*NGN*	HE	77217	62863	71752	77237
317 367		N	*NGN*	HE	77218	62864	71751	77238
317 368		N	*NGN*	HE	77219	62865	71753	77239
317 369		N	*NGN*	HE	77280	62886	71762	77284
317 370		N	*NGN*	HE	77281	62887	71763	77285
317 371		N	*NGN*	HE	77282	62888	71764	77286
317 372		N	*NGN*	HE	77283	62889	71765	77287

Class 318 — 3-Car

Built: BREL Derby and York 1986
Design: BR saloons, with sliding doors, gangwayed throughout. Driver only operation, Driver/guard and public address sytems fitted
Supply: 25kV ac overhead
Traction motors (DMS): Four 332hp (249kW) GECG 315 BZ
Dimensions: *Driving coaches:* 20.13m L × 2.82m W × 3.77m H; *Trailer coach:* 20.18m L × 2.82m W × 3.78m H. Pantograph housed
AWS: Driving vehicles fitted

Diagram	*Type*	*Weight*	*Seats*	*Toilets*
Motor Standard				
EC2.07.0A	MS	50.9t	79	—
Driving Trailer Standard:				
EE2.27.0A	DTS (A)	30.1t	66	1 Invalid area
EE2.28.0A	DTS (B)	29.6t	71	—

Unit No	Liv	Pool	Dep	DTS EE2270A	MS EC2070A	DTS EE2280A
318 250	S	*PGW*	GW	77240	62866	77260
318 251	S	*PGW*	GW	77241	62867	77261
318 252	S	*PGW*	GW	77242	62868	77262
318 253	S	*PGW*	GW	77243	62869	77263
318 254	S	*PGW*	GW	77244	62870	77264
318 255	S	*PGW*	GW	77245	62871	77265
318 256	S	*PGW*	GW	77246	62872	77266
318 257	S	*PGW*	GW	77247	62873	77267
318 258	S	*PGW*	GW	77248	62874	77268
318 259	S	*PGW*	GW	77249	62875	77269
318 260	S	*PGW*	GW	77250	62876	77270
318 261	S	*PGW*	GW	77251	62877	77271
318 262	S	*PGW*	GW	77252	62878	77272
318 263	S	*PGW*	GW	77253	62879	77273
318 264	S	*PGW*	GW	77254	62880	77274
318 265	S	*PGW*	GW	77255	62881	77275
318 266	S	*PGW*	GW	77256	62882	77276
318 267	S	*PGW*	GW	77257	62883	77277
318 268	S	*PGW*	GW	77258	62884	77278
318 269	S	*PGW*	GW	77259	62885	77279
318 270	S	*PGW*	GW	77288	62890	77289

Class 319 — 4-Car

Built: BREL York 1987 for Thameslink cross-London duties from Bedford to Brighton and Orpington via Snow Hill tunnel
Design: BR, Saloons, with sliding doors, gangwayed within unit and emergency end doors
Supply: 25kV ac overhead, 750V dc third rail
Traction motors: Four 332hp (249kW) GEC G315 BZ
Dimensions: 20.18m L × 2.82m W × 3.77m H; **MS** 3.78m H Pantograph housed
Maximum Speed: 100mph

Diagram	*Type*	*Weight*	*Seats*	*Toilet*
Motor Standard				
EC2.09.0A	MS	49.2t	81	—
Driving Trailer Standard:				
EE2.33.0A	DTS (A)	28.2t	81	—
EE2.34.0A	DTS (B)	28.1t	78 incl 8 tip-up	—
Trailer Standard:				
EH2.34.0A	TS	31t	76	2

Unit No	Liv	Pool	Dep	BDTS *EE2340A*	MS *EC2090A*	TS *EH2340A*	DTS *EE2330A*
319 001	N	*NML*	SU	77290	62891	71772	77291
319 002	N	*NSX*	SU	77292	62892	71773	77293
319 003	N	*NSX*	SU	77294	62893	71774	77295
319 004	N	*NSX*	SU	77296	62894	71775	77297
319 005	N	*NSX*	SU	77298	62895	71817	77299
319 006	N	*NSX*	SU	77300	62896	71777	77301
319 007	N	*NSX*	SU	77302	62897	71778	77303
319 008	N	*NSX*	SU	77304	62898	71779	77305
319 009	N	*NSX*	SU	77306	62899	71780	77307
319 010	N	*NSX*	SU	77308	62900	71781	77309
319 011	N	*NSX*	SU	77310	62901	71782	77311
319 012	N	*NML*	SU	77312	62902	71783	77313
319 013	N	*NML*	SU	77314	62903	71784	77315
319 014	N	*NML*	SU	77316	62904	71785	77317
319 015	N	*NML*	SU	77318	62905	71786	77319
319 016	N	*NML*	SU	77320	62906	71787	77321
319 017	N	*NML*	SU	77322	62907	71788	77323
319 018	N	*NML*	SU	77324	62908	71789	77325
319 019	N	*NML*	SU	77326	62909	71790	77327
319 020	N	*NML*	SU	77328	62910	71791	77329
319 021	N	*NML*	SU	77330	62911	71792	77331
319 022	N	*NML*	SU	77332	62912	71793	77333
319 023	N	*NML*	SU	77334	62913	71794	77335
319 024	N	*NML*	SU	77336	62914	71795	77337
319 025	N	*NML*	SU	77338	62915	71796	77339
319 026	N	*NML*	SU	77340	62916	71797	77341
319 027	N	*NML*	SU	77342	62917	71798	77343
319 028	N	*NML*	SU	77344	62918	71799	77345
319 029	N	*NML*	SU	77346	62919	71800	77347
319 030	N	*NML*	SU	77348	62920	71801	77349
319 031	N	*NML*	SU	77350	62921	71802	77351
319 032	N	*NML*	SU	77352	62922	71803	77353
319 033	N	*NML*	SU	77354	62923	71804	77355
319 034	N	*NML*	SU	77356	62924	71805	77357
319 035	N	*NML*	SU	77358	62925	71806	77359
319 036	N	*NML*	SU	77360	62926	71807	77361
319 037	N	*NML*	SU	77362	62927	71808	77363
319 038	N	*NML*	SU	77364	62928	71809	77365
319 039	N	*NML*	SU	77366	62929	71810	77367
319 040	N	*NML*	SU	77368	62930	71811	77369
319 041	N	*NML*	SU	77370	62931	71812	77371
319 042	N	*NML*	SU	77372	62932	71813	77373
319 043	N	*NML*	SU	77374	62933	71814	77375
319 044	N	*NML*	SU	77376	62934	71815	77377
319 045	N	*NML*	SU	77378	62935	71816	77379

Unit No	Liv	Pool	Dep	BDTS	MS	TS	DTS
319 046	N	*NML*	SU	77380†	62936	71776	77381†
319 047	N	*NML*	SU	77430	62961	71866	77431
319 048	N	*NML*	SU	77432	62962	71867	77433
319 049	N	*NML*	SU	77434	62963	71868	77435
319 050	N	*NML*	SU	77436	62964	71869	77437
319 051	N	*NML*	SU	77438	62965	71870	77439
319 052	N	*NML*	SU	77440	62966	71871	77441
319 053	N	*NML*	SU	77442	62967	71872	77443
319 054	N	*NML*	SU	77444	62968	71873	77445
319 055	N	*NML*	SU	77446	62969	71874	77447
319 056	N	*NML*	SU	77448	62970	71875	77449
319 057	N	*NML*	SU	77450	62971	71876	77451
319 058	N	*NML*	SU	77452	62972	71877	77453
319 059	N	*NML*	SU	77454	62973	71878	77455
319 060	N	*NML*	SU	77456	62974	71879	77457
319 061	N	*NML*					
319 062	N	*NML*					
319 063	N	*NML*					
319 064	N	*NML*					
319 065	N	*NML*					
319 066	N	*NML*					
319 067	N	*NML*					
319 068	N	*NML*					
319 069	N	*NML*					
319 070	N	*NML*					
319 071	N	*NML*					
319 072	N	*NML*					
319 073	N	*NML*					
319 074	N	*NML*					
319 075	N	*NML*					
319 076	N	*NML*					
319 077	N	*NML*					
319 078	N	*NML*					
319 079	N	*NML*					
319 080	N	*NML*					

† BDTS and DTS vehicles in reverse positions.

Class 320 — 3-Car

New units for Strathclyde (Glasgow) PTA
Built: BREL York (due 1990)
Design: BR, saloons with sliding doors, gangwayed within unit. Equipped for one man operation and public address system

Supply: 25kV ac overhead
Traction motors: Four 332hp (249kW) Brush
Maximum speed: 100mph

Dimensions: *Driving coaches:* 19.95m L × 2.82m W × 3.78m H; *Trailer coach:* 19.92m L × 2.82m W × 3.78m H (Pantograph housed within body height)
AWS: Driving vehicles fitted

Diagram	*Type*	*Weight*	*Seats*	*Toilet*
Motor Standard Pantograph:				
EC	MS	49.2t	81	—
Driving Trailer Standard:				
EE2	DTS (A)	38.2t	74	1
EE2	DTS (B)	38.2t	78	—

Unit No	Liv	Pool	Dep	DTS	MS	DTS
				EE2	*EC2*	*EE2*
320 01	S	*PGW*				
320 02	S	*PGW*				
320 03	S	*PGW*				
320 04	S	*PGW*				
320 05	S	*PGW*				
320 06	S	*PGW*				
320 07	S	*PGW*				
320 08	S	*PGW*				
320 09	S	*PGW*				
320 10	S	*PGW*				
320 11	S	*PGW*				
320 12	S	*PGW*				
320 13	S	*PGW*				
320 14	S	*PGW*				
320 15	S	*PGW*				
320 16	S	*PGW*				
320 17	S	*PGW*				
320 18	S	*PGW*				
320 19	S	*PGW*				
320 20	S	*PGW*				
320 21	S	*PGW*				
320 22	S	*PGW*				

Class 321 4-Car

Built: BREL York 1988
Design: BR, saloons with sliding doors, gangwayed within unit. Equipped for one man operation, driver/guard communication and public address system
Supply: 25kV ac overhead
Traction Motors: Four 332hp (249kW) Brush
Maximum speed: 100mph
Dimensions: *Driving coaches:* 19.95m L × 2.82m W × 3.78m H; *Trailer coaches:* 19.92m L × 2.82m W × 3.78m H (Pantograph housed within body height)
AWS: Driving vehicles fitted

Diagram	*Type*	*Weight*	*Seats 1st*	*Seats Std*	*Toilet*
Motor Standard, Pantograph:					
EC2.10.0A	MS	49.2t	—	81	—
Battery Driving Trailer Standard:					
EE2.36.0A	DTS	28.2t	—	78	—
Driving Trailer Composite:					
EE3.08.0A	DTC	28.2t	19	58	—
Trailer Standard:					
EH2.35.0A	TS	31t	—	76	2

Unit No	Liv	Pool	Dep	BDTS	MS	TS	DTC
				EE236	*EC210*	*EH235*	*EE308*
321 301	N	*NNE*	IL	77853	62975	71880	78049
321 302	N	*NNE*	IL	77854	62976	71881	78050
321 303	N	*NNE*	IL	77855	62977	71882	78051
321 304	N	*NNE*	IL	77856	62978	71883	78052
321 305	N	*NNE*	IL	77857	62979	71884	78053
321 306	N	*NNE*	IL	77858	62980	71885	78054

Unit No	Liv	Pool	Dep	BDTS	MS	TS	DTC
321 307	N	*NNE*	IL	77859	62981	71886	78055
321 308	N	*NNE*	IL	77860	62982	71887	78056
321 309	N	*NNE*	IL	77861	62983	71888	78057
321 310	N	*NNE*	IL	77862	62984	71889	78058
321 311	N	*NNE*	IL	77863	62985	71890	78059
321 312	N	*NGE*	IL	77864	62986	71891	78060
321 313	N	*NGE*	IL	77865	62987	71892	78061
321 314	N	*NGE*	IL	77866	62988	71893	78062
321 315	N	*NGE*	IL	77867	62989	71894	78063
321 316	N	*NGE*	IL	77868	62990	71895	78064
321 317	N	*NGE*	IL	77869	62991	71896	78065
321 318	N	*NGE*	IL	77870	62992	71897	78066
321 319	N	*NGE*	IL	77871	62993	71898	78067
321 320	N	*NGE*	IL	77872	62994	71899	78068
321 321	N	*NGE*	IL	77873	62995	71900	78069
321 322	N	*NGE*	IL	77874	62996	71901	78070
321 323	N	*NGE*		77875	62997	71902	78071
321 324	N	*NGE*		77876	62998	71903	78072
321 325	N	*NGE*		77877	62999	71904	78073
321 326	N	*NGE*		77878	63000	71905	78074
321 327	N	*NGE*		77879	63001	71906	78075
321 328	N	*NGE*		77880	63002	71907	78076
321 329	N	*NGE*		77881	63003	71908	78077
321 330	N	*NGE*		77882	63004	71909	78078
321 331	N	*NGE*		77883	63005	71910	78079
321 332	N	*NGE*		77884	63006	71911	78080
321 333	N	*NGE*		77885	63007	71912	78081
321 334	N	*NGE*		77886	63008	71913	78082
321 335	N	*NGE*		77887	63009	71914	78083
321 336	N	*NGE*		77888	63010	71915	78084
321 337	N	*NGE*		77889	63011	71916	78085
321 338	N	*NGE*		77890	63012	71917	78086
321 339	N	*NGE*		77891	63013	71918	78087
321 340	N	*NGE*		77892	63014	71919	78088
321 341	N	*NGE*		77893	63015	71920	78089
321 342	N	*NNW*		77894	63016	71921	78090
321 343	N	*NNW*		77895	63017	71922	78091
321 344	N	*NNW*		77896	63018	71923	78092
321 345	N	*NNW*		77897	63019	71924	78093
321 346	N	*NNW*		77898	63020	71925	78094
321 347	N	*N*					
321 348	N	*N*					
321 349	N	*N*					
321 350	N	*N*					
321 351	N	*N*					
321 352	N	*N*					
321 353	N	*N*					

Unit No	Liv	Pool	Dep	BDTS	MS	TS	DTC
321 354	N	*N*					
321 355	N	*N*					
321 356	N	*N*					
321 357	N	*N*					
321 358	N	*N*					
321 359	N	*N*					
321 360	N	*N*					
321 361	N	*N*					
321 362	N	*N*					
321 363	N	*N*					
321 364	N	*N*					
321 365	N	*N*					
321 366	N	*N*					
321 367	N	*N*					
321 368	N	*N*					
321 369	N	*N*					
321 370	N	*N*					
321 371	N	*N*					
321 372	N	*N*					
321 373	N	*N*					
321 374	N	*N*					
321 375	N	*N*					
321 376	N	*N*					

Class 322 — 4-Car

New units for Stansted Airport link service
Built: BREL York (due 1989)
Design: BR, saloons with sliding doors, gangwayed within unit. Equipped for one man operaiton, driver/guard and public address systems
Supply: 25kV ac overhead
Traction motors (MBS): Four 332hp (249kW) Brush
Maximum speed: 100mph
Dimensions: *Driving coaches:* 19.95m L × 2.82m W × 3.78m H. *Trailer coaches:* 19.92m L × 2.82m W × 2.78m H. (Pantograph housed within body height)

Diagram	*Type*	*Weight*	*Seats 1st*	*Seats Std*	*Toilets*
Motor Sandard, Pantograph:					
EC2.	MS	49.2t			
Battery Driving Trailer Standard:					
EE2.	DTS	28.5t			
Driving Trailer Composite:					
EE3.	DTC	28.5t			
Trailer Standard:					
EH2.	TS	31t			2

Unit No	Liv	Pool	Dep	BDTS *EE2*	MS *EC2*	TS *EH2*	DTC *EE3*
322 01	N	*N*					
322 02	N	*N*					

Unit No	Liv	Pool	Dep	BDTS	MS	TS	DTC
322 03	N	*N*					
322 04	N	*N*					
322 05	N	*N*					

DC ELECTRIC MULTIPLE UNITS

Class 421 4-CIG 4-Car

Built: *Class 421/1:* British Railways York 1964. *Class 421/2:* BREL York 1970
Design: BR gangwayed throughout. Driver-guard communication fitted
Power supply: 750/850V dc third rail
Traction motors (MBS): Four 250hp (185kW) dc English Electric
Maximum speed: 90mph
Dimensions: 20.19m L × 2.82m W × 3.86m H
AWS: Driving vehicles fitted

DMEE Diagram	*SR Design*	*Type*	*Weight*	*Seats 1st*	*Seats Std*	*Toilets*
Motor Brake Standard, Pantograph:						
ED2.60.0A	EA	MBS	49t	—	56	
ED2.60.1B	EA1A	MBS	49t	—	56	
ED2.60.2B	EA2A	MBS	49t	—	56	
Driving Trailer Composite (Compartment/Saloon):						
EE3.63.3B	FA1A	DTC	36t	24	28	2
EE3.63.4B	FA2A	DTC	36t	24	28	2
EE3.63.5A	FA	DTC	36t	24	28	2
EE3.64.4B	FA1A	DTC	35.5t	18	36	2
EE3.64.5B	FA2A	DTC	35.5t	18	36	2
EE3.64.6A	FA	DTC	35.5t	18	36	2
EE3.71.0B†. See Class 423						
Trailer Standard:						
EH2.75.0A	BO	TS	31.5t	—	72	
EH2.75.1B	BO1A	TS	31.5t	—	72	

Class 421/1

Fitted with electric parking brake.

Unit No	SC	Liv	Pool	Dep	DTC *EE36*		MBS *ED2600A*	TS *EH275*		DTC *EE36*	
1100			*NSX*	BI	76125	*46A*	62066	71051	*1B*	76071	*35A*
1105	F		*NSX*	BI	76080	*46A*	62021	70699	*0A*	76039	*35A*
1110	F	N	*NSX*	BI	76085	*46A*	62026	70704	*0A*	76031	*46A*
1111	F	N	*NSX*	BI	76086	*46A*	62027	70705	*0A*	76032	*35A*
1114	F	N	*NSX*	BI	76089	*46A*	62030	70708	*0A*	76035	*35A*
1116	F	N	*NSX*	BI	76091	*46A*	62032	70710	*0A*	76037	*35A*

Unit No	SC	Liv	Pool	Dep	DTC	MBS	TS	DTC
1118	F	N	*NSX*	BI	76026 *35A*	62034	70712 *0A*	76093 *46A*
1123	F		*NSX*	BI	76119 *46A*	62060	70717 *0A*	76065 *35A*
1127	F		*NSX*	BI	76102 *46A*	62043	70721 *0A*	76048 *35A*

Class 421/2

Not fitted with electric parking brake.

Unit No	Liv	Pool	Dep	DTC	MBS	TS	DTC
				EE3645B	*ED2602B*	*EH2751B*	*EE3634B*
1201	N	*NSX*	BI	76751	62389	71069	76822
1202	N	*NSX*	BI	76752	62390	71070	76823
1203	N	*NSX*	BI	76753	62391	71071	76824
1204	N	*NSX*	BI	76754	62392	71072	76825
1205	N	*NSX*	BI	76755	62393	71073	76826
1206	N	*NSX*	BI	76756	62394	71074	76827
1208	N	*NSS*	FR	76758	62396	71076	76829
1209	N	*NSS*	FR	76759	62397	71077	76830
1210	N	*NSS*	FR	76760	62398	71078	76831
1211	N	*NSS*	FR	76761	62399	71079	76832
1212	N	*NSS*	FR	76762	62400	71080	76833
1213	N	*NSS*	FR	76763	62401	71081	76834
1214	N	*NSS*	FR	76764	62402	71082	76835
1215	N	*NSS*	FR	76765	62403	71083	76836
1216		*NSS*	FR	76766	62404	71084	76266N†
1217		*NSS*	FR	76767	62405	71085	76838
1218	N	*NSS*	FR	76768	62406	71086	76839
1219		*NSS*	FR	76769	62407	71087	76840
1220		*NSS*	FR	76770	62408	71088	76841
1221		*NSS*	FR	76771	62409	71089	76842
1222		*NSS*	FR	76772	62410	71090	76843
1223		*NSS*	FR	76773	62411	71091	76844
1224		*NSS*	FR	76774	62412	71092	76845
1225		*NSS*	FR	76775	62413	71093	76846
1226		*NSS*	FR	76776	62414	71094	76847
				EE3644B	*ED2601B*	*EH2751B*	*EE3633B*
1238		*NSS*	FR	76582	62288	70968	76612
1241		*NSS*	FR	76585	62291	70971	76615
1243		*NSS*	FR	76587	62293	70973	76617
1244	N	*NSS*	FR	76588	62294	70974	76618
1245	N	*NSS*	FR	76589	62295	70975	76619
1246	N	*NSS*	FR	76590	62296	70976	76620
1247	N	*NSS*	FR	76591	62297	70977	76621
1249	N	*NSS*	FR	76593	62299	70979	76623
1252	N	*NSS*	FR	76596	62302	70982	76626
1253	N	*NSS*	FR	76597	62303	70983	76627

Unit No	Liv	Pool	Dep	DTC	MBS	TS	DTC
1254		*NSS*	FR	76598	62304	70984	76628
1255	N	*NSS*	FR	76599	62305	70985	76629
1256	N	*NSS*	FR	76600	62306	70986	76630
1257	N	*NSS*	FR	76601	62307	70987	76631
1258	N	*NSX*	BI	76566	62282	70988	76576
1259	N	*NSX*	BI	76603	62309	70989	76633
1260	N	*NSX*	BI	76604	62310	70990	76634
1261	N	*NSX*	BI	76605	62311	70991	76635
1262	N	*NSX*	BI	76606	62312	70992	76636
1263		*NSX*	BI	76607	62313	70993	76637
1264		*NSX*	BI	76608	62314	70994	76638
1266	N	*NSX*	BI	76610	62316	70996	76640
				EE3645B	*ED2602B*	*EH2751B*	*EE3634B*
1268	N	*NSX*	BI	76718	62356	71036	76789
1269	N	*NSX*	BI	76719	62357	71037	76790
1270	N	*NSX*	BI	76720	62358	71038	76791
1271	N	*NSX*	BI	76721	62359	71039	76792
1272		*NSX*	BI	76722	62360	71040	76793
1274		*NSX*	BI	76724	62362	71042	76795
1275	N	*NSX*	BI	76725	62363	71043	76796
1276	N	*NSX*	BI	76726	62364	71044	76797
1277	N	*NSX*	BI	76727	62365	71045	76798
1278	N	*NSX*	BI	76728	62366	71046	76799
1279	N	*NSX*	BI	76729	62367	71047	76800
1280	N	*NSX*	BI	76730	62368	71048	76801
1281	N	*NSX*	BI	76731	62369	71049	76802
1282	N	*NSX*	BI	76732	62370	71050	76803
1284	N	*NSX*	BI	76734	62372	71052	76805
1285	N	*NSX*	BI	76735	62373	71053	76806
1286	N	*NSX*	BI	76736	62374	71054	76807
1287	N	*NSX*	BI	76737	62375	71055	76808
1288	N	*NSX*	BI	76738	62376	71056	76809
1289	N	*NSX*	BI	76739	62377	71057	76810
1290	N	*NSX*	BI	76740	62378	71058	76811
1291	N	*NSX*	BI	76741	62379	71059	76812
1292	N	*NSX*	BI	76742	62380	71060	76813
1293	N	*NSX*	BI	76743	62381	71061	76814
1294	N	*NSX*	BI	76744	62382	71062	76815
1295	N	*NSX*	BI	76745	62383	71063	76816
1296	N	*NSX*	BI	76746	62384	71064	76817
1297	N	*NSX*	BI	76747	62385	71065	76818
1298	N	*NSX*	BI	76748	62386	71066	76819
1299	N	*NSX*	BI	76749	62387	71067	76820
1300	N	*NSX*	BI	76750	62388	71068	76821

Class 411 4-CEP 4-Car

Built: British Railways, Eastleigh 1956
Introduced: 1975. Prototype refurbished unit
Design: BR gangwayed throughout, driver/guard communitcation and public address equipment fitted
Supply: 750/850V dc third rail
Traction motors (DMS): Two 250hp (185kW) dc English Electric
Maximum speed: 90mph
Dimensons: 20.34m L × 2.82m W × 3.83m H
AWS: Fitted to driving vehicles

DMEE Diagram	*SR Design*	*Type*	*Weight*	*Seats 1st*	*Seats Std*	*Toilets*
Driving Motor Standard						
EA2.61.1A	AK1A	DMS	41.5t	—	64	
EA2.62.1A	AL1K	DMS	41.5t	—	64	
EA2.63.0A	A0	DMS	41t	—	64	
EA2.63.1A*	A01A	DMS	41t	—	64	
EA2.64.0A	AK	DMS	41t	—	64	
EA2.64.1A	AM	DMS	41t	—	64	
EA2.64.2B	AM1A	DMS	41t	—	64	
EA2.64.3A	AL	DMS	41t	—	64	
EA2.64.4B	AN	DMS	41t	—	64	
EA2.64.5A	AN1A	DMS	41t	—	64	
Trailer Standard						
EH2.77.0A	BX3D	TS	31.5t	—	64	2
EH2.82.0A	BZ	TS	31.5t	—	64	2
EH2.82.1A	BX	TS	31.5t	—	64	2
EH2.82.2A	BX1A	TS	31.5t	—	64	2
EH2.82.4A*	BX1B	TS	31.5t	—	64	2
EH2.84.0A	BX4E	TS	33.5t	—	64	2
Trailer Brake Composite: (Compartment)						
EJ3.60.0A	BW3D	TBC	31.5t	24	6	2
EJ3.61.0A	BY	TBC	31.5t	24	6	2
EJ3.61.1A	BW	TBC	31.5t	24	6	2
EJ3.61.2A	BW1A	TBC	31.5t	24	6	2
EJ3.61.4A*	BW1B	TBC	31.5t	24	6	2

*Unofficial code

CLASS 411/3

Prototype refurbished unit, modified 1975

Unit No	SC	Liv	Pool	Dep	DMS	TBC	TS	DMS
					EA261	*EJ360*	*EH277*	*EA262*
1500		L	*NKC*	RE	61389	70345	70302	61388

Class 411/4

Unit No	SC	Liv	Pool	Dep	DMS	TBC	TS		DMS
					EA2630A	*EJ3610A*	*EH28*		*EA2631A*
1501			*NKC*	RE	61041	70041	70034	*20A*	61042
1502		L	*NKC*	RE	61040	70040	70036	*20A*	61039
1503		L	*NKC*	RE	61033	70037	70033	*20A*	61034
1504		L	*NKC*	RE	61043	70042	71712	*40A*	61037
1505		N	*NKC*	RE	61044	70039	70035	*20A*	61038

Unit No	SC	Liv	Pool	Dep	DMS		TBC		TS		DMS	
					EA264		*EJ361*		*EH28*		*EA2643*	
1506			*NKC*	RE	61349	*0A*	70325	*1A*	70282	*21A*	61348	*3A*
1507			*NKC*	RE	61363	*0A*	70332	*1A*	70289	*21A*	61362	*3A*
1508			*NKC*	RE	61305	*0A*	70303	*1A*	70260	*21A*	61304	*3A*
1509			*NKC*	RE	61335	*0A*	70318	*1A*	70275	*21A*	61334	*3A*
1510			*NKC*	RE	61365	*0A*	70333	*1A*	70290	*21A*	61364	*3A*
1511			*NKC*	RE	61367	*0A*	70334	*1A*	70291	*21A*	61366	*3A*
1512		L	*NKC*	RE	61321	*0A*	70311	*1A*	70268	*21A*	61320	*3A*
1513			*NKC*	RE	61796	*1A*	70321	*1A*	70278	*21A*	61340	*3A*
1514			*NKC*	RE	61327	*0A*	70314	*1A*	70271	*21A*	61326	*3A*
1515		L	*NKC*	RE	61345	*0A*	70323	*1A*	70280	*21A*	61344	*3A*
1516			*NKC*	RE	61319	*0A*	70310	*1A*	70267	*21A*	61318	*3A*
1517		L	*NKC*	RE	61317	*0A*	70309	*1A*	70266	*21A*	61316	*3A*
1518		L	*NKC*	RE	61333	*0A*	70317	*1A*	70274	*21A*	61332	*3A*
1519		L	*NKC*	RE	61403	*0A*	70352	*1A*	70516	*22A*	61402	*3A*
1520		L	*NKC*	RE	61343	*0A*	70327	*1A*	70284	*21A*	61380	*3A*
1521		L	*NKC*	RE	61353	*0A*	70324	*1A*	70281	*21A*	61352	*3A*
1522		L	*NKC*	RE	61347	*0A*	70341	*1A*	70665	*24A*	61346	*3A*
1523		L	*NKC*	RE	61383	*0A*	70342	*1A*	70299	*21A*	61382	*3A*
1524		L	*NKC*	RE	61309	*0A*	70305	*1A*	70262	*21A*	61308	*3A*
1525		L	*NKC*	RE	61235	*0A*	70238	*1A*	70232	*21A*	61236	*3A*
1526		L	*NKC*	RE	61239	*0A*	70240	*1A*	70234	*21A*	61240	*3A*
1527		L	*NKC*	RE	61237	*0A*	70239	*1A*	70233	*21A*	61238	*3A*
1528		L	*NKC*	RE	61379	*0A*	70340	*1A*	70297	*21A*	61378	*3A*
1529		L	*NKC*	RE	61355	*0A*	70328	*1A*	70285	*21A*	61354	*3A*
1530		L	*NKC*	RE	61331	*0A*	70316	*1A*	70273	*21A*	61330	*3A*
1531		L	*NKC*	RE	61233	*0A*	70237	*1A*	70231	*21A*	61234	*3A*
1532		L	*NKC*	RE	61391	*0A*	70346	*1A*	71626	*40A*	61390	*3A*
1533		L	*NKC*	RE	61393	*0A*	70347	*1A*	71627	*40A*	61385	*3A*
1534		L	*NKC*	RE	61405	*0A*	70353	*1A*	71628	*40A*	61404	*3A*
1535		L	*NKC*	RE	61397	*0A*	70349	*1A*	71629	*40A*	61396	*3A*
1536		L	*NKC*	RE	61399	*0A*	70350	*1A*	71631	*40A*	61398	*3A*
1537		L	*NKC*	RE	61229	*0A*	70235	*1A*	70229	*21A*	61230	*3A*
1538		L	*NKC*	RE	61307	*0A*	70304	*1A*	70261	*21A*	61306	*3A*
1539		L	*NKC*	RE	61401	*0A*	70351	*1A*	71632	*40A*	61400	*3A*
1540		L	*NKC*	RE	61870	*1A*	70343	*1A*	70300	*21A*	61384	*3A*
1541		L	*NKC*	RE	61409	*0A*	70355	*1A*	71633	*40A*	61408	*3A*
1542		L	*NKC*	RE	61395	*0A*	70348	*1A*	71634	*40A*	61394	*3A*

Unit No	SC	Liv	Pool	Dep	DMS		TBC		TS		DMS	
1543		L	*NKC*	RE	61323	*0A*	70312	*1A*	70269	*21A*	61322	*3A*
1544		L	*NKC*	RE	61315	*0A*	70308	*1A*	70265	*21A*	61314	*3A*
1545		L	*NKC*	RE	61359	*0A*	70330	*1A*	70287	*21A*	61358	*3A*
1546		L	*NKC*	RE	61357	*0A*	70329	*1A*	70286	*21A*	61356	*3A*
1547		L	*NKC*	RE	61329	*0A*	70315	*1A*	70272	*21A*	61328	*3A*
1548		L	*NKC*	RE	61375	*0A*	70338	*1A*	70295	*21A*	61374	*3A*
1549		L	*NKC*	RE	61339	*0A*	70320	*1A*	70277	*21A*	61338	*3A*
1550		L	*NKC*	RE	61313	*0A*	70307	*1A*	70264	*21A*	61312	*3A*
1551		L	*NKC*	RE	61325	*0A*	70313	*1A*	70270	*21A*	61324	*3A*
1552		L	*NKC*	RE	61373	*0A*	70337	*1A*	70294	*21A*	61372	*3A*
1553		L	*NKC*	RE	61351	*0A*	70306	*1A*	70263	*21A*	61350	*3A*
1554		L	*NKC*	RE	61369	*0A*	70335	*1A*	70292	*21A*	61368	*3A*
1555		L	*NKC*	RE	61311	*0A*	70326	*1A*	70283	*21A*	61310	*3A*
1556		L	*NKC*	RE	61371	*0A*	70336	*1A*	70293	*21A*	61370	*3A*
1557		L	*NKC*	RE	61337	*0A*	70331	*1A*	70288	*21A*	61360	*3A*
1558		L	*NKC*	RE	61361	*0A*	70319	*1A*	70276	*21A*	61336	*3A*
1559		L	*NKC*	RE	61377	*0A*	70339	*1A*	70296	*21A*	61376	*3A*
1560		N	*NSS*	FR	61387	*0A*	70344	*2A*	70301	*21A*	61386	*3A*
1561		N	*NSS*	FR	61231	*0A*	70604	*2A*	70230	*21A*	61232	*3A*
1562		N	*NSS*	RE	61407	*0A*	70236	*1A*	70241	*22A*	61406	*3A*
1563		L	*NKC*	RE	61740	*1A*	70575	*2A*	70526	*22A*	61741	*4B*
1564		L	*NKC*	RE	61788	*1A*	70599	*2A*	70550	*22A*	61789	*4B*
1565		L	*NKC*	RE	61762	*1A*	70586	*2A*	71711	*40A*	61763	*4B*
1566		L	*NKC*	RE	61722	*1A*	70566	*2A*	70517	*22A*	61723	*4B*
1567		L	*NKC*	RE	61786	*1A*	70598	*2A*	70549	*22A*	61787	*4B*
1568		L	*NKC*	RE	61766	*1A*	70588	*2A*	70539	*22A*	61767	*4B*
1569		L	*NKC*	RE	61782	*1A*	70596	*2A*	70547	*22A*	61783	*4B*
1570		L	*NKC*	RE	61738	*1A*	70574	*2A*	70525	*22A*	61739	*4B*
1571		L	*NKC*	RE	61806	*1A*	70608	*2A*	71636	*40A*	61807	*4B*
1572		L	*NKC*	RE	61734	*1A*	70572	*2A*	70523	*22A*	61735	*4B*
1573		L	*NKC*	RE	61726	*1A*	70568	*2A*	70519	*22A*	61727	*4B*
1574		L	*NKC*	RE	61792	*1A*	70601	*2A*	71635	*40A*	61793	*4B*
1575		L	*NKC*	RE	61768	*1A*	70583	*2A*	70540	*22A*	61769	*4B*
1576		L	*NKC*	RE	61770	*1A*	70590	*2A*	70541	*22A*	61771	*4B*
1577		L	*NKC*	RE	61718	*1A*	70564	*2A*	70515	*22A*	61719	*4B*
1578		L	*NKC*	RE	61700	*1A*	70555	*2A*	70506	*22A*	61701	*4B*
1579		L	*NKC*	RE	61772	*1A*	70591	*2A*	70542	*22A*	61773	*4B*
1580		L	*NKC*	RE	61756	*1A*	70589	*2A*	70534	*22A*	61757	*4B*
1581		L	*NKC*	RE	61784	*1A*	70597	*2A*	70548	*22A*	61785	*4B*
1582		L	*NKC*	RE	61748	*1A*	70603	*2A*	71630	*40A*	61797	*4B*
1583		L	*NKC*	RE	61746	*1A*	70578	*2A*	70529	*22A*	61747	*4B*
1584		L	*NKC*	RE	61752	*1A*	70581	*2A*	70532	*22A*	61753	*4B*
1585		L	*NKC*	RE	61710	*1A*	70560	*2A*	70511	*22A*	61711	*4B*
1586		L	*NKC*	RE	61714	*1A*	70562	*2A*	70513	*22A*	61715	*4B*
1587		L	*NKC*	RE	61764	*1A*	70587	*2A*	71625	*40A*	61765	*4B*
1588		L	*NKC*	RE	61720	*1A*	70044	*2A*	70520	*22A*	61721	*4B*
1589		L	*NKC*	RE	61742	*1A*	70576	*2A*	70527	*22A*	61743	*4B*

Unit No	SC	Liv	Pool	Dep	DMS		TBC		TS		DMS	
1590		L	*NKC*	RE	61696	*1A*	70553	*2A*	70504	*22A*	61697	*4B*
1591		L	*NKC*	RE	61790	*1A*	70600	*2A*	70551	*22A*	61791	*4B*
1592		L	*NKC*	RE	61778	*1A*	70594	*2A*	70545	*22A*	61779	*4B*
1593		L	*NKC*	RE	61730	*1A*	70570	*2A*	70521	*22A*	61731	*4B*
1594		L	*NKC*	RE	61754	*1A*	70582	*2A*	70533	*22A*	61755	*4B*
1595		L	*NKC*	RE	61704	*1A*	70557	*2A*	70508	*22A*	61705	*4B*
1596		L	*NKC*	RE	61716	*1A*	70563	*2A*	70514	*22A*	61717	*4B*
1597		L	*NKC*	RE	61708	*1A*	70559	*2A*	70510	*22A*	61709	*4B*
1598		L	*NKC*	RE	61780	*1A*	70595	*2A*	70546	*22A*	61781	*4B*
1599		L	*NKC*	RE	61706	*1A*	70558	*2A*	70509	*22A*	61707	*4B*
1600		L	*NKC*	RE	61724	*1A*	70567	*2A*	70518	*22A*	61725	*4B*
1601		L	*NKC*	RE	61776	*1A*	70593	*2A*	70544	*22A*	61777	*4B*
1602		L	*NKC*	RE	61958	*2B*	70565	*2A*	70279	*21A*	61959	*5A*
1603			*NKC*	RE	61728	*1A*	70569	*2A*	70298	*21A*	61729	*4B*
1604			*NKC*	RE	61732	*1A*	70571	*2A*	70522	*22A*	61733	*4B*
1605			*NKC*	RE	61712	*1A*	70561	*2A*	70512	*22A*	61713	*4B*
1606			*NKC*	RE	61694	*1A*	70552	*2A*	70503	*22A*	61695	*4B*
1607		N	*NKC*	RE	61698	*1A*	70554	*2A*	70505	*22A*	61699	*4B*
1608			*NKC*	RE	61960	*2B*	70659	*4A*	70666	*24A*	61961	*5A*
1609		L	*NKC*	RE	61744	*1A*	70577	*2A*	70528	*22A*	61745	*4B*
1610		L	*NKC*	RE	61750	*1A*	70580	*2A*	70531	*22A*	61751	*4B*
1611		L	*NKC*	RE	61758	*1A*	70584	*2A*	70537	*22A*	61759	*4B*
1612		L	*NKC*	RE	61794	*1A*	70602	*2A*	70535	*22A*	61795	*4B*
1613		L	*NKC*	RE	61760	*1A*	70585	*2A*	70536	*22A*	61761	*4B*
1614		L	*NBT*	RE	61702	*1A*	70556	*2A*	70507	*22A*	61703	*4B*
1615		L	*NBT*	RE	61956	*2B*	70657	*4A*	70664	*24A*	61957	*5A*
1616		L	*NBT*	RE	61950	*2B*	70654	*4A*	70543	*22A*	61951	*5A*
1617		L	*NBT*	RE	61800	*1A*	70605	*2A*	70661	*24A*	61801	*4B*
1618		L	*NBT*	RE	61868	*1A*	70043	*2A*	70663	*24A*	61869	*4B*
1619		L	*NBT*	RE	61952	*2B*	70655	*4A*	70662	*24A*	61953	*5A*
1620		N	*NBT*	RE	61948	*2B*	70653	*4A*	70660	*24A*	61949	*5A*
1621		N	*NBT*	RE	61810	*1A*	70610	*2A*	70524	*22A*	61811	*4B*

Class 421 — 4-CIG 4-Car

Built: Class 421/3: British Railways York 1964; **Class 421/4:** BREL York 1970

Facelifted 1985-89
For full details see Class 421

DMEE Diagram	*SR Design*	*Type*	*Weight*	*Seats 1st*	*Seats Std*	*Toilets*
Motor Brake Standard						
ED2.64.0A	EA3B	MBS	49t	—	56	
ED2.64.1B	EA5B	MBS	49t	—	56	
ED2.64.2C*	EA4B	MBS	49t	—	56	

Driving Trailer Composite: (Compartment/Saloon)						
EE3.69.0A	FA4B	DTC	35.5t	18	36	2
EE3.69.1A	FA6B	DTC	35.5t	18	36	2
EE3.69.2B*	FA5B	DTC	35.5t	18	36	2
EE3.69.3C*	FA7B	DTC	35.5t	18	36	2
EE3.69.4D*	FA8B	DTC	35.5t	18	36	2
Trailer Standard						
EH2.87.0A	BO2B	TS	31.5t	—	72	
EH2.87.1A	BO4B	TS	31.5t	—	72	
EH2.87.2B	BO3B	TS	31.5t	—	72	
EH2.87.3C	BO4B	TS	31.5t	—	72	†

*Official codes not issued

Class 421/3

Equipped with electronic parking brake

Unit No	SC	Liv	Pool	Dep	DTC	MBS	TS	DTC
					EE3690A	*ED2640A*	*EH2870A*	*EE3690A*
1701		N	*NSX*	BI	76087	62028	70706	76033
1702		N	*NSX*	BI	76101	62042	70720	76047
1703		N	*NSX*	BI	76097	62038	70716	76043
1704		N	*NSX*	BI	76092	63033	70711	76038
1705		N	*NSX*	BI	76076	62017	70695	76022
1706		N	*NSX*	BI	76094	62035	70713	76040
1707		N	*NSX*	BI	76084	62025	70703	76030
1708		N	*NSX*	BI	76110	62051	70729	76056
1709		N	*NSX*	BI	76103	62044	70722	76049
1710		N	*NSX*	BI	76078	62019	70697	76024
1711		N	*NSX*	BI	76114	62055	71766	76060
1712			*NSX*	BI	76079	62020	70698	76025
1713			*NSX*	BI	76128	62069	71767	76074
1714			*NSX*	BI	76028	62018	70696	76023
1715			*NSX*	BI	76082	62023	70701	76077
1716		N	*NSX*	BI	76100	62041	71768	76046
1717		N	*NSX*	BI	76083	62024	70702	76029
1718		N	*NSX*	BI	76081	62022	70700	76027
					EE3690A	*ED2643C*	*EH2870A*	*EE3690A*
1719		N	NSX	BI	76116	62057	70719	76062
					EE2690A	*ED2640A*	*EH2870A*	*EE3690A*
1720		N	*NSX*	BI	76098	62039	71769	76044
1721		N	*NSX*	BI	76090	62031	70709	76036
1722		N	*NSX*	BI	76106	62047	70725	76052
1723		N	*NSX*	BI	76107	62048	70726	76053
1724		N	*NSX*	BI	76120	62061	71770	76066
1725		N	*NSX*	BI	76088	62029	70707	76034
1726		N	*NSX*	BI	76109	62050	70728	76055
1727		N	*NSX*	BI	76111	62052	70730	76057

Unit No	SC	Liv	Pool	Dep	DTC	MBS	TS	DTC
					EE3692B	*ED2642C*	*EH2872B*	*EE3692B*
1728		N	*NSX*	BI	76099	62040	70718	76045
1729		N	*NSX*	BI	76104	62045	70723	76050
1730		N	*NSX*	BI	76105	62046	70724	76113
1731		N	*NSX*	BI	76095	62036	70714	76041
					EE3693C	*ED2642C*	*EH2872B*	*EE3693C*
1732		N	*NSX*	BI	76096	62037	70715	76042

Class 421/4

Unit No	SC	Liv	Pool	Dep	Former Unit No	DTC	MBS	TS	DTC
						EE3691A	*ED2641B*	*EH2871A*	*EE3691A*
1801			*NSX*	BI	—	76777	62415	71095	76848
1802			*NSX*	BI	—	76779	62417	71097	76850
1803			*NSX*	BI	—	76780	62418	71098	76851
1804			*NSX*	BI	—	76778	62416	71096	76849
1805			*NSX*	BI	—	76782	62420	71100	76853
1806			*NSX*	BI	—	76783	62421	71101	76854
1807		N	*NSX*	BI	—	76784	62422	71102	76855
1808		N	*NSX*	BI	—	76785	62423	71103	76856
1809		N	*NSX*	BI	—	76786	62424	71104	76857
1810		N	*NSX*	BI	—	76787	62425	71105	76858
1811		N	*NSX*	BI	—	76781	62419	71099	76852
1812		N	*NSX*	BI	—	76757	62395	71075	76828
1813		N	*NSX*	BI	—	76789	62430	71106	76860
						EE3694D	*ED2641B*	*EH2871A*	*EE3694D*
1814		N	*NSS*	FR	(1251)	76595	62301	70981	76625
1815		N	*NSS*	FR	(1240)	76584	62290	70970	76614
1816		N	*NSS*	FR	(1237)	76581	62287	70967	76611
1817		N	*NSS*	FR	(1239)	76583	62289	70969	76613
1818		N	*NSS*	FR	(1267)	76717	62355	71035	76788
1819		N	*NSS*	FR	(1273)	76723	62361	71041	76794
1820		N	*NSS*	FR	(1242)	76586	62292	70972	76616
1821		N	*NSS*	FR	(1248)	76592	62298	70978	76622
1822		N	*NSS*	FR	(1250)	76594	62300	70980	76624
						EE3694D	*ED2641B*	*EH2873C*	*EE3694D*
1823		N	*NSS*	FR	(2207)	76567	62283	71926	76577
1824		N	*NSS*	FR	(2201)	76561	62277	71927	76571
1825		N	*NSS*	FR	(2202)	76562	62278	71928	76572

†Coach Nos 71826/27/28 formerly TRBS Nos 69315/30/31 respectively

Class 431 — 4REP — 4-Car

Built: British Railways, York 1966
Design: BR, gangwayed throughout, Driver/guard communication equipped
Supply: 750/850V dc third rail
Traction Motors (DMS): Two 365hp (300kW) dc English Electric EE546
Maximum speed: 90mph
Dimensions: 20.35m L × 2.83m W × 3.90m H
AWS: Driving vehicles fitted
Note: Tractor unit to work in conjunction with Class 438 TC units. Reformed from Class 432 4-REP during 1988/89

DMEE Diagram	*SR Design*	*Type*	*Weight*	*Seats 1st*	*Seats Std*	*Toilets*
Driving Motor Standard:						
EA2.60.1A	AJ	DMS	55.5t	—	64	—
Trailer Composite (Compartment):						
EH3.--.2B	BU2B	TC	33.5t	36	8	2
Trailer Brake Standard (Compartment):						
EJ2.60.0A	BT	TBS	35.5t	—	32	1 PA fitted

*Unofficial code

Unit No	**Old No**	**Liv**	**Pool**	**Dep**	**DMS** *EA260*	**TBS** *EJ260*	**TC** *EH3--*	**DMS** *EA260*
1901	(2001 R)	N	*NSS*	BM	62141	70830	71163	62142
1902	(2007 R)	N	*NSS*	BM	62154	70824	70845	62153

Class 422 — 4-BIG 4-Car

Built: British Railways, York 1965
Design: BR, gangwayed throughout. All refurbished. Driver/guard communication and public address equipment fitted
Supply: 750/850V dc third rail
Traction Motors: Four 250hp (185kW) dc English Electric
Maximum speed: 90mph
Dimensions: 20.19m L × 2.82m W × 3.86m H
AWS: Driving vehicles fitted

DMEE Diagram	*SR Design*	*Type*	*Weight*	*Seats 1st*	*Seats Std*	*Toilet*
Motor Brake Standard:						
ED2.60.0A	EA	MBS	49t	—	56	—
ED2.60.1B	EA1A	MBS	49t	—	56	—

Driving Trailer Composite (Compartment):						
EE3.63.3B	FA1A	DTC	36t	24	28	2
EE3.63.5A	FA	DTC	36t	24	28	2
EE3.64.4B	FA1A	DTC	35.5t	18	36	2
EE3.64.6A	FA	DTC	35.5t	18	36	2
Trailer Brake Standard:						
EN2.60.0A	BP	TBS	35t	—	40	—
EN2.60.1B	BP1A	TBS	35t	—	40	—

Class 422/1

Fitted with electric parking brakes

Unit No	Liv	Pool	Dep	DTC	MBS	TRBS	DTC
				EE3646A	*ED2600A*	*EN2600A*	*EE3635A*
2101	N	*NSX*	BI	76063	62054	69302	76059
2102	N	*NSX*	BI	76129	62064	69312	76069
2103	N	*NSX*	BI	76124	62065	69313	76070
2104	N	*NSX*	BI	76117	62058	69306	76051
2105	N	*NSX*	BI	76121	62062	69310	76067
2106	N	*NSX*	BI	76118	62059	69307	76064
2107	N	*NSX*	BI	76122	62063	69311	76068
2108	N	*NSX*	BI	76127	62068	69316	76073
2109	N	*NSX*	BI	76123	62070	69318	76075
2110	N	*NSX*	BI	76115	62056	69304	76061
2111	N	*NSX*	BI	76112	62053	69301	76058
				EE3646A	*ED2600A*	*EN2601B*	*EE3635A*
2112	N	*NSX*	BI	76126	62067	69333	76072

Class 422/2

Not fitted with electric parking brakes.

Unit No	Liv	Pool	Dep	DTC	MBS	TRBS	DTC
				EE3644B	*ED2601B*	*EN2601B*	*EE3633B*
2203		*NSX*	BI	76563	62279	69332	76573
2204		*NSX*	BI	76564	62280	69336	76574
2205		*NSX*	BI	76565	62281	69339	76575
2206		*NSX*	BI	76602	62308	69338	76632
2208		*NSX*	BI	76568	62284	69334	76578
2209	N	*NSX*	BI	76569	62285	69335	76579
2210	N	*NSX*	BI	76570	62286	69337	76580

Class 412/3 — 4-BEP 4-Car

Built: British Railways, Eastleigh 1961
Design: BR, gangwayed throughout. Driver/guard communication and public address equipment fitted. Refurbished 1982
Supply: 750/850V dc third rail
Traction Motors (DMS): Two 250hp (185kW) dc English Electric
Maximum speed: 90mph
Dimensions: 20.34m L × 2.82m W × 3.83m H
AWS: Driving coaches fitted

DMEE Diagram	*SR Design*	*Type*	*Weight*	*Seats 1st*	*Seats Std*	*Toilet*
Driving Motor Standard:						
EA2.64.1A	AM	DMS	41t	—	64	—
EA2.64.2B	AM1A	DMS	41t	—	64	—
EA2.64.4B	AN	DMS	41t	—	64	—
EA2.64.5A	AN1A	DMS	41t	—	64	—
Trailer Brake Composite (Corridor):						
EJ3.61.1A	BW	TBC	31.5t	24	6	2
EJ3.61.2A	BW1A	TBC	31.5t	24	6	2
EJ3.61.4A*	BW1B	TBC	31.5t	24	6	2
Trailer Buffet Standard:						
EN2.61.0A	BL3C	TBS	35.5t	—	33	1

*Unofficial code

Unit No	**Liv**	**Pool**	**Dep**	**DMS** *EA264*	**TBC** *EJ361*	**TRBS** *EN261*	**DMS** *EA264*
2301	N	*NSS*	FR	61804 *1A*	70607 *2A*	69341	61805 *4B*
2302	N	*NSS*	FR	61774 *1A*	70592 *2A*	69342	61775 *4B*
2303	N	*NSS*	FR	61954 *2B*	70656 *4A*	69343	61955 *5A*
2304	N	*NSS*	FR	61736 *1A*	70573 *2A*	69344	61737 *4B*
2305		*NSS*	FR	61798 *1A*	70354 *1A*	69345	61799 *4B*
2306		*NSS*	FR	61808 *1A*	70609 *2A*	69346	61809 *4B*
2307		*NSS*	FR	61802 *1A*	70606 *2A*	69347	61803 *4B*

Class 442 — 5-WES 5-Car

Built: BREL, Derby-Litchurch Lane 1987
WESSEX ELECTRIC UNITS
Design: BR, gangwayed Mk3. Power operated swing-plug doors. Sliding doors each end of driving trailers. Air conditioned
Supply: 750/850V dc third rail
Traction Motors (MBLS): Four 365hp (300kW) dc English Electric EE546
Maximum speed: 100mph
Dimensions: 22.15m L × 2.74m W × 3.81m H
AWS: Driving coaches fitted

DMEE Diagram	*SR Design*	*Type*	*Weight*	*Seats 1st*	*Seats Std*	*Toilet*
Motor Buffet Luggage Standard (Modular Catering):						
ED2.65.0A	EC	MBLS	51t	—	14	—
ED2.65.1B*	EC	MBLS	51t	—	14	—
Additional seating in buffet lounge area						
Driving Trailer Standard/First:						
EE2.73.0A	FE	DTS	34t	—	78	1
EE1.60.0A	FD	DTF	34t	50	—	1
Trailer Standard:						
EH2.88.0A	BV	TS	34t	—	80	2
EH2.89.0A	BV-1A	TS	34t	—	78	2 Wheelchair position

*Official code not issued

Unit No	**Liv**	**Pool**	**Dep**	**DTF**	**TS**	**MBLS**	**TS**	**DTS**
				EE1600A	*EH2880A*	*ED2650A*	*EH2890A*	*EE2730A*
2401	N	*NSS*	BM	77382	71818	62937	71842	77406
2402	N	*NSS*	BM	77383	71819	62938	71843	77407
2403	N	*NSS*	BM	77384	71820	62939	71844	77408
2404	N	*NSS*	BM	77385	71821	62940	71845	77409
2405	N	*NSS*	BM	77386	71822	62941	71846	77410
2406	N	*NSS*	BM	77387	71823	62942	71847	77411
2407	N	*NSS*	BM	77388	71824	62943	71848	77412
2408	N	*NSS*	BM	77389	71825	62944	71849	77413
2409	N	*NSS*	BM	77390	71826	62945	71850	77414
2410	N	*NSS*	BM	77391	71827	62946	71851	77415
2411	N	*NSS*	BM	77392	71828	62947	71852	77416
2412	N	*NSS*	BM	77393	71829	62948	71853	77417
				EE1600A	*EH2880A*	*ED2651B*	*EH2890A*	*EE2730A*
2413	N	*NSS*	BM	77394	71830	62949	71854	77418
2414	N	*NSS*	BM	77395	71831	62950	71855	77419
2415	N	*NSS*	BM	77396	71832	62951	71856	77420
2416	N	*NSS*	BM	77397	71833	62952	71857	77421
2417	N	*NSS*	BM	77398	71834	62953	71858	77422
2418	N	*NSS*	BM	77399	71835	62954	71859	77423
2419	N	*NSS*	BM	77400	71836	62955	71860	77424
2420	N	*NSS*	BM	77401	71837	62956	71861	77425
2421	N	*NSS*	BM	77402	71838	62957	71862	77426
2422	N	*NSS*	BM	77403	71839	62958	71863	77427
2423	N	*NSS*	BM	77404	71840	62959	71864	77428
2424	N	*NSS*	BM	77405	71841	62960	71865	77429

Class 492 5-TCB 5-Car

Built: British Railways York 1966. Present formation introduced in 1986-88 from Class 438 4-TC adding TRB to Class 432 4-REP units
Design: BR gangwayed throughout. Driver/guard and public address equipment fitted
Supply: From Class 431, 432 or locomotive
Maximum speed: 90mph
AWS: Driving vehicles fitted
Dimensions: 22.15m L × 2.74m W × 3.81m H

DMEE Diagram	*SR Design*	*Type*	*Weight*	*Seats 1st*	*Seats Std*	*Toilets*
Driving Trailer Standard						
EE2.66.0A	FC	DTS	32.5t	—	64	
EE2.66.1A	FC1A	DTS	32.5t	—	64	
Trailer First: (Compartment)						
EH1.60.0A	BU	TF	33.5t	42	—	2
EH1.60.1B	BU1A	TF	33.5t	42	—	2
Trailer Brake First/Standard: (Compartment)						
EJ1.60.1B	BR1A	TBF	35.5t	24	—	1
EJ2.60.0A	BT	TBS	35.5t	—	32	1
Trailer Buffet Unclass						
EN4.63.0A	BS1A	TRB	35t	—	23	2
Built 1974						

Unit No	**Old No**	**SC**	**Liv**	**Pool**	**Dep**	**DTS** *EE266*	**TF** *EH160*	**TRB** *EN463*	**TBF/TBS**	**DTC** *EE266*
2804	(8009 R)			*NSS*	BM	76286 *0A*	70846 *0A*	69024 #	70820 *EJ2*	76285 *0A*
2807	(8033 R)			*NSS*	BM	76945 *1A*	70854 *0A*	69022	71156 *EJ1*	76946 *1A*
2809	(8031 R)			*NSS*	BM	76329 *0A*	71164 *1B*	69023 #	70842 *EJ2*	76330 *0A*

Class 423/0 4-VEP 4-Car

Built: British Railways Derby and York 1967
Design: BR gangwayed throughout. Driver-guard communication fitted
Power Supply: 750/850V dc
Traction motors: Four 250hp (185kW) English Electric
Maximum speed: 90mph
Dimensions: 20.18m L × 2.82m W × 3.84m H
AWS: Driving vehicles fitted

DMEE Diagram	SR Design	Type	Weight	Seats 1st	Seats Std	Toilet
Motor Brake Standard						
ED2.61.0A	EB	MBS	49t	—	58	
ED2.61.1A	EB1A	MBS	49t	—	58	
ED2.62.0A	EB2A	MBS	49t	—	58	
ED2.63.0A	EV1A	MBS	49t	—	58	
ED2.63.1A	EB2A	MBS	49t	—	58	
ED2.63.2A	EB3A	MBS	49t	—	58	
ED2.63.3A	EB4A	MBS	49t	—	58	
ED2.63.5A	EB6A	MBS	49t	—	58	
Driving Trailer Composite: (Compartment/Saloon)						
EE3.63.4B† See Class 421/2 (not N)						
EE3.65.1A	FB	DTC	32.5t	24	38	1
EE3.66.1A	FB3A	DTC	35t	24	34	1
EE3.67.4A	FB	DTC	35.5t	24	38	1
EE3.67.6A	FB3A	DTC	35.5t	24	38	1
EE3.68.1B	FB1B	DTC	35.5t	18	46	1
EE3.68.2B	FB3B	DTC	35.5t	18	46	1
EE3.68.3B	FB2B	DTC	35.5t	18	46	1
EE3.71.0A	FB	DTC	32.5t	18	46	1
EE3.71.0B	FB4B	DTC	32.5t	18	46	1
Trailer Standard						
EH2.76.0A	BQ	TS	31.5t	—	98	
EH2.78.0A	BQ	TS	31.5t	—	90	
EH2.83.0A	BQ	TS	31.5t	—	98	

Unit No	SC	Liv	Pool	Dep	DTC *EE3710*		MBS *ED2610A*	TS *EH2760A*	DTC *EE3710*	
3001		N	*NSS*	BM	76230	*B*	62121	70781	76231	*B*
3002			*NSS*	BM	76233	*A*	62122	70782	76232	*A*
3003		N	*NSS*	BM	76234	*A*	62123	70783	76235	*A*
3005		N	*NSS*	BM	76239	*A*	62125	70785	76238	*A*
3006		N	*NSS*	BM	76241	*B*	62126	70786	76240	*B*
3007		N	*NSS*	BM	76243	*A*	62127	70787	76242	*A*
3008		N	*NSS*	BM	76244	*A*	62128	70788	76245	*A*
3009		N	*NSS*	BM	76246	*B*	62129	70789	76247	*B*
3010		N	*NSS*	BM	76369	*B*	62130	70790	76249	*B*
3011		N	*NSS*	BM	76251	*B*	62131	70791	76250	*B*
3012		N	*NSS*	BM	76252	*B*	62132	70792	76253	*B*
3013		N	*NSS*	BM	76255	*B*	62133	70793	76254	*B*
3014		N	*NSS*	BM	76257	*B*	62134	70794	76248	*B*
3015		N	*NSS*	BM	76258	*B*	62135	70795	76259	*B*
3016		N	*NSS*	BM	76261	*B*	62136	70796	76260	*B*
3017		N	*NSS*	BM	76262	*A*	62137	70797	76263	*A*
3018		N	*NSS*	BM	76265	*B*	62138	70875	76264	*B*
3019		N	*NSS*	BM	76267	*B*	62139	70799	76837†	*B*
3020		N	*NSS*	BM	76269	*B*	62140	70800	76268	*B*

Unit No	SC	Liv	Pool	Dep	DTC		MBS	TS	DTC	
					EE3710		*ED2611A*	*EH2760A*	*EE3710*	
3026		N	*NSX*	BI	76344	*B*	62187	70877	76343	*B*
3030		N	*NSS*	BM	76352	*B*	62191	70881	76351	*B*
3032		N	*NSS*	BM	76356	*B*	62193	70883	76355	*B*
3034		N	*NSS*	BM	76360	*B*	62195	70885	76359	*B*
3035		N	*NSS*	BM	76362	*B*	62196	70890	76361	*B*
3037		N	*NSS*	BM	76366	*B*	62198	70888	76365	*B*
3046		N	*NSS*	BM	76384	*A*	62207	70897	76383	*A*
					EE3674A		*ED2611A*	*EH2830A*	*EE3674A*	
3058			*NSS*	FR	76446		62219	70909	76445	
					EE36		*ED2631A*	*EH2830A*	*EE36*	
3067			*NSS*	WDs	76464	*76A*		70918	76463	*76A*
3068		N	*NSS*	FR	76466	*82B*	62229	70919	76370	*82B*
3069			*NSS*	WD	76468	*76A*	62230	70920	76467	*76A*
					EE3676A		*ED2631A*	*EH2760A*	*EE3710A*	
3070			*NSS*	WD	76470		62231	70900	76339	
					EE36		*ED2631A*	*EH2830A*	*EE36*	
3071		N	*NSS*	WD	76472	*82B*	62232	70922	76471	*82B*
3072			*NSS*	WD	76474	*76A*	62233	70923	76473	*76A*
3073			*NSS*	WD	76476	*76A*	62234	70924	76475	*76A*
3074			*NSS*	WD	76478	*76A*	62235	70925	76477	*76A*
3075		N	*NSS*	WD	76480	*82B*	62236	70926	76479	*82B*
3076			*NSS*	WD	76482	*76A*	62237	70927	76481	*76A*
3077		N	*NSS*	WD	76484	*82B*	62238	70928	76483	*82B*
3078		N	*NSS*	WD	76486	*82B*	62239	70929	76485	*82B*
3080		N	*NSX*	BI	76490	*82B*	62241	70931	76489	*82B*
3083			*NSX*	BI	76496	*82B*	62244	70934	76495	*82B*
3084			*NSX*	BI	76498	*76A*	62245	70935	76497	*76A*
3085			*NSX*	BI	76500	*76A*	62246	70936	76499	*76A*
3086			*NSX*	BI	76502	*76A*	62247	70937	76501	*76A*
3087			*NSX*	BI	76504	*76A*	62248	70938	76503	*76A*
					EE3661A		*ED2620A*	*EH2780A*	*EE3661A*	
3088			*NSX*	BI	76506		62249	70939	76505	
3089			*NSX*	BI	76508		62250	70940	76507	
3090			*NSX*	BI	76510		62251	70941	76509	
3091		N	*NSX*	BI	76512		62252	70942	76511	
3092		N	*NSX*	BI	76514		62253	70943	76513	
3093		N	*NSX*	BI	76516		62254	70944	76515	
3094		N	*NSX*	BI	76518		62255	70945	76517	
3095		N	*NSX*	BI	76520		62256	70946	76519	
3096		N	*NSX*	BI	76522		62257	70947	76521	
3097		N	*NSX*	BI	76524		62258	70948	76523	

Unit No	SC	Liv	Pool	Dep	DTC		MBS	TS	DTC	
					EE3651A		*ED2620A*	*EH2780A*	*EE3661A*	
3098			*NSX*	BI	76364		62259	70949	76525	
					EE3661A		*ED2620A*	*EH2780A*	*EE3661A*	
3099		N	*NSX*	BI	76528		62260	70950	76527	
					EE36		*ED2632A*	*EH2830A*	*EE36*	
3107		N	*NSX*	BI	76544	*82B*	62268	70958	76543	*82B*
3109			*NSX*	BI	76548	*76A*	62270	70960	76547	*76A*
3110			*NSX*	BI	76550	*76A*	62271	70961	76549	*76A*
3111			*NSX*	BI	76552	*76A*	62272	70962	76551	*76A*
3112		N	*NSX*	BI	76554	*81B*	62273	70963	76553	*81B*
3113		N	*NSB*	WD	76556	*81B*	62274	70964	76555	*81B*
3114		N	*NSX*	WD	76558	*81B*	62275	70965	76557	*81B*
3115		N	*NSX*	WD	76560	*81B*	62276	70966	76559	*81B*
					EE36		*ED2633A*	*EH2830A*	*EE36*	
3116		N	*NSX*	WD	76641	*81B*	62317	70997	76642	*81B*
3117		N	*NSX*	WD	76643	*81B*	62318	70998	76644	*81B*
3118		N	*NSX*	WD	76645	*81B*	62319	70999	76646	*81B*
3119		N	*NSX*	WD	76647	*81B*	62320	71000	76648	*81B*
3120			*NSX*	WD	76649	*75A*	62321	71001	76650	*75A*
3121		N	*NSX*	WD	76651	*81B*	62322	71002	76652	*81B*
3122			*NSX*	WD	76653	*75A*	62323	71003	76654	*75A*
3123		N	*NSX*	WD	76655	*81B*	62324	71004	76656	*81B*
3124			*NSX*	WD	76657	*75A*	62325	71005	76658	*75A*
3125		N	*NSX*	WD	76659	*81B*	62326	71006	76660	*81B*
3126			*NSX*	WD	76661	*75A*	62327	71007	76662	*75A*
3127			*NSX*	WD	76663	*75A*	62328	71008	76664	*75A*
3128			*NSX*	WD	76665	*75A*	62329	71009	76666	*75A*
3129			*NSX*	WD	76667	*75A*	62330	71010	76668	*75A*
3130			*NSX*	WD	76669	*75A*	62331	71011	76670	*75A*
3131			*NSX*	WD	76671	*75A*	62332	71012	76672	*75A*
3132			*NSX*	WD	76673	*75A*	62333	71013	76674	*75A*
3133			*NSX*	WD	76675	*75A*	62334	71014	76676	*75A*
3134		N	*NSX*	BI	76677	*81B*	62335	71015	76678	*81B*
3135		N	*NSX*	BI	76679	*81B*	62336	71016	76680	*81B*
3136			*NSX*	BI	76681	*75A*	62337	71017	76682	*75A*
3137		N	*NSX*	BI	76683	*81B*	62338	71018	76684	*81B*
3138		N	*NSX*	BI	76685	*81B*	62339	71019	76686	*81B*
3139		N	*NSX*	BI	76687	*81B*	62340	71020	76688	*81B*
					EE3681B		*ED2633A*	*EH2760A*	*EE3710B*	
3140		N	*NSX*	BI	76689		62341	70887	76363	
					EE3681B		*ED2633A*	*EH2830A*	*EE3681B*	
3141		N	*NSB*	WD	76691		62342	71022	76692	

Unit No	SC	Liv	Pool	Dep	DTC	MBS	TS	DTC
3142		N	*NSB*	WD	76693	62343	71023	76694
3143			*NSB*	WD	76695	62344	71024	76696
3144		N	*NSB*	WD	76697	62345	71025	76698
3145			*NSS*	BM	76699	62346	71026	76700
3146		N	*NSS*	BM	76701	62347	71027	76702
3147		N	*NSS*	BM	76703	62348	71028	76704
3148		N	*NKC*	RE	76705	62349	71029	76706
3149		N	*NKC*	RE	76707	62350	71030	76708
3150		N	*NKC*	RE	76709	62351	71031	76710
3151			*NKC*	RE	76711	62352	71032	76712
					EE3682B	*ED2633A*	*EH2830A*	*EE3681B*
3152		N	*NKC*	RE	76465	62353	71033	76714
					EE3681B	*ED2633A*	*EH2830A*	*EE3681B*
3153		N	*NKC*	RE	76715	62354	71034	76716
					EE36838	*ED2635A*	*EH2830A*	*EE3683B*
3154		N	*NKC*	RE	76861	62435	71115	76862
3155		N	*NKC*	RE	76863	62436	71116	76864
3156		N	*NKC*	RE	76865	62437	71117	76866
3157		N	*NKC*	RE	76867	62438	71118	76868
3158		N	*NKC*	RE	76869	62439	71119	76870
3159		N	*NKC*	RE	76871	62440	71120	76872
3160		N	*NKC*	RE	76873	62441	71121	76874
3161		N	*NKC*	RE	76875	62442	71122	76876
3162		N	*NKC*	RE	76877	62443	71123	76878
3163		N	*NKC*	RE	76879	62444	71124	76880
3164		N	*NKC*	RE	76881	62445	71125	76882
3165		N	*NKC*	RE	76883	62446	71126	76884
3166		N	*NKC*	RE	76885	62447	71127	76886
3167		N	*NKC*	RE	76887	62448	71128	76888
3169		N	*NKC*	RE	76891	62450	71130	76892
3170		N	*NKC*	RE	76893	62451	71131	76894
3171		N	*NKC*	RE	76895	62452	71132	76896
3172		N	*NKC*	RE	76897	62453	71133	76998
3173		N	*NKC*	RE	76899	62454	71134	76900
3174			*NKC*	RE	76901	62455	71135	76902
3175		N	*NKC*	RE	76903	62456	71136	76904
3176		N	*NKC*	RE	76905	62457	71137	76906
3177		N	*NKC*	RE	76907	62458	71138	76908
3178		N	*NKC*	RE	76909	62463	71139	76910
3179		N	*NKC*	RE	76911	62460	71140	76912
3180		N	*NKC*	RE	76913	62461	71141	76914
3181		N	*NKC*	RE	76915	62462	71142	76916
3182		N	*NKC*	RE	76917	62459	71143	76918
3183		N	*NKC*	RE	76919	62464	71144	76920

Unit No	SC	Liv	Pool	Dep	DTC	MBS	TS	DTC
3184		N	*NKC*	RE	76921	62465	71145	76922
3185		N	*NKC*	RE	76923	62466	71146	76924
3186		N	*NKC*	RE	76925	62467	71147	76926
3187		N	*NKC*	RE	76927	62468	71148	76928
3188		N	*NKC*	RE	76929	62469	71149	76930
3189		N	*NKC*	RE	76931	62470	71150	76932
3190		N	*NKC*	RE	76933	62471	71151	76934
3191		N	*NKC*	RE	76935	62472	71152	76936
3192		N	*NKC*	RE	76937	62473	71153	76938
3193		N	*NKC*	RE	76939	62474	71154	76940
3194		N	*NKC*	RE	76941	62475	71155	76942

Class 413 — 4-CAP 4-car

Built: BR, Eastleigh 1957. Present formations introduced 1982 by pairing Class 414 stock.
Design: BR, non-gangwayed. Driver/guard communication fitted. Controls of power cars not used
Supply: 750/850V dc
Traction Motors (MBS, MLS): Two 250hp (185kW) English Electric

Maximum speed: 90mph
Dimensions: *Motor coaches:* 20.04m L × 2.82m W × 3.86m H (over Periscopes). *Driving coaches:* 20.44m L × 2.82m W × 3.77m H
AWS: See below

DMEE Diagram	*SR Design*	*Type*	*Weight*	*Seats 1st*	*Seats Std*	*Toilet*	*AWS*
Motor Brake Standard:							
EB2.69.2B	CQ2B	MBS	42t	—	84	—	—
EB2.69.3B	CQ3A	MBS	42t	—	84	—	—
EB2.69.6B	CQ3A	MBS	42t	—	84	—	Isolated
EB2.70.0A	CR	MBS	42t	—	84	—	—
EB2.70.3A	CR	MBS	42t	—	84	—	Isolated
Motor Luggage Standard (MLS):							
Details as MBS above							
Driving Trailer Composite/Standard (Compartment/Saloon):							
EE2.21.1A	DX	DTS	32.5t	—	69	2	Fitted
EE2.22.1A	DZ	DTS	32.5t	—	69	2	Fitted
EE3.61.2A	DX	DTC	32.5t	19	50	2	Fitted
EE3.61.3A*	DX1A	DTC	32.5t	19	50	2	Fitted
EE3.62.3A	DZ	DTC	32.5t	19	50	2	Fitted

*Official code not issued

Class 413/2

Unit No	Liv	Pool	Dep	DTC	MBS	MLS	DTS
				EE361	*EB269*	*EB269*	*EE2211A*
3201	N	*NKC*	RE	77120 *3A*	65398 *2B*	65401 *3B*	77123

Unit No	Liv	Pool	Dep	DTC	MBS	MLS	DTS
3202	N	*NKC*	RE	77118 *2A*	65396 *3B*	65412 *3B*	77134
3203	N	*NKC*	RE	77117 *2A*	65395 *6B*	65424 *3B*	77146
3204	N	*NKC*	RE	77132 *2A*	65410 *6B*	65420 *6B*	77142
3205		*NKC*	RE	77135 *2A*	65413 *3B*	65422 *3B*	77144
3206		*NKC*	RE	77141 *2A*	65419 *6B*	65423 *6B*	77145
3207		*NKC*	RE	77126 *2A*	65404 *3B*	65428 *3B*	77150
3208		*NKC*	RE	77147 *2A*	65425 *3B*	65429 *3B*	77151
3209		*NKC*	RE	77129 *2A*	65407 *6B*	65430 *6B*	77152
3210		*NKC*	RE	77124 *2A*	65402 *3B*	65434 *3B*	77156
3211		*NKC*	RE	77115 *2A*	65393 *3B*	65427 *3B*	77149
3212		*NKC*	RE	77128 *2A*	65406 *3B*	65433 *3B*	77155
3213		*NKC*	RE	77119 *2A*	65397 *3B*	65432 *3B*	77154

Class 413/3

Unit No	Liv	Pool	Dep	DTC	MBS	MLS	DTS
				EE3622A	*EB270*	*EB270*	*EE2211A*
3301	N	*NKC*	RE	75373	61253 *0A*	61255 *0A*	75375
3302		*NKC*	RE	75361	61241 *0A*	61244 *0A*	75364
3303		*NKC*	RE	75370	61250 *3A*	61252 *0A*	75372
3304		*NKC*	RE	75402	61282 *3A*	61283 *3A*	75403
3305		*NKC*	RE	75399	61279 *3A*	61302 *3A*	75422
3306		*NKC*	RE	75374	61254 *0A*	61256 *3A*	75376
3307		*NKC*	RE	75378	61258 *0A*	61271 *0A*	75391
3308		*NKC*	RE	75366	61246 *3A*	61264 *3A*	75384
3309		*NKC*	RE	75371	61251 *0A*	61257 *0A*	75377
3310		*NKC*	RE	75363	61243 *0A*	61259 *3A*	75386
3311		*NKC*	RE	75411	61291 *0A*	61297 *3A*	75417

Class 423/1 — 4-VEP 4-Car

For full details see Class 423 4-VEP. Facelifted and Public address fitted: BRML Eastleigh, 1988-90.

DMEE Diagram	*SR Design*	*Type*	*Weight*	*Seats 1st*	*Std*	*Toilet*
Motor Brake Standard:						
ED2.--.0A*	ED6A	MBS	c49t	—	76	—
ED2.--.1A*	ED1A	MBS	c49t	—	76	—
ED2.--.2A*	ED2A	MBS	c49t	—	76	—
Driving Trailer Composite (Compartment):						
EE3.71.5B*	FB5B	DTC	32.5t	18	46	1
EE3.71.7B*	FB7B	DTC	32.5t	18	46	1
Trailer Standard:						
EH2.83.1B*	BQ1B	TS	31.5t	—	96	—

*Official Codes not yet issued

3401-19 to be formed from Unit Nos 3001/02/03/05-20.

Unit No	Old Unit No	Liv	Pool	Dep	DTC	MBS		TS	DTC
					EE3717B	*ED2-0A*		*EQ2831B*	*EE3717B*
3421	(3168)	N	*NKC*	RE	76889	62449		71129	76890
					EE3715B	*ED2-*		*EQ2831B*	*EE3715B*
3422	(3040)	N	*NKC*	RE	76372	62201	*1A*	70891	76371
3423	(3061)	N	*NKC*	RE	76452	62222	*2A*	70912	76451
3424	(3031R)	N	*NKC*	RE	76354	62185	*1A*	70882	76353
3425	(3023R)	N	*NSS*	BM	76338	62192	*1A*	70874	76337
3426	(3047)	N	*NSS*	BM	76386	62208	*1A*	70898	76385
3427	(3041R)	N	*NSS*	BM	76374	62184	*1A*	70892	76373
3428	(3062)	N	*NSS*	BM	76454	62223	*2A*	70913	76453
3429	(3021R)	N	*NSS*	BM	76334	62202	*1A*	70872	76333
3430	(3028)	N	*NSB*	WD	76348	62189	*1A*	70879	76347
3431	(3064R)	N	*NSB*	WD	76458	62182	*1A*	70915	76457
3432	(3054R)	N	*NSB*	WD	76400	62225	*2A*	70905	76399
3433	(3057R)	N	*NSB*	WD	76444	62215	*1A*	70908	76443
3434	(3066R)	N	*NSB*	WD	76462	62218	*1A*	70917	76461
3435	(3025R)	N	*NSX*	BI	76342	62228	*2A*	70876	76341
3436	(3029R)	N	*NSX*	BI	76350	62186	*1A*	70880	76349
3437	(3027R)	N	*NSX*	BI	76346	62190	*1A*	70878	76345
3438	(3100R)	N	*NSX*	BI	76530	62262	*2A*	70951	76329
3439	(3055R)	N	*NSX*	BI	76402	62227	*2A*	70906	76401
3440	(3102R)	N	*NSX*	BI	76534	62188	*1A*	70953	76533
3441	(3043R)	N	*NSX*	BI	76378	62261	*2A*	70894	76377
3442	(3081R)	N	*NSX*	BI	76492	62216	*1A*	70932	76491
3443	(3082R)	N	*NSX*	BI	76494	62263	*2A*	70933	76493
3444	(3038R)	N	*NSX*	BI	76368	62204	*1A*	70889	76367
					EE3715B	*ED2-2A*		*EQ2831C*	*EE3715B*
3445	(3060R)	N	*NKC*	RE	76450	62242		70911	76449
3446	(3101R)	N	*NKC*	RE	76532	62243		70952	76531
3447	(3044R)	N	*NKC*	RE	76380	62199		70895	76379
3448	(3042R)	N	*NKC*	RE	76376	62221		70886	76375
3449	(3022R)	N	*NKC*	RE	76336	62205		70873	76335
3450	(3065R)	N	*NKC*	RE	76460	62203		70916	76459
3451	(3079)	N	*NKC*	RE	76488	62240		70930	76487
3452	(3024R)	N	*NKC*	RE	76340	62183		71021	76690
3453	(3045R)	N	*NKC*	RE	76382	62226		70896	76381
3454	(3049R)	N	*NKC*	RE	76390	62200		70798	76389
3455	(3048R)	N	*NSS*	FR	76388	62206		70899	76387
3456	(3063R)	N	*NSS*	FR	76456	62210		70914	76455
3457	(3050R)	N	*NSS*	FR	76392	62197		70901	76391
3458	(3051R)	N	*NSS*	FR	76394	62209		70902	76393
3459	(3052R)	N	*NSS*	FR	76396	62224		70903	76395
3460	(3105)	N	*NSX*	BI	76540	62211		70956	76539

Unit No	Old Unit No	Liv	Pool	Dep	DTC	MBS	TS	DTC
3461	(3104)	N	*NSX*	BI	76538	62212	70955	76537
3462	(3103R)	N	*NSX*	BI	76536	62213	70954	76535
3463	(3053R)	N	*NSX*	BI	76398	62266	70904	76397
3464	(3056R)	N	*NSX*	BI	76442	62265	70907	76441
3465	(3106R)	N	*NSX*	BI	76542	62264	70957	76541
3466	(3067)	N	*NSS*	WD	76464	62214	70918	76463
3467	(3158)	N	*NSS*	FR	76446	62217	70909	76445
3468	(3059)	N	*NSS*	FR	76448	62267	70910	76447
3469	(3108)	N	*NSX*	BI	76546	62219	70958	76545
3470	(3083)	N	*NSX*	BI	76496	62220	70934	76495
3471	(3084)	N	*NSX*	BI	76498	62269	70935	76497
3472		N				62244		
3473		N				62245		
3474								
3475								
3476								
3477								
3478								
3479								
3480								
3481								
3482								
3483								
3484								
3485								
3486								
3487								
3488								
3489								
3490								
3491								
3492								
3493								
3494								
3495								
3496								
3497								
3498								
3499								
3500								
3501								
3502								
3503								
3504								
3505								
3506								
3507								

Unit No	Old Unit No	Liv	Pool	Dep	DTC	MBS	TS	DTC
3508								
3509								
3510								

Unit Nos 3511-91 to be formed from Class 423/0 1990 onwards.

Class 414 — 2-HAP 2-Car

Built: British Railways Eastleigh 1958
Design: BR non-gangwayed
Power supply: 750/850V dc third rail
Traction motors (DMBS): Two 250hp (185kW) English Electric
Maximum speed: 90mph
Dimensions: *Motor coaches:* 20.04m L × 2.82m W × 3.86m H (over periscopes); *Trailer coaches:* 20.44m L × 2.82m W × 3.77m H
AWS: All vehicles fitted

DMEE Diagram	*SR Design*	*Type*	*Weight*	*Seats 1st*	*Seats Std*	*Toilet*
Driving Motor Brake Standard (Semi-Open)						
EB2.69.6B	CQ3A	DMBS	42t	—	84	
EB2.70.1B	CU	DMBS	42t	—	84	
EB2.70.3A	CR	DMBS	42t	—	84	
Driving Trailer Composite (Compartment/Saloon)						
EE3.61.2A	DX	DTC	32.5t	19	50	2
EE3.62.1B	DAD	DTC	32.5t	19	50	2
EE3.62.3A	DZ	DTC	32.5t	19	50	2

Class 414/2

Unit No	SC	Liv	Pool	Dep	DMBS	DTC
					EE2696B	*FE3612A*
4201			*NSB*	WD	65405	77127

Class 414/3

Unit No	SC	Liv	Pool	Dep	DMBS	DTC
					EE2703A	*EE3623A*
4301			*NSB*	WD	61249	75369
4302			*NSB*	WD	61260	75379
4303			*NSB*	WD	61261	75381
4304			*NSB*	WD	61262	75382
4305			*NSB*	WD	61268	75388
4306			*NSB*	WD	61270	75390
4307			*NSB*	WD	61273	75393
4308			*NSB*	WD	61275	75395
4309			*NSB*	WD	61276	75396
4310			*NSB*	WD	61278	75398
4311			*NSB*	WD	61287	75407
4312			*NSB*	WD	61288	75408
4313			*NSB*	WD	61290	75410

Unit No	SC	Liv	Pool	Dep	DMBS	DTC
4314			*NSB*	WD	61294	75414
4315			*NSB*	WD	61295	75415
4316			*NSB*	WD	61296	75416
4317			*NSB*	WD	61298	75418
4318			*NSB*	WD	61300	75420
4319			*NSB*	WD	61303	75423
					EB2701B	*EE3621B*
4320				WD	61654	75706
4321				WD	61668	75720
4322		N		WD	61683	75735

Class 465 'NETWORKER 1'

A new fleet of suburban trains for Network SouthEast London-Kent services is due to be ordered during 1989 for deliveries commencing in late 1990. Equipment and seating trials are being conducted in Class 455/9 unit No 5920 and Class 457 unit No 7001.

Class 415 4-EPB 4-Car

Built: Southern Region Eastleigh 1951
Design: SR non-gangwayed
Supply: 750/850V dc third rail
Traction motors (DMBS): Two 250hp (185kW) English Electric (E Express gear ratio)
Maximum speed: 75mph (E 90mph)
Dimensions: See below
AWS: Driving vehicles fitted

Driving Motor Brake Standard
Classes 415/1 & 415/5

DMEE Diagram	*SR Design*	*Type*	*Weight*	*Seats*		*Dimensions L × W × H m (over periscopes where fitted)*
EB2.66.2A	CP	DMBS	40t	82		19.23 × 2.82 × 3.99
EB2.66.3A	CP1A	DMBS	40t	82		19.23 × 2.82 × 3.99
EB2.66.4A*	CP3A	DMBS	40t	82		19.23 × 2.82 × 3.99
EB2.66.5A*	CP4A	DMBS	40t	82		19.23 × 2.82 × 3.99
EB2.67.1A	CP1AS	DMBS	40t	84	(semi-open)	19.23 × 2.82 × 3.99
EB2.69.4A	CQ	DMBS	42t	84		20.03 × 2.82 × 3.86
EB2.69.5A	CQ1A	DMBS	42t	84		20.03 × 2.82 × 3.86

Class 415/4 (Facelifted)

DMEE Diagram	*SR Design*	*Type*	*Weight*	*Seats*	*Dimensions L × W × H m (over periscopes where fitted)*
EB2.77.1A*	CX	DMBS	40t	82	19.23 × 2.82 × 3.99

EB2.77.2A*	CX2A	DMBS	40t	82		19.23 × 2.82 × 3.99
EB2.77.3A*	CX3A	DMBS	40t	82		19.23 × 2.82 × 3.99
EB2.77.4A*	CX4A	DMBS	40t	82		19.23 × 2.82 × 3.99
EB2.77.5A*	CX5A	DMBS	40t	82		19.23 × 2.82 × 3.99
EB2.77.6A*	CX6A	DMBS	40t	82		19.23 × 2.82 × 3.99
EB2.78.0A	CX1A	DMBS	40t	82		19.23 × 2.82 × 3.99

Trailer Standard

Class 415/5 (Compartment)

DMEE Diagram	*SR Design*	*Type*	*Weight*	*Seats*		*Dimensions L × W × H m*
EH2.67.0A	DU	TS	28t	108	(9 compt)	18.96 × 2.82 × 3.77
EH2.67.1B	DU1A	TS	28t	108	(9 compt)	18.96 × 2.82 × 3.77
EH2.68.0A	DU	TS	28t	120	(10 compt)	18.96 × 2.82 × 3.77
EH2.68.1B	DU1A	TS	28t	120	(10 compt)	18.96 × 2.82 × 3.77
EH2.68.2C*	DU3A	TS	28t	120	(10 compt)	18.96 × 2.82 × 3.77

Class 415/1

DMEE Diagram	*SR Design*	*Type*	*Weight*	*Seats*	*Dimensions L × W × H m*
EH2.70.0A	DS	TS	27t	102	18.96 × 2.82 × 3.77
EH2.70.1A*	DS1A	TS	27t	102	18.96 × 2.82 × 3.77

Class 415/4 (Facelifted)

DMEE Diagram	*SR Design*	*Type*	*Weight*	*Seats*		*Dimensions L × W × H m*
EH2.79.0A	DAK1B	TS	26t	102		18.96 × 2.82 × 3.77
EH2.79.0B	DAK1B	TS	26t	102	Non-smoking	18.96 × 2.82 × 3.77
EH2.79.3A*	DAK3A	TS	26t	102		18.96 × 2.82 × 3.77
EH2.79.3B*	DAK3B	TS	26t	102		18.96 × 2.82 × 3.77
EH2.80.1B	DAK1B	TS	28t	102	Non-smoking	18.96 × 2.82 × 3.77
EH2.80.1C*	DAK1B	TS	28t	102		18.96 × 2.82 × 3.77
EH2.80.2B*	DAK2B	TS	28t	102	Non-smoking	18.96 × 2.82 × 3.77
EH2.80.3A*	DAK3A	TS	28t	102		18.96 × 2.82 × 3.77
EH2.80.3B*	DAK3B	TS	28t	102		18.96 × 2.82 × 3.77
EH2.81.0A	DAK1A	TS	27t	102		18.96 × 2.82 × 3.77
EH2.81.1A	DAK2A	TS	27t	102		18.96 × 2.82 × 3.77
EH2.81.2B	DAH	TS	27t	102	Prototype	18.96 × 2.82 × 3.77
EH2.81.2D	DAH	TS	27t	102	Prototype, non-smoking	18.96 × 2.82 × 3.77
EH2.81.3A*	DAK3A	TS	27t	102		18.96 × 2.82 × 3.77
EH2.81.3B*	DAK3B	TS	27t	102		18.96 × 2.82 × 3.77
EH2.81.4A*	DAK4A	TS	27t	102		18.96 × 2.82 × 3.77

*Official codes not issued

Class 415/1

Unit No	SC	Liv	Pool	Dep	DMBS	TS	TS	DMBS
					EB2662A	*EH2700A*	*EH2700A*	*EB2662A*
5104			*NKS*	SG	14207	15409	15157	14208
5107			*NKS*	SG	14213	15153	15235	14214
5113			*NKS*	SG	14225	15376	15241	14226
5114			*NKS*	SG	14227	15426	15242	14228
					EB2662A	*EH2701A*	*EH2700A*	*EB2662A*
5115			*NKS*	SG	14230	15350	15243	14229
					EB2662A	*EH2700A*	*EH2700A*	*EB2662A*
5121			*NKS*	SG	14242	15247	15249	14241
5124			*NKS*	SG	14248	15248	15252	14247
5126			*NKS*	SG	14252	15244	15254	14376
5131			*NKS*	SG	14261	15412	15259	14262
5133			*NKS*	SG	14265	15132	15261	14266
					EB2695A	*EH2700A*	*EH2700A*	*EB2662A*
5134			*NKS*	SG	65383	15444	15262	14268
					EB2662A	*EH2700A*	*EH2700A*	*EB2662A*
5138			*NKS*	SG	14275	15423	15266	14276
5139			*NKS*	SG	14277	15442	15267	14278
5145			*NKS*	SG	14290	15158	15273	14289
5146			*NKS*	SG	14291	15133	15274	14292
5148			*NKS*	SG	14296	15343	15276	14295
5150			*NKS*	SG	14099	15370	15278	14299
5153			*NKS*	SG	14305	15256	15281	14306
5154			*NKS*	SG	14308	15279	15282	14307
5155			*NKS*	SG	14309	15107	15283	14310
5156			*NKS*	SG	14311	15272	15334	14312
5157			*NKS*	SG	14313	15381	15335	14314
5159			*NKS*	SG	14317	15105	15337	14318
5160			*NKS*	SG	14319	15268	15338	14320
5163			*NKS*	SG	14325	15260	15341	14326
5166			*NKS*	SG	14331	15253	15344	14332
5168			*NKS*	SG	14335	15340	15346	14336
					EB2694A	*EH2700A*	*EH2700A*	*EB2662A*
5169			*NKS*	SG	65303	15109	15347	14338
					EE2662A	*EH2700A*	*EH2700A*	*EE2662A*
5170			*NKS*	SG	14339	15245	15348	14340
5173			*NKS*	SG	14345	15116	15120	14346
5174			*NKS*	SG	14348	15138	15352	14347
5176			*NKS*	SG	14352	15396	15354	14351
5177			*NKS*	SG	14354	15257	15355	14353

Unit No	SC	Liv	Pool	Dep	DMBS	TS	TS	DMBS
5182			*NKS*	SG	14364	15357	15360	14363
5185			*NKS*	SG	14369	15277	15363	14370
5189			*NKS*	SG	14377	15339	15367	14378
5190			*NKS*	SG	14380	15361	15368	14379
5191			*NKS*	SG	14381	15108	15369	14382
5194			*NKS*	SG	14388	15275	15372	14387
5195			*NKS*	SG	14389	15239	15373	14390
5196			*NKS*	SG	14392	15399	15374	14391
5201			*NKS*	SG	14402	15126	15379	14401
5202			*NKS*	SG	14404	15362	15380	14403
5209			*NKS*	SG	14418	15395	15397	14417
5210			*NKS*	SG	14420	15263	15398	14419
5213			*NKS*	SG	14425	15353	15401	14426
					EB2663A	*EH2700A*	*EH2700A*	*EB2663A*
5217			*NKS*	SG	14434	15366	15405	14433
					EB2663A	*EH2700A*	*EH2700A*	*EB2662A*
5220			*NKS*	SG	14439	15349	15408	14260
					EB2663A	*EH2700A*	*EH2700A*	*EB2663A*
5222			*NKS*	SG	14490	15421	15410	14444
5223			*NKS*	SG	14446	15427	15411	14445
5226			*NKS*	SG	14451	15280	15414	14452
5228			*NKS*	SG	14455	15415	15416	14456
					EB2662A	*EH2700A*	*EH2700A*	*EB2663A*
5229			*NKS*	SG	14333	15435	15417	14457
					EB2663A	*EH2700A*	*EH2700A*	*EB2663A*
5230			*NKS*	SG	14460	15110	15418	14459
5231			*NKS*	SG	14461	15264	15419	14462
5232			*NKS*	SG	14464	15422	15420	14463
					EB2662A	*EH2700A*	*EH2700A*	*EB2663A*
5240			*NKS*	SG	14103	15425	15428	14480
					EB2663A	*EH2700A*	*EH2700A*	*EB2663A*
5242			*NKS*	SG	14483	15402	15430	14484
					EB2662A	*EH2700A*	*EH2700A*	*EB2663A*
5243			*NKS*	SG	14405	15375	15356	14485
					EB2663A	*EH2700A*	*EH2700A*	*EB2663A*
5248			*NKS*	SG	14492	15443	15436	14510

Unit No	SC	Liv	Pool	Dep	DMBS	TS	TS	DMBS
					EB2694A	EH2700A	EH2700A	EB2694A
5261			NKS	SG	65300	15154	15413	65310
					EB2671A	EH2700A	EH2700A	EB2671A
5264	E		NKS	SG	14522	15258	15147	14523

Unit No	Former No	SC	Liv	Pool	Dep	DMBS	TS	TS	DMBS
						EB2662A	EH2700A	EH2700A	EB2662A
5265	(5001)			NKS	SG	14001	15429	15101	14002
5266	(5020)			NKS	SG	14039	15234	15382	14040
5267	(5027)			NKS	SG	14053	15123	15127	14042
5268	(5035)			NKS	SG	14069	15113	15135	14070
5269	(5039)			NKS	SG	14078	15118	15139	14094
5270	(5040)			NKS	SG	14080	15122	15140	14079
5271	(5042)			NKS	SG	14083	15130	15142	14084
5272	(5044)			NKS	SG	14087	15345	15144	14088
5273	(5045)			NKS	SG	14090	15129	15145	14089
5274	(5046)			NKS	SG	14091	15364	15146	14092
5275	(5049)			NKS	SG	14098	15271	15149	14097
5276	(5051)			NKS	SG	14101	15143	15151	14102
						EB2662A	EH2700A	EH2700A	EB2663A
5277	(5052)			NKS	SG	14104	15103	15152	144208

Class 415/4

Built: 1951, facelifted 1979-86

Design: Driver-guard communication and public address system fitted

Unit No	SC	Liv	Pool	Dep	DMBS		TS		TS		DMBS	
					EB2772A		EH2812B		EH2812D		EB2772A	
5401	E		NSL	SU	14556		15449		15450		14521	
					EB2772A		EH2810A		EH2790B		EB2771A	
5402			NSL	SU	14449		15464		15465		14407	
					EB27		EH28B		EH28		EB27	
5403			NSL	SU	14286	71A	15174	01C	15221	01B	14285	71A
5404			NSL	SU	14435	80A	15036	01B	15406	10A	14436	80A
5405			NSL	SU	14470	72A	15053	01B	15216	10A	14469	72A
5406			NSL	SU	14303	71A	15230	01B	15285	10A	14356	71A
5407			NSL	SU	14428	71A	15392	01B	15060	10A	14427	71A
5408			NSL	SU	14297	71A	15227	01B	15313	10A	14298	71A
5409			NSL	SU	14494	72A	15065	01B	15047	10A	14206	71A
5410			NSL	SU	14540	72A	15386	01B	15304	10A	14528 E	71A
5411			NSL	SU	14475	72A	15056	01B	15192	10A	14476	72A

Unit No	SC	Liv	Pool	Dep	DMBS		TS		TS		DMBS	
					EB2771A		*EH2790B*		*EH2810A*		*EB2772A*	
5412			*NSL*	SU	14415		15451		15452		14304	
					EB27		*EH28*		*EH2810A*		*EB27*	
5413			*NSL*	SU	14396	*71A*	15326	*01B*	15191		14395	*71A*
5414			*NSL*	SU	14441	*72A*	15039	*01B*	15182		14442	*72A*
5415			*NSL*	SU	14465	*72A*	15040	*01B*	15051		14466	*72A*
5416			*NSL*	SU	14421	*71A*	15389	*01B*	15324		14422	*71A*
5417			*NSL*	SU	14478	*72A*	15057	*01B*	15041		14477	*72A*
5418			*NSL*	SU	14443	*72A*	15063	*01B*	15219		14282	*71A*
5419			*NSL*	SU	14473	*72A*	15055	*01B*	15058		14474	*72A*
5420			*NSL*	SU	14240	*71A*	15198	*01B*	15202		14239	*71A*
5421			*NSL*	SU	14500	*72A*	15068	*01B*	15073		14499	*72A*
5422			*NSL*	SU	14467	*72A*	15209	*01B*	15050		14468	*72A*
5423			*NSL*	SU	14511	*72A*	15074	*01B*	15212		14512	*72A*
5424			*NSL*	SU	14447	*72A*	15042	*01B*	15052		14448	*72A*
					EB2772A		*EH2790B*		*EH2810A*		*EB2775A*	
5425	E		*NSL*	SU	14538		15453		15454		14570	
					EB27		*EH28*		*EH28*		*EB27*	
5426			*NSL*	SU	14517	*72A*	15077	*01B*	15066	*10A*	14518	*72A*
5427			*NSL*	SU	14453	*72A*	15045	*01B*	15046	*10A*	14454	*72A*
5428			*NSL*	SU	14430	*73A*	15393	*01B*	15061	*10A*	14429	*73A*
5429			*NSL*	SU	14410	*71A*	15333	*01B*	15383	*10A*	14409	*71A*
5430			*NSL*	SU	14496	*72A*	15438	*01B*	15437	*10A*	14509	*72A*
5431			*NSL*	SU	14423	*71A*	15390	*01B*	15400	*10A*	14424	*71A*
5432			*NSL*	SU	14486	*72A*	15044	*01B*	15447	*10A*	14416	*71A*
5433			*NSL*	SU	14472	*72A*	15054	*01B*	15424	*10A*	14471	*72A*
5434			*NSL*	SU	14498	*72A*	15067	*02B*	15455	*11A*	14497	*72A*
5435			*NSL*	SU	14491	*72A*	15403	*01B*	15431	*10A*	14267	*71A*
5436			*NSL*	SU	14534	*72A*	15456	*01B*	15457	*10A*	14543	*72A*
5437			*NSL*	SU	14411	*71A*	15384	*01B*	15394	*10A*	14412	*71A*
5438			*NSL*	SU	14530	*72A*	15459	*02B*	15458	*11A*	14547	*72A*
5439			*NSL*	SU	14487	*72A*	15062	*01B*	15432	*10A*	14488	*72A*
5440			*NSL*	SU	14514	*72A*	15075	*01B*	15445	*10A*	14513	*72A*
5441			*NSL*	SU	14397	*71A*	15327	*01B*	15377	*10A*	14398	*71A*
5442			*NSL*	SU	14537	*72A*	15460	*02B*	15461	*11A*	14554	*72A*
5443			*NSL*	SU	14504	*72A*	15070	*10A*	15440	*01B*	14503	*72A*
5444			*NSL*	SU	14535	*72A*	15463	*11A*	15462	*02B*	14553	*72A*
5445			*NSL*	SU	14527	*72A*	15020	*01B*	15351	*10A*	14529	*72A*
					EB2772A		*EH2810A*		*EH2790B*		*EB2772A*	
5446	E		*NSL*	SU	14531		15466		15467		14541	
5447			*NSL*	SU	14532		15468		15469		14550	
5448			*NSL*	SU	14539		15470		15471		14548	

Unit No	SC	Liv	Pool	Dep	DMBS		TS		TS		DMBS	
					EB2772A		*EH2810A*		*EH2810B*		*EB2772A*	
5449			*NSL*	SU	14438		15037		15407		14437	
					EB27		*EH279*		*EH279*		*EB27*	
5450			*NSL*	SU	14533	*76A*	15472	*3B*	15473	*3A*	14552	*76A*
5451	E		*NSL*	SU	14526	*76A*	15474	*3A*	15475	*3B*	14551	*76A*
5452			*NKS*	SG	14536 E	*76A*	15477	*3A*	15476	*3B*	14563	*75A*
5453	E		*NKS*	SG	14545	*76A*	15479	*3B*	15478	*3A*	14525	*76A*
5454	E		*NKS*	SG	14555	*76A*	15481	*3A*	15480	*3B*	14524	*76A*
					EB27		*EH28*		*EH28*		*EB27*	
5455			*NKS*	SG	14062	*74A*	15023	*03B*	15027	*03A*	14054	*74A*
5456			*NKS*	SG	14481	*75A*	15001	*03A*	15059	*03B*	14482	*75A*
5457			*NKS*	SG	14501	*75A*	15439	*14A*	15069	*03B*	14502	*75A*
5458			*NKS*	SG	14431	*74A*	15034	*03B*	15404	*13A*	14432	*74A*
5459			*NKS*	SG	14506	*75A*	15441	*14A*	15071	*03B*	14505	*75A*
5460			*NKS*	SG	14516	*75A*	15446	*14A*	15076	*03B*	14515	*75A*
5461			*NKS*	SG	14520	*75A*	15448	*14A*	15078	*03B*	14519	*75A*
5462			*NKS*	SG	14021	*74A*	15011	*03B*	15111	*13A*	14022	*74A*
5463			*NKS*	SG	14037	*74A*	15019	*03B*	15119	*13A*	14038	*74A*
5464			*NKS*	SG	14081	*74A*	15166	*03B*	15159	*03A*	14082	*74A*
5465			*NKS*	SG	14236	*74A*	15196	*03B*	15208	*03A*	14350	*74A*
5466			*NKS*	SG	14004	*74A*	15002	*03B*	15220	*03A*	14003	*74A*
5467			*NKS*	SG	14006	*74A*	15003	*03B*	15177	*03A*	14005	*74A*
5468			*NKS*	SG	14211	*74A*	15332	*03A*	15184	*03B*	14212	*74A*
5469			*NKS*	SG	14007	*74A*	15004	*03B*	15201	*03A*	14008	*74A*
5470			*NKS*	SG	14315	*74A*	15286	*03B*	15215	*03A*	14316	*74A*
5471			*NKS*	SG	14255	*74A*	15206	*03B*	15231	*03A*	14256	*74A*
5472			*NKS*	SG	14508	*75A*	15295	*03B*	15169	*03A*	14458	*75A*
5473			*NKS*	SG	14493	*75A*	15029	*03B*	15170	*03A*	14058	*74A*
5474			*NKS*	SG	14065	*74A*	15033	*03B*	15224	*03A*	14066	*74A*
5475			*NKS*	SG	14019	*74A*	15010	*03B*	15048	*03A*	14020	*74A*
5476			*NKS*	SG	14016	*74A*	15316	*03B*	15319	*03A*	14015	*74A*
5477			*NKS*	SG	14013	*74A*	15180	*03B*	15233	*03A*	14057	*74A*
5478			*NKS*	SG	14059	*74A*	15030	*03B*	15167	*03A*	14060	*74A*
5479			*NKS*	SG	14322	*74A*	15289	*03B*	15317	*03A*	14321	*74A*
5480			*NKS*	SG	14264	*74A*	15210	*03B*	15291	*03A*	14263	*74A*
5481			*NKS*	SG	14330	*74A*	15293	*03B*	15226	*03A*	14329	*74A*
5482			*NKS*	SG	14017	*74A*	15009	*03B*	15297	*03A*	14018	*74A*
5483			*NKS*	SG	14052	*74A*	15175	*03B*	15329	*03A*	14051	*74A*
5484			*NKS*	SG	14061	*74A*	15031	*03B*	15308	*03A*	14046	*74A*
5485			*NKS*	SG	14105	*74A*	15178	*03B*	15185	*03A*	14106	*74A*
5486			*NKS*	SG	14071	*74A*	15161	*03B*	15125	*13A*	14072	*74A*
5487			*NKS*	SG	14361	*74A*	15309	*03B*	15359	*13A*	14362	*74A*
5488			*NKS*	SG	14386	*74A*	15321	*03B*	15371	*13A*	14385	*74A*
5489			*NKS*	SG	14024	*74A*	15012	*03B*	15112	*13A*	14023	*74A*
5490			*NKS*	SG	14205	*74A*	15433	*13B*	15128	*13A*	14056	*74A*

Unit No	SC	Liv	Pool	Dep	DMBS		TS		TS		DMBS	
5491			*NKS*	SG	14029	*74A*	15136	*13B*	15115	*13A*	14030	*74A*
5492			*NKS*	SG	14223	*74A*	15246	*13B*	15240	*13A*	14224	*74A*
5493			*NKS*	SG	14028	*74A*	15237	*13B*	15114	*13A*	14027	*74A*
5494			*NKS*	SG	14073	*74A*	15236	*13B*	15137	*13A*	14074	*74A*
5495			*NKS*	SG	14095	*74A*	15265	*13B*	15148	*13A*	14096	*74A*
5496			*NKS*	SG	14400	*74A*	15336	*13B*	15378	*13A*	14399	*74A*
5497			*NKS*	SG	14246	*74A*	15104	*13B*	15251	*13A*	14245	*74A*

Class 415/5

Unit No	Old Unit Nos	SC	Liv	Pool	Dep	DMBS *EB266*		TS *EH26*		TS *EH26*		DMBS *EB266*	
5501	(5125/5166)			*NKS*	SG	14250	*2A*	15015	*80A*	15294	*81B*	14249	*2A*
5502	(5183/5190)			*NKS*	SG	14366	*2A*	15311	*81B*	15318	*81B*	14365	*2A*
5503	(5140/5160)			*NKS*	SG	14359	*2A*	15218	*81B*	15288	*81B*	14279	*2A*
5504	(5038/5174)			*NKS*	SG	14076	*2A*	15163	*81B*	15302	*81B*	14075	*2A*
5505	(5162/5168)			*NKS*	SG	14323	*2A*	15290	*81B*	15296	*81B*	14324	*2A*
5506	(5151/5154)			*NKS*	SG	14302	*2A*	15229	*81B*	15232	*81B*	14301	*2A*
5507	(5171/5220)			*NKS*	SG	14341	*2A*	15299	*81B*	15038	*70A*	14342	*2A*
5508	(5018/5039)			*NKS*	SG	14036	*2A*	15018	*80A*	15164	*81B*	14035	*2A*
5509	(5119/5121)			*NKS*	SG	14238	*2A*	15197	*81B*	15199	*81B*	14237	*2A*
5510	(5172/5115)			*NKS*	SG	14344	*4A*	15193	*82C*	15084	*71B*	14343	*5A*
5511	(5016/5173)			*NKS*	SG	14031	*2A*	15016	*80A*	15301	*81B*	14032	*2A*
5512	(5105/5145)			*NKS*	SG	14210	*2A*	15183	*81B*	15223	*81B*	14209	*2A*
5513	(5179/5182)			*NKS*	SG	14357	*2A*	15307	*81B*	15310	*81B*	14358	*2A*
5514	(5184/5202)			*NKS*	SG	14367	*2A*	15312	*81B*	15330	*81B*	14368	*2A*
5515	(5207/5209)			*NKS*	SG	14413	*2A*	15385	*81B*	15387	*81B*	14414	*2A*
5516	(5032/5133)			*NKS*	SG	14063	*2A*	15032	*80A*	15211	*81B*	14064	*2A*
5517	(5022/5040)			*NKS*	SG	14043	*2A*	15022	*80A*	15165	*81B*	14044	*2A*
5518	(5147/5194)			*NKS*	SG	14294	*2A*	15225	*81B*	15322	*81B*	14293	*2A*
5519	(5137/5139)			*NKS*	SG	14274	*2A*	15320	*81B*	15217	*81B*	14383	*2A*
5520	(5111/5195)			*NKS*	SG	14221	*2A*	15189	*81B*	15323	*81B*	14222	*2A*
5521	(5135/5210)			*NKS*	SG	14050	*2A*	15213	*81B*	15388	*81B*	14270	*2A*
5522	(5197/5243)			*NKS*	SG	14394	*2A*	15325	*81B*	15306	*81B*	14393	*2A*
5523	(5116/5126)			*NKS*	SG	14232	*2A*	15194	*81B*	15204	*81B*	14231	*2A*
5524	(5144/5156)			*NKS*	SG	14287	*2A*	15222	*81B*	15284	*81B*	14288	*2A*
5525	(5136/5231)			*NKS*	SG	14272	*2A*	15214	*81B*	15049	*80A*	14271	*2A*
5526	(5187/5213)			*NKS*	SG	14374	*2A*	15315	*81B*	15391	*81B*	14349	*2A*
5527	(5117/5170)			*NKS*	SG	14234	*2A*	15195	*81B*	15298	*81B*	14233	*2A*
5528	(5129/5177)			*NKS*	SG	14257	*2A*	15207	*81B*	15305	*81B*	14258	*2A*
5529	(5043/5051)			*NKS*	SG	14085	*2A*	15168	*81B*	15176	*81B*	14086	*2A*
5530	(5101/5261)			*NKS*	SG	14201	*2A*	15179	*81B*	15081	*80A*	14202	*2A*
5531	(5005/5159)			*NKS*	SG	14010	*2A*	15005	*70A*	15287	*81B*	14009	*2A*
5532	(5013/5035)			*NKS*	SG	14025	*2A*	15013	*80A*	15160	*81B*	14026	*2A*

Class 415 4-Car

Built: British Railways Eastleigh 1960, facelifted 1982-4
Design: BR non-gangwayed
Driver-guard communication and public address systems fitted
Power Supply: 750/850V dc third rail
Traction Motors (DMBS): Two 250hp (185kW) English Electric. (E Express gear ratio).
Maximum speed: 75mph. *Classs 415/7:* 90mph.
Dimensions: See below.
AWS: Driving vehicles fitted.

DMEE Diagram	*SR Design*	*Type*	*Weight*	*Seats*	*Dimensions L × W × H (m)*
Driving Motor Brake Standard:					
EB2.71.3A*	CAA	DMBS	41t	84	20.04 × 2.82 × 3.86
EB2.72.3A*	CAB	DMBS	41t	84	20.04 × 2.82 × 3.86
Trailer Standard:					
EH2.71.2A*	DAN	TS	29.5t	112	20.43 × 2.82 × 3.77
EH2.71.2B*	DAN2B	TS	29.5t	112	20.43 × 2.82 × 3.77
EH2.71.3A*	DAO	TS	29.5t	112	20.43 × 2.82 × 3.77

*Official codes not issued.

Class 415/6

Unit No	Liv	Pool	Dep	DMBS *EB2713A*	TS *EH2712A*	TS *EH2713A*	DMBS *EB2723A*
5601		*NKS*	SG	61550	70409	70410	61551
5602	N	*NKS*	SG	61582	70441	70442	61583
5603		*NKS*	SG	61538	70397	70398	61539
5604		*NKS*	SG	61588	70447	70448	61589
5605		*NKS*	SG	61540	70399	70400	61541
5606		*NKS*	SG	61536	70395	70396	61537
5610		*NKS*	SG	61566	70425	70426	61567
5611		*NKS*	SG	61570	70429	70430	61571
5612		*NKS*	SG	61542	70401	70402	61543
5613		*NKS*	SG	61532	70391	70392	61533
5614		*NKS*	SG	61546	70405	70406	61547
5615		*NKS*	SG	61612	70471	70472	61613
5616		*NKS*	SG	61576	70435	70436	61577
5617		*NKS*	SG	61592	70451	70452	61593
5618		*NKS*	SG	61584	70443	70444	61585
5619		*NKS*	SG	61562	70421	70422	61563
5620		*NKS*	SG	61602	70461	70462	61603
5621		*NKS*	SG	61520	70380	70379	61521
5622		*NKS*	SG	61560	70419	70420	61561

Class 415/7

Unit No	Old Unit No	SC	Liv	Pool	Dep	DMBS	TS	TS	DMBS
						EB2713A	*EH2712A*	*EH2713A*	*EB2723A*
5623	—	E		*NKC*	RE	61578	70437	70438	61579
5624	—	E		*NKC*	RE	61572	70431	70432	61573
						EB2713A	*EH2712B*	*EH2713A*	*EB2723A*
5625	—	E		*NKC*	RE	61608	70455	70468	61609
						EB2713A	*EH2712A*	*EH2713A*	*EB2723A*
5626	(5607)	E	N	*NKC*	RE	61590	70449	70450	61591
5627	(5608)	E		*NKC*	RE	61600	70460	70459	61601
5628	(5609)	E		*NKC*	RE	61604	70464	70463	61605

Class 455 4-Car

Built: BREL York 1982
Design: BR with sliding doors, gangwayed throughout. All equipped with pressure heating and ventilation, driver-guard communication and public address equipment.
Power supply: 750V dc third rail
Traction motors (MS): Four 205hp (155kW) dc GEC 507-20J. *Diagram EC211:* Two 220hp (165kW) ac GEC G350. (Converted from Class 210 TS at RTC, Derby, 1988).
Maximum speed: 75mph
AWS: Driving vehicles fitted

DMEE Diagram	*SR Design*	*Type*	*Weight*	*Seats*	*Electrical Equipment*	*Dimensions L × W × H (m)*
Motor Standard:						
EC2.03.0A	YA	MS	45.6t	84	GEC	19.92 × 2.82 × 3.77
EC2.03.0B*	YA1A	MS	45.6t	84	GEC	19.92 × 2.82 × 3.77
EC2.03.0C*	YA2A	MS	45.6t	84	GEC	19.92 × 2.82 × 3.77
EC2.03.1A	YA3A	MS	45.6t	84	Brush	19.92 × 2.82 × 3.77
EC2.06.0A	YA4B	MS	45.6t	84	Brush	19.92 × 2.82 × 3.77
EC2.06.1A*	YA5B	MS	45.6t	84	Brush	19.92 × 2.82 × 3.77
EC2.06.2A*	YA6B	MS	45.6t	84	Brush	19.92 × 2.82 × 3.77
EC2.11.0A	—	MS	—	84	GEC	19.92 × 2.82 × 3.77
Driving Trailer Standard:						
EE2.18.0A	ZA	DTS	29.5t	74	—	19.92 × 2.82 × 3.77
EE2.18.0B*	ZB	DTS	29.5t	74	—	19.92 × 2.82 × 3.77
EE2.18.1A*	ZA-1A	DTS	29.5t	74	—	19.92 × 2.82 × 3.77
EE2.26.0A	ZB-1A	DTS	29.5t	74	—	19.92 × 2.82 × 3.77
Trailer Standard:						
EH2.19.0A	XB1A	TS	25.5t	86	—	19.92 × 2.82 × 3.58
EH2.19.2B*	XB2B	TS	25.5t	86	—	19.92 × 2.82 × 3.58
EH2.21.0A	XC	TS	27.1t	84	—	19.92 × 2.82 × 3.77
EH2.21.1A*	XC1A	TS	27.1t	84	—	19.92 × 2.82 × 3.77
EH2.24.0A	XC2B	TS	27.1t	84	—	19.92 × 2.82 × 3.77

† *Modified interiors. Experimental for Class 465 Networker EMUs.*
‡ Experimental Dot-Matrix indicators on interior and exterior.
* Official codes not issued.

Class 455/7

Phase III units

Unit No	Liv	Pool	Dep	DTS	MS	TS	DTS
				EE2180B	*EC2031A*	*EH2190A*	*EE2180B*
5701	N	*NSB*	WD	77727	62783	71545	77728
5702	N	*NSB*	WD	77729	62784	71547	77730
5703	N	*NSB*	WD	77731	62785	71540	77732
5704		*NSB*	WD	77733	62786	71548	77734
5705		*NSB*	WD	77735	62787	71565	77736
5706		*NSB*	WD	77737	62788	71534	77738
5707		*NSB*	WD	77739	62789	71536	77740
5708		*NSB*	WD	77741	62790	71560	77742
5709		*NSB*	WD	77743	62791	71532	77744
5710		*NSB*	WD	77745	62792	71566	77746
5711		*NSB*	WD	77747	62793	71542	77748
5712		*NSB*	WD	77749	62794	71546	77750
5713		*NSB*	WD	77751	62795	71567	77752
5714		*NSB*	WD	77753	62796	71539	77754
5715		*NSB*	WD	77755	62797	71535	77756
5716		*NSB*	WD	77757	62798	71564	77758
5717		*NSB*	WD	77759	62799	71528	77760
5718		*NSB*	WD	77761	62800	71557	77762
5719		*NSB*	WD	77763	62801	71558	77764
5720		*NSB*	WD	77765	62802	71568	77766
				EE2180B	*EC2031A*	*EH2192B*	*EE2180B*
5721		*NSB*	WD	77767	62803	71553	77768
5722		*NSB*	WD	77769	62804	71533	77770
5723		*NSB*	WD	77771	62805	71526	77772
5724		*NSB*	WD	77773	62806	71561	77774
5725		*NSB*	WD	77775	62807	71541	77776
5726		*NSB*	WD	77777	62808	71556	77778
5727		*NSB*	WD	77779	62809	71562	77780
5728		*NSB*	WD	77781	62810	71527	77782
5729		*NSB*	WD	77783	62811	71550	77784
5730		*NSB*	WD	77785	62812	71551	77786
5731		*NSB*	WD	77787	62813	71555	77788
5732		*NSB*	WD	77789	62814	71552	77790
5733		*NSB*	WD	77791	62815	71549	77792
5734		*NSB*	WD	77793	62816	71531	77794
5735		*NSB*	WD	77795	62817	71563	77796
5736		*NSB*	WD	77797	62818	71554	77798
5737		*NSB*	WD	77799	62819	71544	77800
5738		*NSB*	WD	77801	62820	71529	77802
5739		*NSB*	WD	77803	62821	71537	77804
5740		*NSB*	WD	77805	62822	71530	77806
5741		*NSB*	WD	77807	62823	71559	77808

Unit No	Liv	Pool	Dep	DTS	MS	TS	DTS
5742		*NSB*	WD	77809	62824	71543	77810
5743		*NSB*	WD	77811	62825	71538	77812

Class 455/8

Phase I Units

Unit No	Liv	Pool	Dep	DTS	MS	TS	DTS
				EE2180A	*EC2030A*	*EH2210A*	*EE2180A*
5801	N	*NSL*	SU	77579	62709	71637	77580
5802	N	*NSL*	SU	77581	62710	71638	77582
5803	N	*NSL*	SU	77583	62711	71639	77584
5804	N	*NSL*	SU	77585	62712	71640	77586
5805	N	*NSL*	SU	77587	62713	71641	77588
5806	N	*NSL*	SU	77589	62714	71642	77590
				EE2180A	*EC2030B*	*EH2210A*	*EE2180A*
5807	N	*NSL*	SU	77591	62715	71643	77592
				EE2180A	*EC2030A*	*EH2210A*	*EE2180A/ EE2181A**
5808	N	*NSL*	SU	77593	62716	71644	77594
5809	N	*NSL*	SU	77595	62717	71645	77596
5810	N	*NSL*	SU	77597	62718	71646	77598
5811	N	*NSL*	SU	77599	62719	71647	77600
5812	N	*NSL*	SU	77601	62720	71648	77602
5813	N	*NSL*	SU	77603	62721	71649	77604
5814	N	*NSL*	SU	77605	62722	71650	77606
5815	N	*NSL*	SU	77607	62723	71651	77608
5816	N	*NSL*	SU	77609	62724	71652	77610
5817	N	*NSL*	SU	77611	62725	71653	77612
5818	N	*NSL*	SU	77613	62726	71654	77614
5819	N	*NSL*	SU	77615	62727	71655	77616
5820	N	*NSL*	SU	77617	62728	71656	77618
5821	N	*NSL*	SU	77619	62729	71657	77620
5822	N	*NSL*	SU	77621	62730	71658	77622
5823	N	*NSL*	SU	77623	62731	71659	77624
5824‡	N	*NSL*	SU	77637	62732	71660†	77626
5825	N	*NSL*	SU	77627	62733	71661	77628
5826	N	*NSL*	SU	77629	62734	71662	77680*
5827	N	*NSL*	SU	77631	62735	71663	77632
5828	N	*NSL*	SU	77633	62736	71664	77634
5829	N	*NSL*	SU	77635	62737	71665	77636
5830	N	*NSL*	SU	77625	62743	71666	77638
5831	N	*NSL*	SU	77639	62739	71667	77640
5832	N	*NSL*	SU	77641	62740	71668	77642
5833	N	*NSL*	SU	77643	62741	71669	77644
5834	N	*NSL*	SU	77645	62742	71670	77646

Unit No	Liv	Pool	Dep	DTS	MS	TS	DTS
5835	N	*NSL*	SU	77647	62738	71671	77648
5836	N	*NSL*	SU	77649	62744	71672	77650
5837	N	*NSL*	WD	77651	62745	71673	77652
5838	N	*NSL*	WD	77653	62746	71674	77654
5839	N	*NSL*	WD	77655	62747	71675	77656
5840	N	*NSL*	WD	77657	62748	71676	77658
5841	N	*NSL*	WD	77659	62749	71677	77660
5842	N	*NSL*	WD	77661	62750	71678	77662
5843	N	*NSL*	WD	77663	62751	71679	77664
5844	N	*NSL*	WD	77665	62752	71680	77666
5845	N	*NSL*	WD	77667	62753	71681	77668
5846	N	*NSL*	WD	77669	62754	71682	77670
5847	N	*NSL*	WD	77671	62755	71683	77672
5848	N	*NSL*	WD	77673	62756	71684	77674
5849	N	*NSL*	WD	77675	62757	71685	77676

Class 455/8

Phase II Units

Unit No	Liv	Pool	Dep	DTS	MS	TS	DTS
				EE2181A	*EC2030C*	*EH2211A*	*EE2181A/ EE2180A**
5850†	N	*NSL*	SU	77677	62758	71686	77678
5851	N	*NSL*	WD	77679	62759	71687	77630*
5852	N	*NSL*	WD	77681	62760	71688	77682
5853	N	*NSL*	WD	77683	62761	71689	77684
5854	N	*NSL*	WD	77685	62762	71690	77686
5855	N	*NSL*	WD	77687	62763	71691	77688
5856	N	*NSL*	WD	77689	62764	71692	77690
5857	N	*NSL*	WD	77691	62765	71693	77692
5858	N	*NSL*	WD	77693	62766	71694	77694
5859	N	*NSL*	WD	77695	62767	71695	77696
5860	N	*NSL*	WD	77697	62768	71696	77698
5861	N	*NSL*	WD	77699	62769	71697	77700
5862		*NSL*	WD	77701	62770	71698	77702
5863		*NSL*	WD	77703	62771	71699	77704
5864	N	*NSL*	WD	77705	62772	71700	77706
5865		*NSL*	WD	77707	62773	71701	77708
5866		*NSL*	WD	77709	62774	71702	77710
5867		*NSL*	WD	77711	62775	71703	77712
5868	N	*NSL*	WD	77713	62776	71704	77714
5869	N	*NSL*	WD	77715	62777	71705	77716
5870		*NSL*	WD	77717	62778	71706	77718
5871		*NSL*	WD	77719	62779	71707	77720
5872†	N	*NSL*	WD	77721	62780	71708	77722
5873		*NSL*	WD	77723	62781	71709	77724
5874		*NSL*	WD	77725	62782	71710	77726

Class 455/9

Phase IV Units

Unit No	Liv	Pool	Dep	DTS	MS	TS	DTS
				EE2260A	*EC2060A*	*EH2240A*	*EE2260A*
5901		*NSL*	WD	77813	62826	71714	77814
5902		*NSL*	WD	77815	62827	71715	77816
5903		*NSL*	WD	77817	62828	71716	77818
5904		*NSL*	WD	77819	62829	71717	77820
5905		*NSL*	WD	77821	62830	71718	77822
5906		*NSL*	WD	77823	62831	71719	77824
5907		*NSL*	WD	77825	62832	71720	77826
5908		*NSL*	WD	77827	62833	71721	77828
5909		*NSL*	WD	77829	62834	71722	77830
5910		*NSL*	WD	77831	62835	71723	77832
5911		*NSL*	WD	77833	62836	71724	77834
				EE2260A	*EC2062A*	*EH2240A*	*EE2260A*
5912		*NSL*	WD	77835	62837	71725	77836
				EE2260A	*EC2060A*	*EH2240A*	*EE2260A*
5913		*NSL*	WD	77837	62838	71726	77838
5914		*NSL*	WD	77839	62839	71727	77840
5915		*NSL*	WD	77841	62840	71728	77842
				EE2260A	*EC2061A*	*EH2240A*	*EE2260A*
5916		*NSL*	WD	77843	62841	71729	77844
5917		*NSL*	WD	77845	62842	71730	77846
5918		*NSL*	WD	77847	62843	71731	77848
5919		*NSL*	WD	77849	62844	71732	77850

Unit No	Liv	Pool	Dep	DTS	MS	MS	DTS
				EE2260A	*EC2060A*	*EC2110A*	*EE2260A*
5920†	N	*NSL*	WD	77851	62845	67400	77852

Note: Vehicle 67400 renumbered from 60400

Class 456 — 2-Car

To be built: BREL, York 1989/90
Design: BR with sliding doors, gangwayed. similar to Class 455
24 units. Full details to be announced

Class 416 — 2-EPB 2-Car

Built: British Railways, Eastleigh 1953
Design: BR, non-gangwayed
Supply: 750V dc third rail
Traction Motors: Two 250hp (185kW) dc English Electric

Maximum speed: 75mph
Dimensions: *Motor vehicles:* 20.03m L × 2.82m W × 3.86m H. *Trailer vehicles:* 20.44m L × 2.82m W × 3.86m H
AWS: All vehicles fitted

DMEE Diagram	*SR Design*	*Type*	*Weight*	*Seats*	*Dimensions L × W × H (m)*
Driving Motor Brake Standard:					
Class 416/2					
EB2.69.4A	CQ	DMBS	42t	84 (Semi-open)	20.03 × 2.82 × 3.86
EB2.69.5A	CQ1A	DMBS	42t	84 (Semi-open)	20.03 × 2.82 × 3.86
EB2.--.0A*	CQ	DMBS	42t	82 (Open)	20.03 × 2.82 × 3.86
Class 416/3					*Over periscopes*
EB2.77.2A*	CX2A	DMBS	40t	82	19.10 × 2.82 × 3.98
EB2.77.5A*	CX5A	DMBS	40t	82	19.10 × 2.82 × 3.98
EB2.77.6A*	CX6A	DMBS	40t	82	19.10 × 2.82 × 3.98
Class 416/4					
EB2.80.0A	CY	DMBS	42t	82	20.03 × 2.82 × 3.86
EB2.80.1A*	CY2A	DMBS	42t	82	20.03 × 2.82 × 3.86
EB2.81.0A	CY3B	DMBS	42t	79	20.03 × 2.82 × 3.86
Driving Trailer Standard:					
Class 416/2					
EE2.64.1A	DV	DTS	32.5t	102 (Semi-Compt)	20.44 × 2.82 × 3.86
EE2.--.0A*	DV	DTS	32.5t	94 (Semi-Open)	20.44 × 2.82 × 3.86
Class 416/3					*Over periscopes*
EE2.69.0A	DAL	DTS	30t	92	19.10 × 2.82 × 3.98
EE2.69.1A*	DAL-1A	DTS	30t	92	19.10 × 2.82 × 3.98
Class 416/4					
EE2.71.0A	DAM1A	DTS	30.5t	92	20.44 × 2.82 × 3.86
EE2.71.1A*	DAM	DTS	30.5t	92	20.44 × 2.82 × 3.86
EE2.74.0A	DAM3B	DTS	30.5t	90	20.44 × 2.82 × 3.86
EE2.74.1B	DAM	DTS	32.5t	90	20.44 × 2.82 × 3.86

*Official codes not issued

Class 416/2

Unit No	Pool	Dep	DMBS *EB2694A*	DTS *EE2641A*
6202	*NKS*	SG	65301	77501
6203	*NKS*	SG	65302	77502
6205	*NKS*	SG	65304	77504
6207	*NKS*	SG	65306	77506
6212	*NKS*	SG	65326	77511
6213	*NKS*	SG	65327	77512
6217	*NKS*	SG	65331	77516
6218	*NKS*	SG	65332	77517
6221	*NKS*	SG	65335	77520
6222	*NKS*	SG	65336	77521

Unit No	Pool	Dep	DMBS	DTS
6223	*NKS*	SG	65337	77522
6224	*NKS*	SG	65338	77523
6225	*NKS*	SG	65339	77524
6226	*NKS*	SG	65340	77525
6227	*NKS*	SG	65341	77526
			EB2--0A	*EE2641A*
6229	*NKS*	SG	65343	77528
6230	*NKS*	SG	65344	77529
6231	*NKS*	SG	65345	77530
6235	*NKS*	SG	65349	77534
6236	*NKS*	SG	65350	77535
6237	*NKS*	SG	65351	77536
			EB2--0A	*EE2--0A*
6238	*NKS*	SG	65352	77537
			EB2694A	*EE2641A*
6239	*NKS*	SG	65353	77538
			EB2--0A	*EE2--0A*
6240	*NKS*	SG	65354	77539
			EB2694A	*EE2641A*
6241	*NKS*	SG	65355	77540
6243	*NKS*	SG	65357	77542
6244	*NKS*	SG	65358	77543
6245	*NKS*	SG	65359	77544
6247	*NKS*	SG	65361	77546
6249	*NKS*	SG	65363	77548
6251	*NKS*	SG	65365	77550
6253	*NKS*	SG	65367	77552
6255	*NKS*	SG	65369	77554
6256	*NKS*	SG	65370	77555
6257	*NKS*	SG	65371	77556
			EB2695A	*EE2641A*
6259	*NKS*	SG	65373	77558
6260	*NKS*	SG	65374	77559
6261	*NKS*	SG	65375	77560
6262	*NKS*	SG	65376	77561
6263	*NKS*	SG	65377	77562
6264	*NKS*	SG	65378	77563
6265	*NKS*	SG	65379	77564
6267	*NKS*	SG	65381	77566
6268	*NKS*	SG	65382	77567
			EB2694A	*EE2641A*
6269	*NKS*	SG	65307	77568
			EB2695A	*EE2641A*
6270	*NKS*	SG	65384	77569
6271	*NKS*	SG	65385	77570
6272	*NKS*	SG	65386	77571
6273	*NKS*	SG	65387	77572
6274	*NKS*	SG	65388	77573
6275	*NKS*	SG	65389	77574
6276	*NKS*	SG	65390	77575
6277	*NKS*	SG	65391	77576
6278	*NKS*	SG	65392	77577

Class 416/3

Built: 1955-59, facelifted 1983-84. Driver/guard communication and public address equipment fitted. Units 6313-28 ftted with window bars for North London line service

Unit No	Liv	Pool	Dep	MBS	DTS
				EB277	*EE2690A*
6301		*NSL*	SU	14577 *2A*	16121
6302		*NSL*	SU	14580 *2A*	16124
6303		*NSL*	SU	14576 *2A*	16120
6304		*NSL*	SU	14589 *2A*	16133
6305		*NSL*	SU	14587 *2A*	16131
6306		*NSL*	SU	14571 *2A*	16115
				EB277	*EE2691A*
6307		*NSL*	SU	14573 *5A*	16117
6308		*NSL*	SU	14564 *5A*	16108
6309		*NSL*	SU	14562 *5A*	16106
6310		*NSL*	SU	14574 *5A*	16118
6311		*NSL*	SU	14565 *5A*	16109
6312		*NSL*	SU	14579 *5A*	16123
6313		*NNL*	SU	14558 *5A*	16102
6314		*NNL*	SU	14586 *5A*	16130
6315		*NNL*	SU	14590 *5A*	16134
6316		*NNL*	SU	14559 *5A*	16103
6317		*NNL*	SU	14578 *5A*	16122
6318		*NNL*	SU	14566 *5A*	16110
6319		*NNL*	SU	14568 *5A*	16112
6320		*NNL*	SU	14561 *5A*	16105
6321		*NNL*	SU	14283 *2A*	16128
6322		*NNL*	SU	14575 *5A*	16119
6323		*NNL*	SU	14581 *5A*	16125
6324		*NNL*	SU	14560 *5A*	16104

Unit No	Liv	Pool	Dep	MBS	DTS
6325		*NNL*	SU	14567 *5A*	16111
6326		*NNL*	SU	14546 *6A*	16129
6327		*NNL*	SU	14572 *5A*	16116
6328		*NNL*	SU	14582 *5A*	16126
6329		*NSL*	SU	14542 *2A*	16114
6330		*NSL*	SU	14588 *5A*	16132
6331		*NSL*	SU	14583 *5A*	16127
6332		*NSL*	SU	14569 *5A*	16113
6333		*NSL*	SU	14557 *5A*	16101
6334		*NSL*	SU	14546 *6A*	16107

Class 416/4

Built: 1953, facelifted 1985-86. Driver/guard communication and public address equipment fitted. Units 6401-09 modified with extra end doorways

Unit No	Liv	Pool	Dep	MBS	DTS
				EB2810A	*EE2740A*
6401	N	*NKS*	SG	65346	77531
6402	N	*NKS*	SG	65362	77547
6403		*NKS*	SG	65356	77541
6404		*NKS*	SG	65329	77514
6405		*NKS*	SG	65347	77532
6406		*NKS*	SG	65305	77505
6407		*NKS*	SG	65330	77515
6408		*NKS*	SG	65342	77527
				EB2810A	*EE2741B*
6409		*NKS*	SG	65309	77113
				EB2800A	*EE2711A*
6410		*NKS*	SG	65334	77519
6411		*NKS*	SG	65333	77518
6412		*NKS*	SG	65364	77549
				EB2801A	*EE2710A*
6413		*NKS*	SG	65372	77557
				EB2800A	*EE2711A*
6414		*NKS*	SG	65368	77553
6415		*NKS*	SG	65348	77533
6416		*NKS*	SG	65328	77513
6417		*NKS*	SG	65366	77551
6418		*NKS*	SG	65360	77545

Class 457 — 4-Car

Built: BREL Derby 1982. Former Class 210 Diesel-Electric Multiple-Unit stock modified at RTC, Derby, 1988. (TS No 71733 see Class 455/9.)
Design: BR with sliding doors, gangwayed throughout. Public address system
Supply: 750V dc third rail

Traction motors: (DMS) Two 220hp (165kW) three phase ac Brush
Maximum speed: 75mph
Dimensions: *Driving vehicles:* 19.83m L × 2.82m W × 3.77m H; *Trailer vehicles:* 19.92m L × 2.82m W × 3.77m H
AWS: Driving vehicles fitted

DMEE Diagram	*SR Design*	*Type*	*Weight*	*Seats*
Driving Motor Standard				
EA2.09.0A	—	DMS(A)	29t	74
EA2.09.1B	—	DMS(B)	29t	74

Trailer Standard

EH2.24.0A	XC2B	TS	27.1t	84
EH2.36.0A	—	TS	26.5t	84

Unit No	SC	Liv	Pool	Dep	DMS	TS	TS	DMS
					EA2090A	*EH2360A*	*EH2240A*	*EA2090B*
7001		N	*NSB*	WD	67300	67401	71733	67301

Note: 67300/01, 67401 renumbered from 60300/01, 60401 during 1988

Class 447 — 4-Car

PRIVATE OWNER — BATTERSEA LEISURE GROUP
To be built: BREL York 1990
Four units based on the Class 319 design for 750/850V dc third rail supply only. To operate service between London Victoria and a new Battersea Leisure Centre

Vehicle Nos: BLL 99470-BLL 99481

Class 438/0 — 4-TC 4-Car

TRAILER UNITS
Built: British Railways York 1966
Design: BR gangwayed throughout. Driver-guard and public address equipment fitted
Maximum speed: 90mph
Dimensions: 22.15m L × 2.74m W × 3.81m H
AWS: Driving vehicles fitted

DMEE Diagram	*SR Design*	*Type*	*Weight*	*Seats 1st*	*Seats Std*	*Toilet*
Driving Trailer Standard						
EE2.66.0A	FC	DTS	32.5t	—	64	
Trailer Brake Standard: (Compartment)						
EJ2.60.0A	BT	TBS	35.5t	—	32	1
Trailer First/Composite: (Compartment)						
EH1.60.0A	BU	TF	33.5t	42	—	2
EH3.—.1A*	BU	TC	33.5t	30	16	2
EH3.—.2B*	BU	TC	33.5t	36	8	2

* Unofficial codes

Unit No	SC	Liv	Pool	Dep	DTS	TF/TC	TBS	DTS
					EE2660A	*EH1600A/EH3–*	*EJ2600A*	*EE2660A*
8001		N	*NSS*	BM	76270	70844 *2B*	70812	76332
8004		N	*NSS*	BM	76275	70847 *0A*	70815	76276
8006		N	*NSS*	BM	76280	70849 *0A*	70817	76279
8007			*NSS*	BM	76281	70850 *0A*	70818	76282
8010		N	*NSS*	BM	76288	70853 *2B*	70821	76287

Unit No	SC	Liv	Pool	Dep	DTS	TF/TC	TBS	DTS
8012		N	*NSS*	BM	76292	70858 *2B*	70828	76291
8014			*NSS*	BM	76295	70857 *0A*	70825	76296
8015		N	*NSS*	BM	76297	70855 *1A*	70823	76298
8017		N	*NSS*	BM	76302	70860 *2B*	70826	76301
8018		N	*NSS*	BM	76303	70861 *2B*	70829	76304
8020			*NSS*	BM	76307	70863 *0A*	70831	76308
8021			*NSS*	BM	76309	70864 *0A*	70832	76310
8023		N	*NSS*	BM	76313	70866 *2B*	70834	76314
8026			*NSS*	BM	76319	70869 *0A*	70837	76320
8027		N	*NSS*	BM	76321	70870 *2B*	70838	76322
8028			*NSS*	BM	76324	70871 *0A*	70839	76323

Class 488 — RAILAIR 2- & 3-Car

TRAILER UNITS
Built: BREL Derby and Eastleigh, 1984
Design: BR rebuilt Mk 2f stock built 1973, gangwayed throughout. Air conditioned. Public address equipment fitted

Maximum speed: 90mph
Dimensions: 20.38m L × 2.84m W × 3.79m H
Livery: InterCity Gatwick Express

DMEE Diagram	*SR Design*	*Type*	*Weight*	*Seats 1st*	*Seats Std*	*Toilet*
Trailer Standard:						
EH2.85.0A	BC	TS	35t	—	56	1
Trailer First/Standard Handbrake:						
EP1.01.1A	BA	TFH	35t	41	—	1 Payphone
EP2.01.0A	BB	TSH	35t	—	56	1

Class 488/2

Unit No	Pool	Dep	TFH *EP1011A*	TSH *EP2010A*
8201	*IVG*	SL	72500	72638
8202	*IVG*	SL	72501	72617
8203	*IVG*	SL	72502	72640
8204	*IVG*	SL	72503	72641
8205	*IVG*	SL	72504	72628
8206	*IVG*	SL	72505	72629
8207	*IVG*	SL	72506	72642
8208	*IVG*	SL	72507	72643
8209	*IVG*	SL	72508	72644
8210	*IVG*	SL	72509	72635

Class 488/3

Unit No	Pool	Dep	TSH *EP2010A*	TS *EH2850A*	TSH *EP2010A*
8302	*IVG*	SL	72602	72701	72604
8303	*IVG*	SL	72603	72702	72608
8304	*IVG*	SL	72606	72703	72611
8305	*IVG*	SL	72605	72704	72609
8306	*IVG*	SL	72607	72705	72610
8307	*IVG*	SL	72612	72706	72613
8308	*IVG*	SL	72614	72707	72615
8309	*IVG*	SL	72616	72708	72639
8310	*IVG*	SL	72618	72709	72619
8311	*IVG*	SL	72620	72710	72621
8312	*IVG*	SL	72622	72711	72623
8313	*IVG*	SL	72624	72712	72625
8314	*IVG*	SL	72626	72713	72627
8315	*IVG*	SL	72636	72714	72645

Unit No	Pool	Dep	TSH	TS	TSH
8316	*IVG*	SL	72630	72715	72631
8317	*IVG*	SL	72632	72716	72633
8318	*IVG*	SL	72634	72717	72637
8319	*IVG*	SL	72646	72718	72647

Class 419 DMLV

Built: British Railways, Eastleigh 1959
Design: BR non-gangwayed. Driving cab each end. These vehicles can work singly, hauling a limited load, or in multiple with EP-type stock. They are equipped with traction batteries for working on non-electrified quay lines at Dover and Folkestone
Power Supply: 750/850V dc third rail or batteries
Traction Motors: Two 250hp (185kW) dc English Electric
Maximum speed: 90mph
Dimensions: 20.45m L × 2.82m W × 3.86m H (over periscopes)

DMEE Diagram	*SR Design*	*Type*	*Weight*
Driving Motor Luggage Van:			
EX5.60.0B*	AF	DMLV	45.5t
EX5.60.1C*	AF1A	DMLV	45.5t

*Official codes not issued

Unit No	Liv	Pool	Dep	DMLV
				EX5600B
9001	L	*RPMD*	RE	68001
9002		*RPMD*	RE	68002
				EX5601C
9003	L	*RPMD*	RE	68003
9004	RR	*RPMD*	RE	68004
9005	L	*RPMD*	RE	68005
9006	L	*NBT*	RE	68006
9007	L	*RPMD*	RE	68007
9008	L	*RPMD*	RE	68008
9009	RR	*RPMD*	RE	68009
9010	L	*NBT*	RE	68010

Class 489 DMLV RAILAIR

Built: BREL, Eastleigh 1984
Design: BR converted from Class 414 DMBS vehicles built 1958. Gangwayed at one end. Public address transmitter equipment
Supply: 750/850V dc third rail
Traction Motors: Two 250hp (185kW) dc English Electric
Maximum speed: 90mph
AWS: Fitted
Dimensions: 20.45m L × 2.82m W × 3.86m H
Livery: InterCity Gatwick Express

DMEE Diagram	*SR Design*	*Type*	*Weight*
Driving Motor Luggage Van:			
EX5.61.0A	AQ	DMLV	45t

Unit No	Pool	Dep	DMLV
			EX5610A
9101	*IVG*	SL	68500
9102	*IVG*	SL	68501
9103	*IVG*	SL	68502
9104	*IVG*	SL	68503

Unit No	Pool	Dep	DMLV
9105	*IVG*	SL	68504
9106	*IVG*	SL	68505
9107	*IVG*	SL	68506
9108	*IVG*	SL	68507
9109	*IVG*	SL	68508
9110	*IVG*	SL	68509

Class 482

An order for 20 Motor Standard coaches is to be placed during 1989 for Network SouthEast Waterloo and City line.

Class 483

Built: Metro-Cammell 1938
Purchased from London Underground 1988 for operation on Network SouthEast Isle of Wight services. Sixteen vehicles to be overhauled at BRML Eastleigh Works to form two-car units
Design: London Transport tube with sliding doors. Cab end-doors sealed, inner-end doors for emergency egress. Fitted with driver/guard communication and public address equipment

Power supply: 630V dc third rail
Traction motors (DMBS):
Dimensions: 15.94m L × 2.60m W × 2.88m H
AWS: Fitted

Driving Motor Brake Second

DMEE	*SR*			
Diagram	*Design*	*Type*	*Weight*	*Seats*
EB2.--.--	CV	DMBS	27.45t	42

Unit No	SC	Liv	Pool	Dep	DMBS *EB2*	DMBS *EB2*
483001		N	*NSS*			
483002		N	*NSS*			
483003		N	*NSS*			
483004		N	*NSS*			
483005		N	*NSS*			
483006		N	*NSS*			
483007		N	*NSS*			
483008		N	*NSS*			

Note: Full details to be advised

Classes 485 & 486 — 5-VEC & 2-TIS

5- and 2-Car Units (Isle of Wight)
Introduced: 1967, rebuilt from london Transport stock built 1935
Design: LT with sliding doors end doors throughout, sealed on cab ends of DMBS vehicles. Fitted with driver-guard communication and public address equipment

Supply: 630V dc third rail
Traction motors (DMBS): Two 240hp (178kW) dc English Electric EE507
Maximum speed: 30mph
AWS: Fitted to DMBS coaches

DMEE Diagram	*SR Design*	*Type*	*Weight*	*Seats*	*Dimensions L × W × H*
Driving Motor Brake Standard					
EB2.61.2A	CV2A	DMBS	32t	26	16.19 × 2.69 × 2.90
EB2.61.2B	CV2B	DMBS	32t	26	16.19 × 2.69 × 2.90
EB2.61.2C	CV2C	DMBS	32t	26	16.19 × 2.69 × 2.90
EB2.61.3A	CV3A	DMBS	32t	26	16.19 × 2.69 × 2.90
EB2.61.3B	CV3B	DMBS	32t	26	16.19 × 2.69 × 2.90
EB2.61.4A	CV4A	DMBS	32t	26	16.19 × 2.69 × 2.90
EB2.61.4B	CV4B	DMBS	32t	26	16.19 × 2.69 × 2.90
Driving Trailer Standard					
EE2.60.0B	DAE1A	DTS	17t	38	15.82 × 2.69 × 2.90
EE2.60.2A	DAF2A	DTS	17t	38	15.82 × 2.69 × 2.90
EE2.60.3A	DAF3A	DTS	17t	38	15.82 × 2.69 × 2.90 Driving compartment not used
Trailer Standard					
EH2.61.1A	DAF1A	TS	18t	42	15.69 × 2.69 × 2.90
EH2.61.1B	DAF1B	TS	18t	42	15.69 × 2.69 × 2.90

All codes not yet official
Formations shown may be varied to suit local operating requirements
i De-icing equipment in unused driving cab

Class 485

Unit No	SC	Liv	Pool	Dep	DMBS	TS	TS	TS	DMBS
					EB2612B	*EE2603A*	*EH2611B*	*EE2603A*	*EB2612C*
485041			*NSS*	RY	1 N	27 N	92	26 N	2
					EB2614B	*EH2611B*	*EH2611B*	*EE2603A*	*EB2614A*
485042			*NSS*	RY	3 N	95 N	47	29 N	4 N
					EB2612A	*EE2602A*	*EE2603A*	*EH2611B*	*EB2612C*
485043			*NSS*	RY	5 N	31 i N	32 N	43	6
					EB2614B	*EH2611B*	*EE2603A*	*EH2611A*	*EB2614A*
485044		N	*NSS*	RY	7	44	33	49	8
					EB2613B	*EH2611B*	*EE2603A*	*EH2611B*	*EB2613A*
485045		N	*NSS*	RY	9	94	34	93	10

Class 486

Unit No	SC	Liv	Pool	Dep	DMBS	DTS
					EB2614B	*EE2600B*
486031		N	*NSS*	RY	11	28

Class 487

Waterloo & City Line Units
Built: English Electric 1940
Design: SR with sliding doors, tube size vehicles end doors throughout. Trains formed of up to 2 Motors and 3 Trailers. Driver-guard communication equipment fitted
Supply: 750/850V dc third rail
Traction Motors: Two 190hp (140kW) dc English Electric
Maximum Speed: 40mph
Dimensions: 14.86m L × 2.64m W × 2.92m H

AWS: Not fitted
Livery: Network and Allied-Lyons sponsorship logo as shown N
DMEE *SR*

Diagram	*Design*	*Type*	*Weight*	*Seats*
Driving Motor Brake Standard				
EB2.60.0B*	CS	DMBS	29t	40
EB2.60.1B*	CW1A	DMBS	29t	40
Trailer Standard				
EH2.60.0B*	DAG	TS	20t	52

*Unofficial codes

DMBS

No	SC	Liv	Pool	Dep
EB2600B				
51		N	*NSB*	WC
53		N	*NSB*	WC
54		N	*NSB*	WC
55			*NXX*	WC (s)
56		N	*NSB*	WC
EB2601B				
57		N	*NSB*	WC
EB2600B				
58		N	*NSB*	WC
59		N	*NSB*	WC
60		N	*NSB*	WC
61		N	*NSB*	WC
62		N	*NSB*	WC

TS

No	SC	Liv	Pool	Dep
EH2600B				
71			*NXX*	WC (s)
72		N	*NSB*	WC
73		N	*NSB*	WC
74		N	*NSB*	WC
75		N	*NSB*	WC
76		N	*NSB*	WC
77		N	*NSB*	WC
78		N	*NSB*	WC
79			*NXX*	WC (s)
80		N	*NSB*	WC
81		N	*NSB*	WC
83		N	*NSB*	WC
84		N	*NSB*	WC
85		N	*NSB*	WC
86		N	*NSB*	WC

Class 504 — 2-CAR

Built: British Railways Wolverton 1959
Design: BR, non-gangwayed
Supply: 1,200V dc, third rail side contact
Traction motors (DMBS): Four 141hp (90kW) dc English Electric
Maximum Speed: 65mph

AWS: All fitted

Diagram	*Type*	*Weight*	*Seats*
Driving Motor Brake Standard			
EB2.04.0A	DMS	50t	84
Driving Trailer Standard			
EE2.15.1A	DTS	33t	94

Dimensions: 20.31m L × 2.82m W × 3.84m H

Note: Unit numbers are not always carried, but formations are normally maintained

Unit No	SC	Liv	Pool	Dep	DMBS	DTS
					EB2040A	*EB2151A*
504 444			*PBQ*	BQ	65444	77165
504 445		M	*PBQ*	BQ	65445	77166
504 446		M	*PBQ*	BQ	65446	77167
504 447			*PBQ*	BQ	65447	77168
504 449		M	*PBQ*	BQ	65449	77170
504 450		M	*PBQ*	BQ	65450	77171
504 451		M	*PBQ*	BQ	65451	77172
504 452			*PBQ*	BQ	65452	77173
504 453		M	*PBQ*	BQ	65453	77174
504 454			*PBQ*	BQ	65454	77175
504 455		M	*PBQ*	BQ	65455	77176
504 456		M	*PBQ*	BQ	65456	77177
504 457		M	*PBQ*	BQ	65457	77178
504 458		M	*PBQ*	BQ	65458	77179
504 459			*PBQ*	BQ	65459	77180
504 460		M	*PBQ*	BQ	65460	77181
504 461		M	*PBQ*	BQ	65461	77182

Class 507 — 3-Car

Built: BREL, York 1978
Design: BR saloon with sliding doors, driver/guard and public address equipment. Units 507.001-008 fitted with de-icing equipment
Supply: 600/750V dc
Traction Motors: Four 110hp (82.5kW) dc GEC G310AZ
Maximum speed: 75mph
Unit No 507009 experimentally equipped additionally with magnetic track brakes. Unit normally used on Wirral Line services

Dimensions: *Motor coaches:* 20.20m L × 3.02m W × 3.58m H. *Trailer coaches:* 19.92m L × 3.02m W × 3.58m H

Diagram	*Type*	*Weight*	*Seats*
Driving Motor Standard:			
EA2.01.0A	DMS	35.5t	74
Trailer Standard:			
EH2.05.0A	TS	25.5t	86
EH2.05.0B	TS	25.5t	86
Battery Driving Motor Standard:			
EI2.02.0A	BDMS	37t	74

Unit No	Liv	Pool	Dep	BDMS	TS	DMS
				EI2020A	*EH2050B*	*EA2010A*
507 001		*PHR*	HR	64367	71342	64405
507 002		*PHR*	HR s	64368	71343	64406
507 003		*PHR*	HR	64369	71344	64407
507 004		*PHR*	HR	64370	71345	64408
507 005		*PHR*	HR	64371	71346	64409
507 006		*PHR*	HR	64372	71347	64410
507 007		*PHR*	HR	64373	71348	64411
507 008		*PHR*	HR	64374	71349	64412
				EI2020A	*EH2050A*	*EA2010A*
507 009		*PHR*	HR	64375	71350	64413
507 010		*PHR*	HR	64376	71351	64414
507 011		*PHR*	HR s	64377	71352	64415

Unit No	Liv	Pool	Dep	BDMS	TS	DMS
507 012		*PHR*	HR	64378	71353	64416
507 013		*PHR*	HR	64379	71354	64417
507 014		*PHR*	HR	64380	71355	64418
507 015		*PHR*	HR	64381	71356	64419
507 016		*PHR*	HR	64382	71357	64420
507 017		*PHR*	HR	64383	71358	64421
507 018		*PHR*	HR	64384	71359	64422
507 019		*PHR*	HR	64385	71360	64423
507 020		*PHR*	HR	64386	71361	64424
507 021		*PHR*	HR	64387	71362	64425
507 022		*PHR*	HR	64388	71363	64426
507 023		*PHR*	HR	64389	71364	64427
507 024		*PHR*	HR	64390	71365	64428
507 025		*PHR*	HR	64391	71366	64429
507 026		*PHR*	HR	64392	71367	64430
507 027		*PHR*	HR	64393	71368	64431
507 028		*PHR*	HR	64394	71369	64432
507 029		*PHR*	HR	64395	71370	64433
507 030		*PHR*	HR	64396	71371	64434
507 031		*PHR*	HR	64397	71372	64435
507 032		*PHR*	HR	64398	71373	64436
507 033		*PHR*	HR	64399	71374	64437

Class 508 — 3-CAR

Built: BREL, York 1979
Design: BR saloon, with sliding doors, gangwayed within unit and end doors, driver-guard communication and public address equipment
Power Supply: 750/850V dc third rail
Traction Motors (DMS & BDMS): Four 110hp (82.5kW) dc GEC G310AZ or Brush TM61-53 (Interchangeable)
Maximum Speed: 75mph
Dimensions: *Driving coaches:* 20.20m L × 2.82m W × 3.58m H; *Trailer coach:* 19.92m L × 2.82m W × 3.58m H

AWS: Driving coaches fitted

Diagram	*Type*	*Weight*	*Seats*
Driving Motor Standard			
EA2.08.0A	DMS	36t	74
Trailer Standard			
EH2.18.0A	TS	26.5t	86
EH2.--.0A*	TS	26.5t	82
Battery Driving Motor Standard			
EI2.03.0A	BDMS	36.5t	74

*Official diagram not issued

Unit No	SC	Liv	Pool	Dep	BDMS	TS	DMS
					EI2030A	*EH2—0A*	*EA2080A*
508 101			*PBD*	BD	64692	71483	64649
508 102			*PBD*	BD	64693	71484	64650
508 103			*PBD*	BD	64694	71485	64651
508 104			*PBD*	BD	64695	71486	64652

Unit No	SC	Liv	Pool	Dep	BDMS	TS	DMS
508 105			*PBD*	BD	64696	71487	64653
508 106			*PBD*	BD	64697	71488	64654
508 107			*PBD*	BD	64698	71489	64655
508 108			*PBD*	BD	64699	71490	64656
508 109			*PBD*	BD	64700	71491	64657
508 110			*PBD*	BD	64701	71492	64658
508 111			*PBD*	BD	64702	71493	64659
508 112			*PBD*	BD	64703	71494	64660
					EI2030A	*EH2—0A*	*EA2080A*
508 113			*PBD*	BD	64704	71495	64661
508 114			*PBD*	BD	64705	71496	64662
508 115			*PBD*	BD	64706	71497	64663
508 116			*PBD*	BDs	64707	71498	64680
508 117			*PBD*	BD	64708	71499	64665
508 118			*PBD*	BD	64709	71500	64666
508 119			*PBD*	BD	64710	71501	64667
					EI2030A	*EH2180A*	*EA2080A*
508 120			*PBD*	BD	64711	71502	64668
					EI2030A	*EH2—0A*	*EA2080A*
508 121			*PBD*	BD	64712	71503	64669
508 122			*PBD*	BD	64713	71504	64670
508 123			*PBD*	BD	64714	71505	64671
508 124			*PBD*	BD	64715	71506	64672
508 125			*PBD*	BD	64716	71507	64673
508 126			*PBD*	BD	64717	71508	64674
508 127			*PBD*	BD	64718	71509	64675
508 128			*PBD*	BD	64719	71510	64676
508 129			*PBD*	BD	64720	71511	64677
508 130			*PBD*	BD	64721	71512	64678
508 131			*PBD*	BD	64722	71513	64679
508 132			*PBD*	BD	64723	71514	64664
508 133			*PBD*	BD	64724	71515	64681
508 134			*PBD*	BD	64725	71516	64682
508 135			*PBD*	BD	64726	71517	64683
508 136			*PBD*	BD	64727	71518	64684
508 137			*PBD*	BD	64728	71519	64685
508 138			*PBD*	BD	64729	71520	64686
508 139			*PBD*	BD	64730	71521	64687
508 140			*PBD*	BD	64731	71522	64688
508 141			*PBD*	BD	64732	71523	64689
508 142			*PBD*	BD	64733	71524	64690
508 143			*PBD*	BD	64734	71525	64691

NB: Units 508134-43 normally operate on Hall Road (HR) duties from Kirkdale depot.

Spare Vehicles. Network SouthEast EMU Stock

Vehicle No	Type	Class	DMEE Diagram	SR Design
61035	MBS	411/4	EA2.63	AP
61342	MBS	411/5	EA2.64	AL
70995	TS	421/2	EH2.75	BO-IA
76108	DTC	421/1	EE3.64	FA
76331	DTS	438	EE2.66	FC
76339	DTC	423	EE3.65	FB
76639	DTC	423	EE3.63.3B	

Service Department Multiple-Unit Stock

SECTOR: *DMEX:* Director of Mechanical and Electrical Engineering.
DRTC: Director of Research.

(Note: Specification codes A-R are shown for cross-reference purposes only for this publication).

DIESEL-ELECTRIC MULITPLE-UNITS

Spec	*Built*	*Type*	*Dimensions L×W×H (m)*	*Weight*	*Max speed*	*Brake*
A	BR Eastleigh 1958	Trailer	20.34×2.74×3.87	31.5t	75mph	Air
B1	BR Eastleigh 1956	Driving Motor	15.94×2.74×3.87	55t	75mph	Air
	Engine: English Electric 4SRKT Mk II, 4cyl, 500hp (375kW) *Traction Motors:* Two nose-suspended, axle-hung. *Main Generator:* EE Type 824.					
B2	BR Eastleigh 1956	Trailer	15.94×2.74×3.87	55t	75mph	Air

DIESEL-MECHANICAL MULITIPLE UNITS

The following vehicles have a number of common features which are summarised as follows:
Engines: (where fitted) Two AEC or Leyland 150hp (114kW) 6cyl, horizontal, except:
Spec **Q:** One Cummins NT855 R5 285hp (213kW)
Spec **R:** Two Rolls-Royce 130D of 180hp (134kW) 6cyl
Transmission: Four-speed epicyclic gearbox, carden shaft. Spec **Q:** Voith.
Maximum speed: 70mph, except Spec **Q:** 75mph.

Spec	*Built*	*Type*	*Dimensions L×W×H (m)*	*Weight*	*Engines*	*Gangway*
C1	BR Derby 1954	Driving Motor B	18.49×2.82×3.85	27t	AEC	Within unit
C2	BR Derby 1954	Driving Trailer	18.49×2.82×3.85	21t	—	Within unit
D	BR Derby 1956	Driving Motor B	18.49×2.82×3.85	—	AEC	Twin-cab
E	Gloucester RCW 1958	Driving Motor B	20.45×2.82×3.86	36.5t	AEC	Twin-cab
F1	Pressed Steel 1960	Driving Motor B	20.45×2.82×3.86	38t	Leyland	Twin-cab
F2	Pressed Steel 1960	Driving Trailer	20.45×2.82×3.86	30t	—	—
G1	Park Royal 1957	Driving Motor B	18.49×2.82×3.85	34t	AEC	Within unit
G2	Park Royal 1957	Driving Trailer	18.49×2.82×3.85	27t	—	Within unit
H1	Gloucester RCW 1957	Driving Motor B	18.49×2.82×3.85	30.5t	AEC	Within unit
H2	Gloucester RCW 1957	Driving Trailer	18.49×2.82×3.85	25.5t	—	Within unit
I	BR Derby 1958	Trailer	19.58×2.82×3.87	28.5t	—	—

K1	Cravens 1956	Driving Motor B	18.49×2.82×3.84	30t	Leyland	Within unit
K2	Cravens 1956	Driving Trailer	18.49×2.82×3.84	23t	—	Within unit
M1	Metro Cammell 1957-59	Driving Motor B	18.49×2.82×3.85	32.5t	Leyland	Within unit
M2	Metro Cammell 1957-59	Driving Motor	18.49×2.82×3.85	32.5t	Leyland	Within unit
N	Pressed Steel 1960	Driving Trailer	20.45×2.82×3.86	29.5t	—	—
P	Wickham 1958	Driving Motor	10.97×2.72×3.84	11t	AEC	Railbus
Q	BREL York 1987	Driving Motor	20.06×2.73×3.77	36.5t	Cummins	Within unit
R1	BRCW 1961	Driving Motor B	18.48×2.82×3.84	32.5t	RR	Within unit
R2	BRCW 1961	Driving Motor	18.48×2.82×3.84	32.5t	RR	Within unit

Veh No	*Former No*	*Spec*	*Type*	*Pool*	*Depot*	*Use*
DB975007	(79018)	C1	QWV(DMB)	DMEX	RG	2-car Ultrasonic Test Train
DB975008	(79612)	C2	QXV(DT)	DMEX	RG	2-car Ultrasonic Test Train
RDB975010	(79900)	D	QWV(DMB)	DRTC	ZQ	RTC Test Coach *Iris*
TDB975023	(55001)	E	QWV(DMB)	DMEX	TS	Route Learning
TDB975025	(60755)	A	QXV(T)	DMEX	SL	SR General Manager's Saloon
TDB975042	(55019)	E	QWV(DMB)	DMEX	TS	Route Learning
RDB975089	(50396)	G1	QWV(DMB)	DRTC	ZQ	RTC Laboratory 5 Trim
RDB975090	(56162)	G2	QXV(DT)	DRTC	ZQ	RTC Laborary No 4
DB975349	(51116)	H1	QWV(DMB)	DMEX	CA	2-car unit RCE Inspection Saloon (a)
RDB975386	(60750)	A	QXV(T)	DRTC	ZQ	RTC (Tilt Tests)
DB975539	(56101)	H2	QXV(DT)	DMEX	CA	2-car unit RCE Inspection Saloon (a)
DB975637	(56300)	H2	QXV(DT)	DMEX	CA	2-car unit RCE Inspection Saloon (b)
TDB975659	(55035)	F1	QWV(DMB)	DMEX	00	Route Learning. Set No L135
DB975664	(51122)	H1	QWV(DMB)	DMEX	CA	2-car unit RCE Inspection Saloon (b)
RDB975964	(59466)	I	QXV(T)	DMEX	ZD	Stores Van
ADB977048	(56142)	K2	QXV(DT)	DMEX	BX	Sandite spray
ADB977052	(56145)	K2	QXV(DT)	DMEX	TS	Sandite spray
TDB977123	(51286)	K1	QWV(DMB)	DMEX	CA	2-car Route Learning unit, (c)
TDB977124	(51296)	K1	QWV(DMB)	DMEX	CA	2-car Route Learning unit, (d)
TDB977125	(56444)	K2	QXV(DMB)	DMEX	CA	2-car Route Learning unit, (c)
TDB977126	(56445)	K2	QXV(DMB)	DMEX	CA	2-car Route Learning unit, (d)
ADB977342	(53475)	L	QWV(DMB)	DRTC	ZQ	RTC Carriage wash test vehicle
ADB977376	(60002)	B1	QWA(DMB)	DMEX	SU	3-car unit SR Sandite train, Unit 066
ADB977377	(60504)	B2	QXA(T)	DMEX	SU	3-car unit SR Sandite train, Unit 066
ADB977379	(60003)	B1	QWA(DMB)	DMEX	SU	3-car unit SR Sandite train, Unit 066
DB977391	(51433)	M1	QWV(DMB)	DRTC	ZQ	2-car unit RTC Track Assessment train
DB977392	(53167)	M1	QWV(DMB)	DRTC	ZQ	For RTC Track Assessment train
DB977393	(53246)	M1	QWV(DMB)	DRTC	ZQ	2-car unit RTC Track Assessment train
TDB977466	(54286)	N	QXV(DT)	DMEX	CF	Sandite trailer coach
TDB977486	(54285)	N	QXV(DT)	DMEX	LA	Sandite trailer coach
TDB977535	(53259)	M1	QWV(DMB)	DMEX	HT	2-car Sandite unit, (f)
TDB977536	(53295)	M1	QWV(DMB)	DMEX	HT	2-car Sandite unit, (f)
ADB977607	(51464)	M1	QWV(DMB)	DMEX	ED	2-car Route Learning/Sandite unit, (g)
ADB977608	(51525)	M1	QWV(DM)	DMEX	ED	2-car Route Learning/Sandite unit, (g)
ADB977611	(51824)	R1	QWV(DMB)	DMEX	NL	2-car Sandite train (j)
ADB977612	(51838)	R1	QWV(DM)	DMEX	NL	2-car Sandite train (j)
ADB977613	(51826)	R1	QWV(DMB)	DMEX	NL	2-car Sandite train (k)
ADB977614	(52076)	R1	QWV(DM)	DMEX	NL	2-car Sandite train (k)
ADB977615	(54281)	F2	QXV(DT)	DMEX	LA	Sandite trailer coach
RDB999507	—	P	QWV(DM)	DRTC	ZQ	RTC Laboratory Track Recorder
DB999600	—	Q	QWA(DM)	DRTC	ZQ	2-car RTC Track Recording Train, (h)
DB999601	—	Q	QWA(DM)	DRTC	ZQ	2-car RTC Track Recording Train, (h)

ELECTRIC MULTIPLE UNIT VEHICLES

Most of the following continue to operate as a 'multiple-unit' of two or more vehicles. Unit numbers in brackets are class numbers, not carried on the vehicle as part of the unit identity. The first three vehicles listed are now in Service Stock use but have not been officially recorded by the BRB, DMEE, Rolling Stock Library. All vehicles are formerly Capital Stock and in most cases seating has been removed and replaced by special equipment appropriate to the vehicles current use. Rail Cleaning units can be used for either De-Icing fluid or Sandite (leaf removal) applications.

Units listed take electricity supply from ac overhead lines at 6.25 and 25kV or dc third rail at 630/750/850V as indicated under Vehicle Type. Traction Motors are all dc manufactured by English Electric (EE), or General Electric Company (GEC).

Diagram	*Built*	*Vehicle type*	*ex-Class*	*Dimensions L×W×H (m)*	*Weight*	*Max*	*Motors*	*Gangway*
ED2.04.0A	1960	AC Motor Brake	305/1	20.27×2.82×3.98	55t	75	4 GEC 200hp	—
EE2.09.1B	1960	AC Driving Trailer	305/1	20.36×2.82×3.84	31.5t	75	—	—
EF2.05.0A	1960	AC Batt Driving Trailer	305/1	20.36×2.82×3.84	35t	75	—	—
EZ5.02.0A	1939	DC Driving Motor Brake	402	19.53×2.74×3.99	44t	70	2 EE 275hp	—
EZ5.03.0A	1940	DC Driving Motor Brake	4-LAV	19.51×2.74×3.99	44t	70	2 EE 275hp	—
EZ5.04.0A	1957	DC Driving Motor Brake	501	18.47×2.82×3.86	47t	70	4 GEC 185hp	—
EZ5.04.1B	1957	DC Driving Motor Brake	501	18.47×2.90×3.86	48t	70	4 GEC 185hp	—
EZ5.06.0A	1957	DC Driving Trailer	501	18.47×2.82×3.86	30t	70	—	—
EZ5.06.1B	1957	DC Driving Trailer	501	18.47×2.90×3.86	30.5t	70	—	—
EZ5.12.0A	1948	DC Driving Motor Brake	405	19.23×2.74×3.99	39t	70	2 EE 250hp	—
EZ5.15.0A	1958	DC Driving Motor Brake	412	19.23×2.74×3.98	40t	90	2 EE 250hp	—
EZ5.16.0A	1958	DC Driving Trailer	412	19.23×2.74×3.98	30t	75	2 EE 250hp	—
EZ5.20.0A	1946	DC Trailer	4-SUB	19.99×2.74×3.99	29t	70	—	—
EZ5.22.2C	1957	DC Driving Motor Brake	414/2	20.42×2.82×3.86	42t	90	2 EE 250hp	—
EZ5.23.0A	1957	DC Driving Trailer	414/2	20.42×2.82×3.86	32.5t	90	—	—
EZ5.25.0A	1953	DC Driving Motor Brake	416/2	20.04×2.82×3.86	40.5t	75	2 EE 250hp	—
EZ5.25.0B	1953	DC Driving Motor Brake	416/2	20.04×2.82×3.86	40.5t	75	2 EE 250hp	—
EZ5.26.0A	1954	DC Driving Trailer	416/2	20.44×2.82×3.86	32.5t	75	—	—
EZ5.28.0A	1967	AC Driving Trailer	302	20.36×2.82×3.86	32.5t	75	—	—
EZ5.29.0A	1967	AC Motor Brake	302	20.27×2.82×3.86	55t	75	4 EE 192hp	
EZ5.--	1966	DC Driving Trailer	438	20.35×2.82×3.86	32.5t	90	—	Throughout

Veh No	*Former No*	*Dia/type*	*Unit No*	*Pool*	*Depot*	*Use*
61463	—	ED2040A(MB)	305935	DMEX	IL	ECML Driver Instruction unit
75496	—	EF2050A(BDT)	305935	DMEX	IL	ECML Driver Instruction unit
75548	—	EE2091B(DT)	305935	DMEX	IL	ECML Driver Instruction unit
ADB975027	(61162)	EZ5040A(DMB)	(930)	DMEX	SH	R&D Test Car
ADB975032	(75165)	EZ5060A(DT)	(930)	DMEX	SH	R&D Test Car *Mars*
ADB975586	(10907)	EZ5120A(DMB)	(930)004	DMEX	EH	Rail Cleaning Unit
ADB975587	(10908)	EZ5120A(DMB)	(930)004	DMEX	EH	Rail Cleaning Unit
ADB975588	(10981)	EZ5120A(DMB)	(930)005	DMEX	WD	Rail Cleaning Unit
ADB975589	(10982)	EZ5120A(DMB)	(930)005	DMEX	WD	Rail Cleaning Unit
ADB975590	(10833)	EZ5120A(DMB)	(930)006	DMEX	WD	Rail Cleaning Unit
ADB975591	(10834)	EZ5120A(DMB)	(930)006	DMEX	WD	Rail Cleaning Unit
ADB975592	(10993)	EZ5120A(DMB)	(930)007	DMEX	GI	Rail Cleaning Unit
ADB975593	(12659)	EZ5120A(DMB)	(930)007	DMEX	GI	Rail Cleaning Unit
ADB975594	(12658)	EZ5120A(DMB)	(930)003	DMEX	SU	Rail Cleaning Unit
ADB975595	(10994)	EZ5120A(DMB)	(930)003	DMEX	SU	Rail Cleaning Unit
ADB975596	(10844)	EZ5120A(DMB)	(930)008	DMEX	GI	Rail Cleaning Unit
ADB975597	(10987)	EZ5120A(DMB)	(930)008	DMEX	GI	Rail Cleaning Unit
ADB975598	(10989)	EZ5120A(DMB)	(930)009	DMEX	BI	Rail Cleaning Unit
ADB975599	(10990)	EZ5120A(DMB)	(930)009	DMEX	BI	Rail Cleaning Unit
ADB975600	(10988)	EZ5120A(DMB)	(930)010	DMEX	BI	Rail Cleaning Unit

ADB975601	(10843)	EZ5120A(DMB)	(930)010	DMEX	BI	Rail Cleaning Unit
ADB975602	(10991)	EZ5120A(DMB)	(930)011	DMEX	RE	Rail Cleaning Unit
ADB975603	(10992)	EZ5120A(DMB)	(930)011	DMEX	RE	Rail Cleaning Unit
ADB975604	(10939)	EZ5120A(DMB)	(930)012	DMEX	FR	Rail Cleaning Unit
ADB975605	(10940)	EZ5120A(DMB)	(930)012	DMEX	FR	Rail Cleaning Unit
ADB975896	(11387)	EZ5120A(DMB)	(930)013	DMEX	RE	Rail Cleaning Unit
ADB975897	(11388)	EZ5120A(DMB)	(930)013	DMEX	RE	Rail Cleaning Unit
ADB977068	(14549)	EZ5150A(DMB)	(931)019	DMEX	SG	Stores unit
ADB977069	(16029)	EZ5160A(DMB)	(931)019	DMEX	SG	Stores unit
ADB977290	(65318)	EZ5250A(DMB)	(931)018	DMEX	SG	Stores unit
ADB977291	(65324)	EZ5250A(DMB)	(931)018	DMEX	SG	Stores unit
ADB977296	(65319)	EZ5250B(DMB)	(932)050	DMEX	SH	RSD Test unit
ADB977297	(77108)	EZ5260A(DT)	(932)050	DMEX	SH	RSD Test unit
ADB977304	(65317)	EZ5250A(DMB)	(936)021	DMEX	WD	Traction shunting unit
ADB977305	(65322)	EZ5250A(DMB)	(936)021	DMEX	WD	Traction shunting unit
DB977335	(76277)	EZ5 (DT)	—	DRTC	ZQ	RTC Track Recording Train
DB977336	(76278)	EZ5 (DT)	—	DRTC	ZQ	RTC Track Recording Train
ADB977345	(61178)	EZ5041B(DMB)	(936)001	DMEX	BD	Rail Cleaning unit
ADB977346	(75178)	EZ5061B(DT)	(936)001	DMEX	BD	Rail Cleaning unit
ADB977347	(61180)	EZ5041B(DMB)	(936)002	DMEX	BD	Rail Cleaning unit
ADB977348	(75180)	EZ5061B(DT)	(936)002	DMEX	BD	Rail Cleaning unit
ADB977349	(61183)	EZ5041B(DMB)	(936)003	DMEX	BD	Rail Cleaning unit
ADB977350	(75183)	EZ5061B(DT)	(936)003	DMEX	BD	Rail Cleaning unit
ADB977362	(10392)	EZ5200A(T)	(930)	DMEX	BI	De-Icing coach
ADB977363	(10399)	EZ5200A(T)	(930)	DMEX	FR	De-Icing coach
ADB977364	(10400)	EZ5200A(T)	(930)	DMEX	RE	De-Icing coach
ADB977365	(10726)	EZ5020A(DMB)	(930)001	DMEX	SU	Rail Cleaning unit
ADB977366	(10500)	EZ5030A(DMB)	(930)002	DMEX	BM	Rail Cleaning unit
ADB977367	(10497)	EZ5030A(DMB)	(930)002	DMEX	BM	Rail Cleaning unit
ADB977368	(10499)	EZ5030A(DMB)	(930)002	DMEX	SU	Rail Cleaning unit
ADB977385	(61148)	EZ50418(DMB)	(936)148	DMEX	WN	Rail Cleaning unit
ADB977386	(75189)	EZ5061B(DT)	(936)148	DMEX	WN	Rail Cleaning unit
ADB977505	(65321)	EZ5250B(DMB)	(932)053*	DMEX	SH	RSD Test unit
ADB977506	(65323)	EZ5250B(DMB)	(932)054*	DMEX	SH	RSD Test unit
ADB977507	(77110)	EZ5260A(DT)	(932)053	DMEX	SH	RSD Test unit
ADB977508	(77112)	EZ5260A(DT)	(932)054	DMEX	SH	RSD Test unit
ADB977531	(14047)	EZ5120A(DMB)	(930)015	DMEX	SU	Sandite unit
ADB977532	(14048)	EZ5120A(DMB)	(930)015	DMEX	SU	Sandite unit
ADB977533	(14273)	EZ5120A(DMB)	(930)016	DMEX	SU	Sandite unit
ADB977534	(14384)	EZ5120A(DMB)	(930)016	DMEX	SU	Sandite unit
ADB977559	(65313)	EZ5250A(DMB)	(931)026	DMEX	SU	Stores unit
ADB977560	(65320)	EZ5250A(DMB)	(931)026	DMEX	SU	Stores unit
ADB977566	(65312)	EZ5250A(DMB)	(931)017	DMEX	SU	Stores unit
ADB977567	(65314)	EZ5250A(DMB)	(931)017	DMEX	SU	Stores unit
ADB977598	(75080)	EZ5280A(DT)	(937)996	DMEX	IL	Rail Cleaning unit
ADB977599	(61073)	EZ5290A(MB)	(937)996	DMEX	IL	Rail Cleaning unit
ADB977600	(75061)	EZ5280A(DT)	(937)996	DMEX	IL	Rail Cleaning unit
ADB977601	(75211)	EZ5280A(DT)	(937)997	DMEX	IL	Rail Cleaning unit
ADB977602	(61228)	EZ5290A(MB)	(937)997	DMEX	IL	Rail Cleaning unit
ADB977603	(75035)	EZ5280A(DT)	(937)997	DMEX	IL	Rail Cleaning unit
ADB977604	(75077)	EZ5280A(DT)	(937)998	DMEX	IL	Rail Cleaning unit
ADB977605	(61062)	EZ5290A(MB)	(937)998	DMEX	IL	Rail Cleaning unit
ABD977606	(75070)	EZ5280A(DT)	(937)998	DMEX	IL	Rail Cleaning unit
ADB977609	(65414)	EZ5222C(DMB)	(930)022	DMEX	WD	Rail Cleaning unit
ADB977610	(77130)	EZ5230A(DT)	(930)022	DMEX	WD	Rail Cleaning unit

*When ADB977505 and ADB977506 run together Unit No to be 055.

Additional Information

The following information updates this publication with notified changes by mid-March 1989.

DIESEL MULTIPLE-UNITS

DELETE (Withdrawn):

51458, 51522, 51809, 52084, 53026/37, 53214/51, 53866/69, 53922, 54013/19, 54375, 59096, 59113, 78722, 78967/69.

SPECIAL CHANGES:

Class 101: *Reinstated, Add:* 51520 2102F *PNL* NL.
Class 114: Delete: 53015/18, 54009/15 (to Parcels stock).
Class 141: 141003 renumbered 141104.
Classes 155/0 and 155/1: Not in public service pending modifications.
Class 158: *add footnote:* Unit Nos 158707-75 ordered January 1989.

SECTOR CODES:

NSB: 51060/62/66/73/74/76/79/86/90/94/99, 51104/07/90, 51211/26, 51425/31/32/34/98/99, 51501/03/04, 59091, 59101/15/17/25/28, 59416/19/21/25/30/35/37, 59526/30/40/43/70.
NNE: 51207/08, 51444.
NSX: 205008/09/12/15/16/18/23/24, 205101.

SECTOR & DEPOT CODE CHANGES (New allocations):

PCF CF: 51449, 53240, 53887, 150233/35/43, 156420/38/48/52/54/55/61-73.
PCH CH: 53626/34/36.
PLA LA: 55004/11 (at Tyseley waiting orders).
PHA HA: 150260, 156445/47/49/50/53/56/74.
PIS IS: 156446/57/58/77/78.
PNH NH: 142071, 150202/04/06/10/16/18/22.
PNL NL: 51197, 51243, 51456/58, 51522, 53162/69/95/96, 53229/35, 53606, 54196, 142050, 150264, 156451/59/60/75/76/79-83.
PTS TS: 53980-83, 54246/53/56/66.
PXXZ: 52043, 53355, 53427/60/74/96, 53501/56, 53812, 54054/71, 54350/98, 54401, 59330, 59748/86, 59812.
PXXZ CP(s): 53355, 53500/18/56, 53812.
Stored: Add to allocation '(s)': 52043, 53427, 54071.

DIAGRAM NUMBER CHANGES:

DQ2.02.2B: **51203.**

SPECIAL CHARACTERISTICS (Add):

†: 51197, 51203, 53139/41.
#: 51446/50/54/55/58/67/95, 51510/15/16/17/19/22/24/26/29/38, 51795, 51801/04, 53141/59/62, 53229, 53335, 59096, 59690.
R 55200, 55300, 150124/28/30.
RP 156445/46/47/50/53/56/57/58/77/78.
V 142015-19/21/24/25/27/34/35/36/47/48/60/71.

LIVERIES (Add):
N: 51332/45/74/87, 51572, 51680, 51912, 53155, 53479, 53539/99, 54194, 54271, 54358, 55023, 59206, 59305, 59484/97, 59565, 59735/36/39, 205030.

PARCELS STOCK

Class 114 Add:
55928 (53018) DX5.13.0B RR *RPXN* CA.
55929 (53015) DX5.13.0B RR *RPXN* CA.
54903 (54009) DX5.14.0A RR *RPXN* CA.
54904 (54015) DX5.14.3B RR *RPXN* CA.

Sector Code on all DMUs *RXXN* to now read *RPXN*.

ELECTRIC MULTIPLE UNITS
New Class 320: Unit Nos to read 320301-320322, coach numbers DTS 77899-77920, MS 63021-63042, DTS 77921-77944.
Seats to read: MS and DTS(A): each 79.

Delete, Withdrawn: 302231/35/37/38/41/43/48/55/76, 8021, ADB 975027.

Renumbered and reclassified: Unit Nos 310048, 310053, 310054, 310062, 310063 officially now 310109, 310108, 310110, 310107, 310111 respectively. (p88 delete footnote).

SECTOR CODES:
NGE: 302245/52.
NNE: 321312-19.
NNL: 321336-46.
RPMA: 308993/94/95.

SECTOR & DEPOT CODES:
NGE IL: 302264/70/82.
NKS SG: 5451.
NNL BY: 321320/21.
NSL SU: 5837.
NTS EM: 308133-39.
NXX PQ(s): 302246/49/54/60/68/69/89/90/91/95, 307101/06.
NXX Shoeburyness(s): 302284.
PXX GW(s): 303005/71.
Stored (s): 1280/95, 3441.

DIAGRAM NUMBERS:
***Class 413:** DTC to DTS, Seats 69-*
EE2.72.1A: * 77120.*
EE2.21.1A: 77117/18/32/35.
EE2.22.1A: 75373.

Additional Information/Notes

Class 415/7: *EB2.71.0J:* 61572/78, 61600.
EB2.71.2J: 61590, 61604/08.
EB2.72.0H: 61573/79, 61601.
EB2.72.2H: 61591, 61605/09.
EH2.71.0E: 70431/37/49/60/64.
EH2.71.1E: 70432/38/50/59/63/68.

SET FORMATIONS:

302269: add 75216 in place of 75242.

302990		*RPMA*	IL	75082	61090	75084	
302991		*RPMA*	IL	75221		75211	

308994: add 75927 (BDTS).
2306 delete 69346.

2308	(1562R)	*NSS*	FR	61407	70236	69346	61406

3466 to 3471 add 'R' to old unit numbers.
3467 to read (3058R).

3472	(3085R)	*NSX*	BI	76500	62244	70936	76499
3473	(3086R)	*NSX*	BI	76502	62245	70937	76501
3474					62246		
3475					62247		

LIVERIES:
Network SouthEast: N: 305502, 307111/20/25, 308135/49, 309612 (delete E), 312799, 1217/20/21/41/64, 4303/21, 5485/86, 5606, 6308, 6403/05; delete 307106, 6401.

SPECIAL CHARACTERISTICS:
F: add 312799.

***Motive Power Monthly* — June 1989**

A full depot by depot listing of all DMU stock, including formations of conventional stock, correct to 1 April 1989 will be included in the above magazine, on sale 8 May 1989.

Also included will be an up to date depot allocation summary for all EMUs.